CAMBRIDGE LATIN AMERICAN STUDIES

EDITORS

MALCOLM DEAS   CLIFFORD T. SMITH
JOHN STREET

25

ALLENDE'S CHILE

THE POLITICAL ECONOMY OF THE RISE AND FALL OF
THE UNIDAD POPULAR

THE SERIES

ALLENDE'S CHILE

The political economy of the rise and fall of the Unidad Popular

STEFAN DE VYLDER

Lecturer at the Stockholm School of Economics

CAMBRIDGE UNIVERSITY PRESS

CAMBRIDGE

LONDON · NEW YORK · MELBOURNE

Published by the Syndics of the Cambridge University Press
The Pitt Building, Trumpington Street, Cambridge CB2 1RP
Bentley House, 200 Euston Road, London NW1 2DB
32 East 57th Street, New York, NY 10022, USA
296 Beaconsfield Parade, Middle Park, Melbourne 3206, Australia

First published in 1974 in Scandinavia as *Chile 1970–73:
The Political Economy of the Rise and Fall of the Unidad Popular*
by UF-Förlaget, Stockholm. This new version first published by
Cambridge University Press in 1976.

Photoset and printed
by Interprint (Malta) Ltd

Library of Congress Cataloguing in Publication Data
De Vylder, Stefan, 1943–
Allende's Chile.
(Cambridge Latin American studies; 25)
Published in 1974 in Stockholm under title: Chile 1970–73.
Bibliography: p.
1. Chile – Economic conditions – 1918 – 2. Unidad Popular.
3. Chile – Economic policy. I. Title. II. Series.
HC192.D48   1976   330.9'83'064   72-27797
ISBN 0 521 21046 1

CONTENTS

Contents

ACKNOWLEDGMENTS

Most of this study was written in 1972 and 1973 during my sixteen-month stay in Chile. The visit to Chile was made possible by generous financial assistance from the Stockholm School of Economics, whose support in this and other respects I gratefully acknowledge.

Numerous friends and colleagues have given invaluable encouragement and support to me in my work. Some have submitted earlier drafts of this study to stimulating and sometimes quite severe criticism; others have helped to reduce the number of errors in my treatment of the English language, typed the final manuscripts or simply given me the indispensable moral support I badly needed to be able to finish the work. I wish to thank them all. But in particular I wish to thank the Chilean people, whose warmth, hospitality and courage impressed me so much while I was their guest and whose struggle against the tyranny installed in their country on 11 September, 1973 deserves not only our sympathy but our active solidarity and support as well.

Stockholm, September 1974

STEFAN DE VYLDER

CHILEAN EXPRESSIONS AND
ABBREVIATIONS USED

afuerino	unattached day-laborers
Asamblea del Pueblo	Peoples Assembly
asentamiento	agrarian cooperative: transitional system of managing expropriated land
asentado	member of an *asentamiento*
b. ha	basic hectare
campesino	smallholder or landless farm worker
canasta popular	'popular basket': a selection of groceries distributed inexpensively by DINAC
CAP	Pacific Steel Company
capas medias	middle strata of society
CELADE	Centro Latinoamericano de Demograffía
CEPRO	Centros de Producción (production centers)
CERA	Centros de la Reforma Agraria (agrarian reform centers)
CEREN	Centro de Estudios de la Realidad Nacional
CESO	Centro de Estudios Socio-Económicos
CG	Contraloría General
CIDA	Comité Interamericano de Desarrollo Agrícola
CODELCO	Corporación de Cobre: the Chilean state's agency for handling copper exports
comando comunal	organs of popular power comprising entire communities
Comité Campesino	transitional system (after 1970) of managing expropriated land
Comité de Vigilancia	worker's committees to supervise administration in private industry
Confederación Democrática	anti-UP coalition
CORA	Agrarian Reform Corporation
cordón industrial	industrial belts, regional groupings of industry
CORFO	Industrial Development Corporation
CORVI	Corporación de la Vivienda (housing corporation)
CUP	Comités de la Unidad Popular
CUT	Central Unica de Trabajadores

ix

Chilean expressions and abbreviations

DC see PDC	
decreto de insistencia	insistency decree: mainly for interventions and requisitions
DINAC	state grocery distributing company
DIRINCO	Dirección Nacional de Industria y Comercio
DR	Democracia Radical (Radical Democrats)
ECLA	Economic Commission for Latin America
fundo	*latifundo*, large estate
gremio	guild
IC	Izquierda Cristiana (Christian Left)
ICIRA	Instituto de Capacitación e Investigación en Reforma Agraria (Institute of Training and Research for Agrarian Reform)
INE	Instituto Nacional de Estadística (National Institute of Statistics)
inquilino	sharecropper
inquilinaje	system of sharecropping
CESO	Centro de Estudios Socio-Económicos
CIDA	Comité Interamericano de Desarrollo Agrícola
intendente	provincial governor
interventor	state manager of privately owned business
JAP	Junta de Abastecimiento y Precios (price and supply committee)
MAPU	Movimiento de Acción Popular Unitaria
mediano	owner of medium-sized farm (20–80 b. ha)
milicia popular	popular militia
MIR	Movimiento de Izquierda Revolucionaria (Movement of the Revolutionary Left)
NACLA	North American Congress on Latin America
ODEPA	Oficina de Planificación Agrícola (agricultural planning agency)
ODEPLAN	Oficina de Planificación Nacional (Chilean planning ministry)
OEA	Organizacion de los Estados Americanos
PC	Partido Communista (Communist Party)
PDC (DC)	Partido Demócrata Cristiano (Christian Democratic Party)
PIR	Partido de Izquierda Radical (Radical Left Party)
PN	Partido Nacional (National Party)
población	squatter settlement
poblador	slum dweller
poder popular	popular power

x

Chilean expressions and abbreviations

PR	Partido Radical (Radical Party)
promoción popular	'popular promotion'
PS	Partido Socialista (Socialist Party)
reserva	80 b. ha allowed to owner of expropriated land
socio	full members of cooperatives
SOCOAGRO	state controlled enterprise for meat distribution
SOFOFA	Chilean Association of Manufacturers
sueldo vital	officially established subsistence wage
toma de fundo	land occupation
UP	Unidad Popular

Introduction

It is easy to understand why the evolution of political events in Chile under Salvador Allende and the Unidad Popular (UP) attracted attention all over the world. The scarcity of previous attempts at a 'constitutional' transition to socialism made the UP experiment pretty well unique, and undoubtedly the political and economic development during the Allende period had a significance which went far beyond the Chilean borders.

Today we all know that the UP's 'Chilean road to socialism' was a blind alley, leading the Chilean people not to socialism by peaceful means but to fascism by violent means. It can also be debated whether the class character and the objectives of the Allende government really were such as to warrant the designation 'socialist'. What is certain, however, is that with the overthrow of Allende and of Chilean democracy the question of the viability of the 'Chilean road' has already been answered: it didn't work. The Unidad Popular was defeated.

But *why* it didn't work remains an important question, and the purpose of this study is to analyze one aspect of the UP's failure, the economic aspect. What was the nature of the UP's economic project? How was it implemented, and with what consequences? In what sense is it correct to say that the Allende government's economic strategy failed, and most important of all: if it did fail – and I will assert that it did – why? To answer these questions is the main object of this study.

In view of the complete military defeat suffered by the Chilean Left on 11 September, 1973, the economic issues discussed below might appear irrelevant. 'So what,' the reader might say to himself when reading about, say, inflation, foreign trade or the production of corn in 1972, 'as long as the working class was unarmed and the enemy armed, the whole UP experiment was doomed to failure.' To this I can only say: the question of the armed forces and the UP's lack of military preparations, despite being of obvious importance, will not be analyzed in what follows. I will concentrate on economic and, to a certain extent, political matters – the latter mainly in so far as they are of importance for an understanding of economic events (and they very often are). Many of the most interesting aspects of the social and political development in 1970–73 will be almost completely neglected; this is, for example, the case with the different forms of mass mobilization and organs of working class power that more or less spontaneously emerged as the political polarization proceeded. And the Right's extra-parliamentary means to precipitate the overthrow of Allende will be dealt with only when they are directly related to the economic situation; strikes, lockouts, capital flight and economic sabotage will thus be subject to analysis – or at least description – while the growth of fascist movements and rightist para-military organizations will not. The international situation and the impact of political events in Chile's neighboring countries is another topic which, for reasons indicated above, largely falls beyond the scope of this study.

In no way do I pretend to cover the whole Chilean process, let alone attempt to explain the UP's eventual defeat with reference to economic factors only.

There are several major themes running through this study. Almost all are connected with the UP's economic program – its theoretical foundations, its political and economic implications, its internal contradictions and the efforts to implement it in a hostile environment in which the government's political adversaries, in addition to holding economic power, controlled most of the vital institutions of the Chilean state apparatus. Although the analysis concentrates on conditions specific to Chile – much space is in fact devoted to lengthy institutional descriptions which I have found necessary to include – the discussion of the above aspects of the UP program might also serve to clarify some questions of importance for our understanding of certain general problems connected with so-called constitutional transitions to socialism.

Disposition

The first three chapters are intended as background information of a political and economic character.

Chapter 1 is a brief survey, without any analytical pretensions, of a few characteristics of the state of the Chilean economy before the Unidad Popular took office. It begins with a description of the Chilean people's living standards prior to 1970, and some of the salient features of Chile's economic structure are then presented. Special attention is paid to aspects which are of interest for an understanding of the UP's economic program. This introductory chapter ends with a summary of major economic achievements – or lack of major achievements – during Eduardo Frei's Christian Democratic administration in 1964–70.

In the next chapter the economic and political climate at the time of the 1970 presidential election is presented, together with a first overview of the main programmatic objectives of the new government. The purpose is to familiarize the reader with the political environment in Chile in 1970 and with some of the most important strategic differences that existed within the ideologically heterogeneous UP coalition.

In chapter 3 some general observations regarding the Allende government's position are made. Emphasis is here put on the institutional framework – in particular on the division of power between the different bodies of the Chilean state apparatus – and on the composition of social and economic forces in Chile by the time the Unidad Popular initiated its task.

In chapter 4 the UP's short-term economic policy is studied: the main objectives and principal results of the drastically expansionary 'reactivation program' launched early in 1971.

The repercussions – inflation, bottlenecks and shortages, and stagnation of output – in 1972 and 1973 of the short-term program and of the sharpening of the political struggle are analyzed in chapter 5: Here we can study how the Allende government tried in vain to cope with the mounting economic difficulties that arose and which were in part self-made, in part created by the rightist opposition and, last but not least, the consequences of the limitations of Chile's rigid, dependent and underdeveloped economic structure.

The last part of the study is devoted to the UP's program of 'structural transformations', i.e. the formation of the state area of the economy and the agrarian reform.

The objectives of the nationalization project and the difficulties encountered in implementing it against fierce resistance are discussed in chapter 6. The internal disagreements within the UP about the question of the size of the state controlled sector and the methods to be applied in the struggle against private capital are here used to analyze further an issue touched upon on several occasions earlier in the study, namely the political and economic implications of the fundamental strategic differences that existed between the 'anti-monopolistic' and the 'anti-capitalistic' factions of the UP.

This divergency within the Chilean Left will also be used to illustrate some of the reasons for the Allende government's relative failure in carrying through a viable land reform. The analysis of the huge difficulties confronting the UP in its agrarian policies adds further support to several of the arguments advanced in the previous chapters. For in the study of the agrarian sector it becomes apparent how almost all contradictions inherent in the UP's program, in the socio-economic structure of Chile and in the general economic and political situation that prevailed during the Allende regime, converged, thus confirming the infeasibility of the strategy advocated by the dominant opinion within the Unided Popular.

A few words should finally be said about the degree of accuracy of the statistical data and other sources used in this study.

A note on the quality of Chilean statistics

The overall reliability of Chilean national accounts is, to begin with, fairly high. Since the early 1940s most of the items have been calculated in accordance with basically the same norms as those applied in the United States and Western Europe, and although the statistical error in the estimates is often appreciably greater – in part due to Chile's endemic inflation, the large distortions in relative prices and the rather crude techniques used in the deflating procedure – there are few serious biases or inconsistencies. Economists in Chile and abroad seldom hesitate to use most of these statistics, although data on physical production volumes are always regarded as preferable when assessing trends in output over time.

The degree of accuracy, however, varies substantially between the different components of the national accounts and in Chile's statistical production in general. It is easy to point out items for which the accuracy is in general regarded as 'high': population and employment statistics for the census years, volume of mineral and industrial production, balance of trade and general government, among others. Figures on agricultural production, construction, income distribution and several other areas could be classified as 'moderately accurate', while population and employment statistics for the intercensus years, in particular from rural provinces, and savings, investments, profits and inventories are among the least reliable of Chilean statistics.

There are also great differences in the methods used to make the estimates. Various survey and sample techniques naturally play a dominant role for all those items for which data covering the whole statistical population cannot easily be obtained. Simple extrapolation of population statistics is often made for the intercensus years, and a kind of regional extrapolation is sometimes used in those cases where results

4

Introduction

from Santiago are extended to cover the rest of the country. The procedures used to correct for the most obvious distortions have gradually
been refined and systematic errors reduced.

A few points specifically related to the present study need to be made.
One problem is rampant inflation. Although, after decades of experience,
Chile's statisticians have become skilled in taking a normal rate of price
increases in the range of twenty to forty per cent a year into account,
the levels reached in 1972 and 1973, and the problems arising out of the
UP's efforts to enforce strict but largely inoperative price controls, made
much of the statistical price indices, and consequently calculations based
on them, almost meaningless. For this reason physical units rather than
escudos have been used below whenever possible.

Another problem has to do with time. Some – for 1973 virtually all –
data I have used are of a preliminary character. This is, for example, the
case with the external sector, where other circumstances also contributed
to render the collection of accurate data difficult: the UP government was
quite reluctant to make certain information about capital movements
and the increasingly deteriorating foreign exchange situation public.
There are, of course, also many sectors from which the official figures had
not yet been gathered, let alone been published, by the time Allende was
ousted.

The question of *whose* figures to use also deserves a brief comment.
The general principle applied has been simple: I have mostly relied upon
official statistics provided by the UP government, in general taken from
publications by the Central Bank, the National Institute of Statistics or
the Chilean Planning Office ODEPLAN. Two studies made at the
Economic Institute of the University of Chile have also been very useful.

During the UP period the rightist opposition often published figures
from, say, Chile's National Association of Manufacturers, which were
less encouraging – or, toward the end of the Allende regime, even more
gloomy – than those from the different ministries and public institutions.
I have almost consistently abstained from making use of these and similar
sources. In the official data released between 1970 and September 1973
there existed, as far as I could judge, a political bias only in the *way* the
UP government presented its economic statistics – not in the material in
itself.

All departures from the above principle for the selection of data have
been indicated in the text or, usually, in the notes. For lack of official
data I have, for example, on a few occasions had to utilize figures on the
economic development in 1973 published in Chile after the military take-

5

over. These are however exceptions; everybody who is the least familiar with the Pinochet regime's grotesque manipulation of information knows that such data should be taken with great care.

Facts and opinions of all kinds have been obtained from Chilean newspapers and magazines, as well as from conversations with public officials, economists, politicians, and Chileans in general. Most of this information is of a qualitative nature – policy statements by leading politicians, documents, newspaper editorials, etc., which perhaps constituted the most valuable sources of all for my understanding of the social, economic and political development in Chile. Sometimes certain economic statistics have, however, also been taken from second or third hand sources such as Chilean mass media. The biases and errors that can be found in this kind of information are well known and need not be repeated here, but I should stress that the very occasional use that has been made of such sources for quantitative data can in no way affect the main conclusions of this study.

CHAPTER I

An introduction to the Chilean economy[1]

LIVING STANDARDS

Chile's *per capita* income has historically been quite respectable. It was once the highest in Latin America, and although Chile lost this position a long time ago the estimated national income of some six hundred US dollars *per capita* in the late 1960s still made Chile a country with one of the highest income levels in the Third World.

For most of the Chilean people this statistical average was out of reach, however. The vast majority of the population received far less than six hundred dollars a year:

Table 1.1   *Income distribution in Chile in 1968. Estimates of relative shares of personal income and of total income-earning population*

Income group	% of income-earning population	% of total personal income	Approximate *per capita* income[a] (US dollars)
Lower	71.5	26.0	220
Middle	24.1	28.5	710
Higher	4.4	45.5	6,200

[a] Based on the assumption of equal family sizes.

The purchasing power of the officially established subsistence wage, the so-called *sueldo vital*, at or below which about half of Chile's income earners used to be paid, was appreciably lower in 1970 than in the early 1950s.

If we look at a selection of 'social indicators' we also find many signs of widespread misery. In 1970 the rate of infant mortality was still 79 per 1,000 live births, or considerably above the average for Latin America as a whole. The availability of medical services was low and stagnating.

Rural areas, as always in Chile, stood out as particularly under-privileged. While, for example, Santiago could count on one physician

7

for every 938 inhabitants in 1969 – close to the national average of the United States – the corresponding figures in rural provinces reached one per several thousand, in Arauco almost 9,000 inhabitants per doctor. Other measures of health standards reveal a similar picture, with extremely high mortality rates and few doctors, nurses and hospitals in the Chilean countryside (as well as in the urban slum districts).

The worst enemy of the Chilean people's health was malnutrition, estimated to have been responsible for the death of at least 7,000 children a year at the end of the 1960s. According to a nation-wide nutrition survey covering the period 1965–9 more than one-third of the adult population consumed less than 2,000 calories *per capita* per day, and women and children especially in the low-income groups suffered from huge deficiencies of calories and proteins.

Various other studies indicate that perhaps half of the youth was underfed at the end of the 1960s. Of a large sample of seven-year-old children, mainly from rural provinces, 60 per cent showed clear signs of undernourishment, often serious enough to cause permanent neurological damage. At the age of two a child from a working class family was, on average, five centimetres shorter than one from the middle and upper classes.

A large and growing housing shortage and inadequate sanitary facilities constituted another problem affecting Chile's low-income groups. The average number of individuals per existing housing unit rose from 6.8 to over 7.0 between 1960 and 1970, and in the latter year the Chilean people disposed of 6.7 per cent fewer square metres of housing space *per capita* than ten years earlier. In 1970, 26.8 per cent of all existing dwellings in the cities lacked drinking water, and in rural areas the corresponding figure was 87.3 per cent.

Considerable progress in educational standards was made during the postwar period. The rate of illiteracy was reduced from 19.6 to 11.4 per cent between 1952 and 1970, and both the government of Jorge Alessandri (1958–64) and, in particular, that of Eduardo Frei (1964–70) managed to keep school enrollment far above the rate of population growth. University education expanded especially rapidly; faster, in fact, than employment opportunities for professionals with university degrees.

Higher education was, however, still a privilege for a very small minority. Although more than 95 per cent of the children entered primary school at the age of six in 1962, only 32 per cent remained enrolled until completion seven years later. Out of every 100 students who did enter secondary school in 1965 sixty-six dropped out before 1969 without

8

having graduated. Conditions outside the classrooms were such that no educational reform, however ambitious it might have been (and the Christian Democrats' reform of 1965 was quite ambitious), could prevent most of the working class youth from leaving school early in order to help support their families.

To find a job was not easy, though. Unemployment and underemployment were high. The Chilean economy continued to be a labor surplus economy, and the excess of people over productive employment opportunities showed a pronounced tendency to grow. Most of the new job seekers ended up in the services sector. The absolute number of farm workers was only insignificantly higher in 1970 than in 1930, but few of the urban immigrants could be absorbed by the industrial sector. In relative terms manufacturing employed less people in 1970 than twenty years earlier. After a marked rise during the interwar period the percentage of the labor force working in manufacturing industry experienced a slight decline in the 1950s and 1960s. The services sector was, in short, bolstered up for lack of other employment alternatives.

Although the postwar process of exclusion of wide sectors of the Chilean population from the regular labor market was mitigated somewhat during the early 1960s, the decade ended with a miserable employment situation. Out of a labor force of some 3.2 million people 260,000 were officially registered as unemployed, and about 600,000 were occupied in what ODEPLAN, the Chilean planning ministry, characterized as 'marginal activities' – that is, mainly various services with extremely low income and productivity levels. Another 150,000 people outside the labor force, appearing as 'inactive' in occupational statistics, constituted a reserve of disguised unemployment; they were willing to work, but knew that no job was available. Thus, without taking the notorious rural underemployment into account, the number of unemployed or marginally employed Chileans comprised about one-third of the economically active population.

STRUCTURAL CHARACTERISTICS

Great but poorly utilized development potentials

A concise depiction of the Chilean economy's achievements during the present century would be 'secular stagnation'. Or, to use an expression currently in vogue, 'stagflation'; the average rate of inflation between

1920 and 1970 exceeded 25 per cent a year. The following appraisal from the mid-1960s could in part illustrate what the poor economic record has signified for most of the Chilean people: 'While a relatively important and prosperous middle sector has developed, average living standards in Chile have not risen much. The conditions of the overwhelming majority of the population have probably not improved at all . . . Some important groups have suffered a substantial deterioration in their living standards.'[2]

At first glance the Chilean economy's secular stagnation might appear astonishing. Generously favored by nature and sparsely populated as it is Chile has more natural resources *per capita* than most nations in the world. A well diversified and easily exploitable physical endowment provides Chile with virtually all the prerequisites for agriculture and for manufacturing and mining industries. In general, other factors to which beneficial development effects are sometimes attributed, such as high export earnings, foreign aid and foreign investment, have not been in short supply.

But the Chilean economy as a whole has never 'taken off'. Ever since the sixteenth century temporary upswings have been followed by crises and stagnation. A wide gulf has always existed between the country's huge development potentials and the living standards that it has actually offered the majority of its inhabitants.[3] Where progress occurred it failed to spread to the other parts of the economy, or else it was of short duration. As formulated by Marto Ballesteros and Tom Davis: 'Even a brief review of Chile's economic history reveals that the growth of a particular sector has not succeeded in eliciting a strong, expansive response from the remaining sectors of the economy.'

Sectoral distribution of output and employment

This is not the place to attempt an analysis of how the above incapacity of the Chilean economy has expressed itself in the course of its history. But it must be stressed that Ballesteros and Davis' observation points to a fundamental structural defect of the economy which has historical roots dating back to colonial times. Time after time certain sectors have experienced temporary 'booms', usually generated by foreign demand and affecting mineral exports (gold and silver during colonial times, nitrates between 1880 and 1930, copper in the 1950s and 1960s). These booms have largely failed to benefit the economy as a whole, however, and once having come to an end they have left stagnation and misery behind.

This *désarticulation*, to borrow an expression introduced by Samir Amin to characterize the economic structure of a typical 'underdeveloped' country,[5] could be illustrated with the huge disparities in labor productivity found both between and within the different sectors of the Chilean economy. As a rough measure of the magnitudes of the inter-sectoral productivity differences we could compare the percentage distribution of Gross Domestic Product and of total employment. Such a comparison for 1952 and 1969 is provided in table 1.2.

From these figures we see how Chile's aggregate employment structure remained comparatively stable, while the different sectors' respective shares in the generation of GDP underwent more drastic changes, a clear symptom of structural rigidities. In particular we notice that labor productivity in mining, manufacturing and construction increased markedly, thus widening further the gap between these industries and agriculture. The relative decline in productivity of the services sector is conspicuous. From having been a 'plus sector' in 1952 services were, as a consequence of the large absorption of labor in combination with the decrease in the share of output generated, converted to a 'minus sector' with a productivity per worker falling short of the national average.

With further disaggregation we would of course find much larger productivity differences than those illustrated in table 1.2. Within agriculture, for example, labor productivity – but not productivity per hectare – was far higher on large estates than on small *minifundios*,[6] and an industrial worker in a modern plant produced several times more than a small artisan also classified as employed in manufacturing. Comparing two extremes of the Chilean labor force, a *minifundista* producing food

Table 1.2 *Distribution of GDP (at market prices) and labor force in 1952 and 1969*

	1952			1969		
	% of:			% of:		
	GDP	Labour force	Difference	GDP	Labour force	Difference
Agriculture, forestry and fishing	17.9	29.7	−11.8	7.5	25.0	−17.5
Mining, manufacturing, construction	31.8	28.7	+3.1	47.9	28.1	+19.8
Services	49.3	41.6	+7.7	44.9	46.9	−2.0

for some 100 dollars a year and a copper miner in Exotica extracting over 250 tons of pure copper a year with a value of several hundred thousand dollars, we get an impression of the vast differences that could occur in Chilean labor productivity.

What happened in postwar Chile was that employment stagnated precisely in those activities which had a high and rising labor productivity (large-scale mining and certain manufacturing industries, above all). Labor force absorption instead took place in the increasingly over-crowded services sector, leading to a concomitant loss of the type of 'transfer gains' encountered in developed, coherent economies where, at least in the long run, people tend to leave the stagnant sectors (sub-sectors, individual firms) in order to find new jobs in the rapidly expanding ones. There is a great difference between being 'pulled' to the computer industry and being 'pushed' to shoe cleaning.

But the purpose of this introduction to the Chilean economy's structure and employment rigidities is not to discuss economic development and make international comparisons. The main reason why the sectoral distribution of GDP and employment is important within the present context is that the situation described above should be kept in mind when we come to the class structure of the society that the Unidad Popular inherited and tried to transform. For the high degree of *désarticulation* of the economy not only produced economic effects, it was also very much reflected in the composition of the social forces stuggling for power in Chile in 1970–73, and its political implications were no doubt considerable. Without some knowledge of the extreme hetero-geneity in productivity and income levels between and within the different sectors of the economy much of what happened in Chile under Allende cannot be properly understood.

A brief description should also be made of two other salient features of the economic structure, features that were to play an important role in the Unidad Popular's economic and political project: the economy's high degree of foreign dependence and its monopolistic character.

Foreign dependence

Chile's formal national independence was won in the 1810s, when Spanish colonial rule was overthrown. The liberation was, however, only political. No social or economic revolution took place, and the groups dominating Chile's social and economic life prior to independence continued to do so, but without the restrictions imposed upon them by the colonial administration. The domestic élite that took over was from the very beginning closely associated with foreign commercial interests, and those who led the revolt against the Spanish Crown by no means abolished the privileges created during colonial rule: they inherited them. Their economic and political power was then used to reimport Europe; not only European consumer goods but modern Europe's current political ideas and 'way of life' as well.

This happened a long time ago. But Chile's status as a dependent country far down in the world economic hierarchy has not undergone any fundamental changes. Despite an increasingly abundant literature on the subject, 'foreign dependence' is no exact and well defined concept, and no attempt will be made here to clarify the theoretical issues involved. The importance for Chile of her vaguely defined dependence should nevertheless be stressed. Historically, foreign trade and foreign investments have had a decisive impact both upon the Chilean economy's law of motion – all its clearly discernible phases have been induced by external impulses – and upon the generation of its most outstanding structural characteristics. Added to this is the more or less indirect influence of foreign commodities and consumption patterns, foreign economic and military aid, foreign know-how and technology, foreign loans, foreign culture, foreign economic and political doctrines, etc.

But to reduce the problem of foreign dependence to manageable proportions we have to leave most of these aspects aside. In what follows only a limited selection of economic facts and figures will be presented, and the purpose is to provide a quantitative overview rather than to interpret the data.

Foreign capital had entrenched itself in many strategic activities by the late 1960s. Most of the rich mineral resources – accounting for over 85 per cent of Chile's export earnings – were directly controlled by foreign interests. Apart from the North American control of large-scale copper mining, foreign interests owned and operated all large-scale iron mining (Bethlehem Steel Co.) and close to a hundred per cent of the nitrate and iodine industry.

Besides its control of the mineral export sector, foreign capital also dominated Chile's import trade, and it is estimated that almost fifty per cent of wholesale trade was handled by foreign companies. Foreign capital monopolized telephone and telegraph services and held a majority interest in the major electricity company, it controlled five banks and had minority interests in several more, and all the main advertising agencies were either subsidiaries of foreign companies or mixed Chilean–foreign enterprises. Thus, important financial and service activities were also thoroughly penetrated by foreign capital.

In manufacturing, foreign ownership was of less importance in quantitative terms, but it was growing rapidly and was strategically distributed. Thus, while foreign interests owned 20.3 per cent of the capital stock in all Chile's industrial joint-stock companies in 1969, the foreign share in industries such as chemical products, transport equipment, rubber products, and electrical machinery and equipment – all with growth rates between two and four times as high as the overall industrial average – reached 38.3, 43.8, 45.1 and 59.9 per cent, respectively, and in all these industries foreign shareholding was so distributed that it rendered possible an effective control of between sixty and eighty per cent of all capital within each sector.

To this concentration in the most dynamic branches we should add another important feature: the heavy predominance of foreign capital in the very largest corporations. Although foreign participation existed in only about one-quarter of all Chile's industrial joint-stock companies (or in 212 out of 833), this quarter accounted for 59.5 per cent of all industrial share capital. Among the 100 largest companies, foreign ownership was found in 61, and in 40 of these the foreign holdings were large enough to guarantee the control of the administration of the company in question.

Among the investing countries the United States dominated, with some two-thirds of the value of total foreign investment in Chile. Over half of the American[7] capital was concentrated in large-scale mining.

Another aspect of foreign investments in Chile that should be observed is their rapid growth during the 1960s. The changes made at the beginning of the decade in the legislation concerning the entry of foreign capital into Chile granted foreign investors a wide range of privileges, which in part explains the dramatic upsurge of foreign investments in the years that followed. Of a total inflow of foreign capital of 1,672 million dollars between 1954 and 1970, 1,457 millions, or 87 per cent, occurred during the period 1962–70.

This massive entry of foreign capital was far from sufficient to prevent a rapid worsening of Chile's balance of foreign investments, however. The large American copper companies alone occasioned a leakage of foreign exchange in the form of profit remittances that exceeded 100 million dollars a year in the late sixties, and Chile's private foreign investment balance deteriorated from a yearly average of −68.5 million

Structural characteristics

dollars in 1955–9 and −87.1 in 1960–4 to −199.1 in 1968–70, the latter corresponding to almost 20 per cent of total export earnings.

There also existed in Chile, as in other underdeveloped, dependent countries, a large foreign dominance even within that part of industry which was not wholly or partially owned by foreign capital. As described by Andre Gunder Frank:

> Through affiliates of metropolitan corporations, through joint metropolitan–Chilean enterprise, through licensing arrangements, through trade marks and patents, through metropolitan owned or controlled advertising agencies, and through a host of other institutional arrangements, much of the Chilean consumer goods industry is also coming to have an ever increasing satellite dependency on the metropolis.[8]

Of the various mechanisms mentioned above those related to technology are of special interest. The type of capital-intensive and 'luxury-intensive' industrialization that Chile embarked upon during the 1950s and 1960s was to a large extent sustained by imports of technology through direct foreign investment and/or through various licensing and royalty arrangements. The importance of the latter was growing rapidly – in part due to an advantageous tax legislation – and while foreign direct investments in Chilean manufacturing were mainly found in the largest corporations within the modern sectors, licensing and royalty arrangements with Chilean industrialists covered a wide range of different industries with different characteristics.

Together with the denationalization of the Chilean economy through direct foreign investment and various forms of technological subordination to foreign capital, Chile also increased her dependence on foreign loans and on foreign exchange in general. In 1970 the public sector had accumulated a foreign debt exceeding 3 thousand million dollars, and the

Table 1.3 *Service payments on foreign capital and ratio of service payments to exports of goods and services 1958–68 (based on annual averages, millions of dollars)*

Period	Service payments[a]	Exports	Ratio of service payments to export earnings
1958–64	237	549	43.1
1965–68	467	953	49.0

[a] Including amortization and interest payments plus profits and depreciations of direct investments.

15

private sector, also increasingly dependent on foreign credits which financed thirty per cent of all private investments, contributed with another 600 million dollars in foreign debt. As a result of this heavy borrowing Chile increased her foreign debt more than sixfold between 1960 and 1970, and amortization and interest payments came to constitute a heavier and heavier burden. At the end of the sixties total payments on foreign capital absorbed almost fifty per cent of Chile's export earnings.

This mounting debt burden had not yet given rise to serious import problems. The difference between export earnings and service payments continued to rise in absolute terms, and as seen in table 1.4 the constantly growing inflow of foreign financial resources made it possible to increase substantially the net capacity to import during the whole postwar period.

The fact that Chile was extremely favored with respect to the terms of trade during the 1960s did not prevent her from having become the most indebted country in the world *per capita*[9] when the copper bonanza was coming to an end in 1970. The high copper incomes served to accelerate the process. Given the Chilean governments' traditionally almost unlimited acceptance of all foreign loans within reach, the creditor countries' confidence in Chile's capacity to pay has, together with strictly political considerations, been the main regulator of the amount of credits granted. It is hardly a coincidence that the periods of huge foreign borrowing (the 1920s and the 1960s) have coincided with palmy days for Chile's mineral exporters.

This pattern has had a destabilizing impact on Chile's import capacity. Debts have been incurred when export earnings have been high and rising, but once balance of payment difficulties have arisen credit lines have been cut and serious adjustment problems have had to be coped with.

It should also be pointed out that an important lesson from Chile's historical experiences in this field is that a powerful 'ratchet effect' of

Table 1.4 *Index of Chile's net capacity to import, selected years (1947–100)*

Year	Import capacity
1947	100.0
1960	215.7
1969	507.8

growing dependence upon imports seems to have been operating whenever the external sector has prospered. The situation described below by Andre Gunder Frank could hardly have occurred in an economy which had not been 'spoilt' by recurrent invasions of foreign exchange and imported commodities:

Having been a producer of capital equipment in the nineteenth century, Chile now has to import 90 per cent of its investment in plant and equipment. Provided by nature with ample coal, petroleum and hydraulic resources, Chile nevertheless has to import fuels. Having been a major exporter of wheat and livestock products, Chile is now highly dependent on food imports.[10]

The only major sector where the Chilean economy, instead of ceding ground to imports, showed a manifest tendency towards self-sufficiency was the consumer goods industry. By 1970 the share of consumer goods other than foodstuffs in total imports had been reduced to less than ten per cent, and the century-long process during which imports changed from being a constant threat to Chile's incipient consumer goods industry to being its vital supplier of raw materials, fuels, and capital goods was practically completed.

But the fact that the process of import substitution of consumer goods was coming to an end also signified that the dynamics with which it had periodically provided the economy were becoming saturated (given existing income distribution and price structure). The basis upon which this apparent success in import substitution rested was, furthermore, exceedingly fragile. Besides the heavy dependence on imports of capital goods and the large import content of the expansive industries, the reliance upon foreign financing and foreign technology had both increased the economy's vulnerability to adverse external conditions and earmarked an appreciable part of export earnings for service payment purposes. The foreign penetration also accentuated the *désarticulation* of the economy as well as its highly monopolistic and inegalitarian character.

The Chilean economy's monopolistic structure

A large number of studies confirm the high degree of concentration of ownership and control of all important sectors of the Chilean economy, as well as the existence of a handful of powerful interest groups, or 'clans', which through their control of a wide range of different financial and industrial activities exercised a dominant influence over the economy as a whole.

An introduction to the Chilean economy

Within manufacturing, the 833 joint-stock companies that existed in 1969 accounted for over two-thirds of the whole output of Chile's industrial establishments (about 35,000, including crafts). Of these 833 joint-stock companies 277, or about one-quarter, controlled 82 per cent of the total capital stock. The individual branches or subsectors were, with very few exceptions, dominated by one to three big corporations whose combined market shares exceeded 50 per cent. In industries controlled by foreign capital the monopolistic structure was especially pronounced.

In wholesale trade conditions were similar. In 1967 twelve companies out of a total of 2,600 accounted for 44 per cent of total sales. Of the commercial banks the largest one, Banco de Chile, provided 32 per cent, and the largest five 57.4 per cent of all private bank credit.

To this concentration of industrial production, banking activity and wholesale trade (not to mention agriculture and mining, which will be dealt with separately in chapters 6 and 7) into a limited number of large units we should add the concentration of ownership that existed. In 59 per cent of the 271 dominant industrial corporations the ten largest shareholders owned over 90 per cent of all shares, and in 85 per cent of the cases their share surpassed 50 per cent. Figures which, of course, indicate a still higher degree of control of the administration of the companies.

The major shareholders tended, furthermore, to be identical in a large number of different corporations, and their economic power embraced all vital sectors of the economy. The 'commanding heights' of the Chilean economy can, in fact, be said to have been in the hands of about fifteen large economic groups which were present in every private industrial, financial and commercial activity of importance. The mightiest of these clans, the Edwards family, intimately linked to the dominant American interests operating in Chile, alone controlled one commercial bank, seven financial and investment corporations, five insurance companies, thirteen industries and two publishing houses. With respect to the latter, of prime importance for the reproduction of the political views and ideology of the extreme Right, the supremacy of the Edwards group in the Chilean market used to be disproportionately large. In the late 1960s its newspaper chain *El Mercurio* alone supplied over half of the total circulation of dailes in the country, and its publishing house Lord Cochrane an even higher share of the supply of weekly magazines. Together with the closely associated Editorial Zig-Zag the Edwards controlled almost 100 per cent of the whole Chilean market for magazines, comics, etc.

The main adversaries of the Unidad Popular were, in short, not only extremely powerful in the economic field, they had a large amount of vital resources in the ideological struggle as well.

To facilitate an understanding of the Allende government's heritage a few words should finally be said about the economic project of the Christian Democratic administration and about the specific situation in which the Chilean economy found itself by the late 1960s.

THE CHRISTIAN DEMOCRATS' 'REVOLUTION IN FREEDOM'

The reform program of Eduardo Frei – marketed as 'Revolution in Freedom' – was ambitious in the sense that it clearly recognized a large number of structural defects of the Chilean economy. It was the first systematic attempt on the continent to implement a development strategy in accordance with the ideology of the most advanced representatives of Latin American bourgeois reformism: the Alliance for Progress and the Economic Commission for Latin America. Its main ingredients – agrarian reform, redistribution of income, emphasis on industrial growth and reliance upon foreign aid, trade and investment – could all be found in expositions from the Alliance for Progress and ECLA from the early 1960s, although with different emphasis, ECLA always giving prominence to the necessity of industrialization and of social reforms and the Alliance for Progress to the foreign ingredients.

Like most other Chilean presidents Frei promised an accelerated rate of economic growth, a gradual cut-back in inflation and unemployment and an improvement of living standards, especially for the poor majority. But unlike most of his predecessors Frei provided a catalogue of means through which this development was to come about. In the field of economic policy the state was to play a far more active role than during the two earlier administrations; public investments were to increase, and through the channelling of financial resources according to state-determined priorities specific targets in the sectoral distribution of GDP were to be achieved. Industry was to be given preferential treatment, and its share of GDP was supposed to increase from some 26 per cent to slightly over 30. The relative share of mining was also to increase, while the expansion of the services sector would be halted and its share of GDP drastically curtailed. The instruments chosen to steer this selective growth were public investment and credit policy and a stimulation of the entry of foreign capital and technology.

To advance towards a solution of the long-standing agrarian problem, the government set up ambitious targets for agrarian reform. The totally insufficient legislation from the Alessandri period would be changed so as to permit a 'revolution' in the land tenure system to take place, and according to initial promises 100,000 new peasants proprietors were to be created in six years.

To improve conditions of life for the Chilean masses and to correct the admittedly distorted pattern of growth a radical redistribution of income was to be undertaken, partly through increase of the legal minimum wage and improvements in the social security system and partly by giving the underprivileged poor access to educational facilities on a massive scale. To counteract the economic, social and political 'marginalization' heavy emphasis was put on encouraging initiatives to stimulate organizations 'from below': and the possibilities of 'participation' – the most commonly used slogan – were to be extended to virtually all categories of powerless Chileans.

The importance of national solidarity was stressed. A condition for the success of the 'Revolution in Freedom' was said to be the 'communitarian cooperation' of all groups and classes. Although being far from anti-imperialistic, the Christian Democrats' program also contained references to 'reduction of the foreign dependence' and 'perfection of the national sovereignty'. Concrete indications of how this was to be attained were few, however, and apart from the much talked about program of 'Chilean-ization' of the large US-owned copper mines, discussed in chapter 6, the struggle for national independence was assumed to be a spiritual rather than tangible process.

Unlike Jorge Alessandri in 1958 and Salvador Allende in 1970, Eduardo Frei and the Christian Democrats took office during a period of rapid economic expansion. The outlook for the Chilean economy looked good. The friendly relations with the United States – which had provided generous financial support to Frei during his election campaign – promised a continuation of the inflow of foreign aid, loans and private investments, and the escalation of the United States' war in South-East Asia guaranteed a good market for Chilean copper.

To these external stimuli which the Chilean economy could count on we should add the dynamic components of Frei's reform program, such as the role of the state as promoter of economic growth. Public invest-ment – including loans to the private sector from state-controlled credit institutions – grew at an annual rate of some ten per cent between 1964 and 1970, thus giving the government the direct or indirect control of about three-quarters of all investment decisions by the end of the period.

The active support of manufacturing provided the economy with another impulse. During the 1960s Chile entered a new stage of import substitution through the creation of new industries producing consumer durables and a rapid expansion of the existing ones. Protected by almost prohibitive tariffs and quantitative restrictions and benefiting from various forms of public subsidies, the industries producing cars, televisions, etc., greatly increased their output, as is shown in table 1.5.

The growth of these and other modern industries entailed a considerable shift in the composition of output within the manufacturing sector.

Exports, public investments and the consumer durables industry continued their rapid, although somewhat erratic, expansion up to 1969. Nevertheless, overall economic activity succeeded in sustaining its high rate of growth during only the first two years of the Frei administration. As from 1967 the Chilean economy once again revealed its inherent tendency toward stagnation. GDP *per capita* increased with only one per cent as an annual average during 1967–70, and in agriculture, manufacturing, construction and basic services output *per capita* in 1970 even fell slightly short of the 1966 levels.

Table 1.5   *Annual production of selected consumer durables, 1964 and 1969 (thousands of units)*

	1964	1969
Televisions	7.2	110.0
Record-players	13.0	81.8
Cars	7.8	22.1

Table 1.6   *Value added in manufacturing, percentage shares 1960 and 1970*

	1960	1970
Traditional industries [a]	54.8	45.5
Intermediate industries [b]	30.4	32.0
Dynamic industries [c]	14.8	22.5

[a] Food, beverages, tobacco, textiles, clothing and footwear, furniture, printing and publishing, and miscellaneous.

[b] Wood, paper and paper products, leather and leather products, rubber products, chemical products, petroleum and coal products, basic metals, and non-metallic mineral products.

[c] Metal products, machinery, electrical products, and transport equipment.

Table 1.7   *Composition of the creation of new employment 1960 – 70 (percentages)*

	1960 – 64	1964 – 7	1967 – 70
Production of goods	44.3	37.4	18.5
Basic services	10.5	4.5	10.3
Other services	45.2	58.1	71.2

After 1966 the recession thus became especially pronounced in the goods-producing sectors, the growth rates of which tended to lag appreciably behind the growth of the economy as a whole. The Christian Democratic government's failure to create new employment in these sectors was conspicuous. As table 1.7 shows, the postwar trend towards services was not reversed but reinforced.

After six years of 'Revolution in Freedom' all the government's major promises remained unfulfilled. The rate of economic growth had declined, as compared with the preceding period; the two good years 1965 and 1966 were followed by four poor ones, and the Chilean economy's inegalitarian pattern of demand and resource allocation had become further accentuated. Despite favorable external conditions and heavy public investment the rate of gross investment had tapered off, to amount to no more than 15–16 per cent of GDP in 1969–70, as against 17–18 per cent in 1965–6 and 26.9 per cent projected in the economic plans of 1965. Like all previous governments during the twentieth century the Christian Democrats also failed to come to grips with inflation, which accelerated throughout the 1967–70 recession when the consumer price index rose 21.9, 27.9, 29.3 and 34.9 per cent a year.

The government had, in short, proved unable to change the fundamental behavior of the economy. All Chile's major social and economic problems remained to be solved, and the immediate economic prospects were far from bright. By the end of the Frei administration Chile exhibited clear symptoms of going through a crisis of the kind experienced in the mid fifties: a combination of galloping inflation and stagnation. In contrast to the previous crisis, however, the foreign debt now amounted to several years' export earnings, and the Chilean people now owed foreign banks and aid organizations more than three hundred US dollars *per capita*.

CHAPTER 2

The Unidad Popular

POLITICAL BACKGROUND AND THE ELECTION OF SALVADOR ALLENDE

Together with Uruguay, Chile used to be presented as the model of democracy in Latin America. On the surface, it displayed an amazing stability and sophisticated parliamentarism. Military coups and other forms of non-constitutional transfers of power have been rare, and in terms of continuity of governments it has been said that Chile's political history between the 1830s and 1973 would make most European countries look like 'banana republics'. Another feature of Chilean politics that made the country stand out as different from most others – developed and under-developed alike – was the apparent lack of political violence. Between 1837 and 1970 no leading Chilean statesman or high-ranking military officer was assassinated.

This was the official picture, but other aspects of Chile's past should be remembered as well. Behind its institutional stability and tranquility Chile's history has always been full of class confrontations, full of violence, repression, massacres and concentration camps. One example can be enough: conservative estimates give a figure of some 5,000 Chilean workers shot dead by police and army in about twenty big massacres between 1900 and 1970.[1]

This is not the place to make an exposition of Chile's political history, but one thing deserves to be emphasized. For an understanding of Chile's political past and the environment in which the forces making up the Unidad Popular grew up and were shaped, the two parallel traditions of almost uninterrupted parliamentarism and of violence, repression and militant mass struggle should be recalled.

Tradition has played an important role in past and present social struggles in Chile, and both the 'establishment' and the popular movements have a history of oft-evoked memorable events, dates and heroes. This historical consciousness helps to explain why such typical Latin American phenomena as populist or right wing movements headed by

23

civil or military *caudillos* have been of such limited importance in Chile; they have been able to dominate the political scene only for very short periods, and they have never managed to destroy the Left's political organizations. The latter remained for several decades, despite periods of repression and recurrent splits, the best organized and most influential working-class parties in the whole of South America. They were supported by one of the continents's most advanced trade union movements and their electoral successes were sometimes remarkable. In the 1941 parliamentary elections, for example, the Marxist parties managed to capture over 30 per cent of the votes.

In view of these circumstances – and many others, of course, which have to be left out in this necessarily meagre overview of Chile's political traditions – it is far from surprising that Chile was to become the first country in the Western Hemisphere to elect a Marxist president. But why in 1970? And why did the non-Marxist majority permit Salvador Allende to take office? And in what state was the country handed over to the new administration? A brief look at the situation in Chile before and immediately after the presidential election can, I hope, serve to clarify these questions, of obvious importance for an understanding of the specific conjuncture in which the new government initiated its work.

The crisis of the late sixties

Although the term general crisis is in no sense absolute but must be identified in terms of origin, degree of intensity and general dissemination throughout the society, there can be little doubt that Chile, during the last years of the Frei government, displayed a wide range of symptoms. The problem of acute economic stagnation has already been discussed. It remains to look at the socio-political atmosphere.

To begin with, a clear sign of widespread discontent was the declining popular support for the governing party as manifested in successive electoral defeats. In 1964 Eduardo Frei received 56.1 per cent of the votes and the support of a quite heterogenous coalition of voters. His successor as presidential candidate, Radomiro Tomic, was abandoned both by the Left and, above all, by the Right, and received in 1970 27.8 per cent, less than half of Frei's percentage. In the parliamentary elections the share of the Christian Democratic Party (Partido Demócrata Cristiano, PDC) fell from 42.3 per cent in 1965 to 29.8 per cent in 1969. Electoral participation declined considerably, possibly indicating dissatisfaction with the system at large. Absenteeism increased from 19.4

(1965) to 29.5 per cent (1969) of registered voters. At the same time, the two big Marxist parties advanced – the Communist Party (Partido Communista, PC) from 12.4 to 16.6 per cent and the Socialist Party (Partido Socialista, PS) from 10.3 to 12.8 per cent between 1965 and 1969.

In the late 1960s Chilean party politics were characterized by a significant swing to the Left and by a pronounced polarization, tendencies which were reflected both between and within the different parties. Within the Christian Democratic Party an internal split became inevitable as the economic and political rule of the rightist faction, headed by Eduardo Frei, turned increasingly repressive. In 1969, after the government's third big massacre,[2] an influential group of members of the PDC repudiated the party and formed a new movement, MAPU (Movimiento de Acción Popular Unitaria), which later became perhaps the most leftist political force within the UP coalition. The Radical Party (Partido Radical, PR), a faithful barometer of Chilean politics,[3] also suffered a split. A conservative minority left the party, began to call themselves Radical Democrats (Democracia Radical, DR) and initiated a rapid march towards the extreme Right, while the majority declared the PR socialist (later on even revolutionary, which occasioned a new split) and integrated itself into the electoral preparations of the UP.

The Socialist and Communist Parties remained by and large intact, but internal discord was growing and for the PS especially the 1960s signified a marked radicalization. The old leadership of the party was replaced by representatives of the by then majority leftist segment, whose political line in several important respects was very close to that of the recently founded Movement of the Revolutionary Left (Movimiento de Izquierda Revolucionaria, MIR), by far the most influential revolutionary group to the Left of the traditional parties. The Socialist Party's National Congress in 1967 adopted, for example, resolutions stating that 'the pacific and electoral struggles can only be accepted as limited forms of action' and emphasized the necessity to prepare the Chilean workers for armed struggle. This was in sharp contrast to the Communist Party, which continued to offer the parliamentary road to socialism as the only viable possibility.[4]

Important changes also occurred outside the realm of the traditional political parties. In the countryside the mass of *campesinos* (smallholders and landless farmworkers) – whose expectations had risen sharply after 1964, only to become frustrated during the latter half of the Christian Democratic administration – began to mobilize and fight for their interests in a way never seen in Chile before. Rural trade unions, which prior to 1964 were subject to a host of legal restrictions and hardly existed at all, proliferated to embrace, by 1970, well over 100,000 members. Strikes and land occupations became increasingly common.[5]

The entire trade union movement in fact underwent a rapid development, after more than a decade of relative stagnation. Thus, while in 1953 there were 2,067 trade unions with 298,000 members and in 1964 1,863 different unions with a total of 271,000 members, in 1970 the corresponding figures had increased to 4,519 and 551,000, respectively,[6] representing about 20 per cent of all wage and salary earners. Within manufacturing industry 36 per cent of the work force – and over 50 per cent of large-scale industry – was organized.[7]

To this quantitative development of the labor movement we should add the tendency toward growing militancy among Chile's organized and unorganized workers. Two general strikes were organized between 1967 and 1970, and in the latter year, when confrontations reached a peak, 5,295 labor conflicts affecting more than 300,000 workers were registered.[8]

A traditionally unorganized and political rather passive group also began to mobilize: the *pobladores*, the slum dwellers living in the vast squatter settlements (*poblaciones*) encircling all Chilean cities, and Santiago in particular. Although earlier signs of social unrest within these areas of widespread misery had not been lacking (in 1957, for example, tens of thousands of poorly dressed and underfed *pobladores* invaded and pillaged the centre of Santiago in a sudden outburst of spontaneous, violent protest[9]), it was not until the late 1960s that conscious, organized political work took root in the urban slum. As in the case of the *campesinos*, the Christian Democrats were initially the most active political party.[10] Under the auspices of the Catholic Church and the PDC a plethora of organizations (Neighborhood Councils, Mothers' Centres, Parents' Centres, etc.) grew up in the *poblaciones*, organizations which constituted the cornerstones of the PDC's ambitious program of 'popular promotion' (*promoción popular*) for the urban poor.[11] But the *pobladores* turned out to be – and here again the parallel with the *campesinos* is obvious – far easier to radicalize than the PDC had originally thought and hoped, and the creation of various 'communitarian organizations' gave the Left an excellent platform that it had failed to create by itself. In 1970 only a handful of Santiago's *poblaciones* were controlled

26

by the PDC, and the 'popular promoters' sent out from the party were to an increasing extent replaced by the riot police, who responded to the more and more common illegal land seizures with tear gas and machine guns. As in many other fields the Christian Democrats' 'Popular Promotion' produced a boomerang effect.[12] The rising expectations among the *pobladores* were bound to clash with a deteriorating social and economic reality, and in a large number of *poblaciones* the PDC organizations for cooptation to society were both taken over by the Left and complemented with 'popular militias' (*milicias populares*).

Thus, the Chilean political scene in 1970 presented clear symptoms of disintegration, reflected both in confusion and splits within the traditional parties and in the upsurge of militant forms of mass struggle such as land occupations, strikes and even armed propaganda attacks *à la Tupamaros* upon banks, supermarkets and public institutions. Student rebellion added to the turmoil. The Left was on the offensive; the Unidad Popular was created in the midst of a prolonged economic, social and political crisis, and Chile's traditional bourgeois institutions were questioned not only by an élite of left-wing politicians but to an increasing extent by the masses themselves. The milieu in which the presidential election was held is well described by Eduardo Labarca:

Not one day elapsed without a strike breaking out, without a new land seizure taking place or without 10, 50 or up to 200 *fundos* remaining occupied by the farm workers. Right in the middle of the election campaign the first general strike of *campesinos* was realized, and 55 days before the elections a general national strike was successfully carried through.[13]

The presidential election

In view of what has been said above we might perhaps expect a convincing victory for the candidate of the Left, but several factors impeded an easy translation of social unrest into votes for Salvador Allende. First, there was the problem of electoral participation. Wide sectors of the recently radicalized groups were excluded from voting, either because they were illiterates or because they simply had not bothered to go through all the bureaucratic formalities required for electoral registration. Second there was the well known phenomenon of a strengthening of the extreme Right in times of a social crisis – 'law and order', etc. The candidature of Radomiro Tomic, finally, served to disseminate confusion among many of the unorganized people vacillating to the Left. Tomic's electoral platform coincided, at least formally, in many vital aspects with that of Salvador Allende, and his terminology, heavily loaded with expressions such as 'capitalism', 'neo-capitalism', 'oligarchy' and 'imperialism', gave quite as radical an impression as Allende's.

What favored Allende was the split of the non-Marxist opposition. In contrast to the 1964 election, which was basically an uneven fight between Frei and Allende, the Chilean people had in 1970 a choice of three apparently equally strong candidates: Allende, Tomic and Jorge Alessandri, the latter backed by the rightists parties, mainly the National Party (Partido Nacional, PN).

But while it is true that this non-Marxist split made it possible for Allende to win a relative majority in a three-cornered fight, it is difficult to imagine how the opposition's split could have been avoided. The still powerful PDC could not withdraw their candidate without a further acceleration of the decomposition of the party, and it was equally impossible for the Chilean Right to accept that Chile would be left with a choice between two candidates whose anti-capitalistic messages were difficult to distinguish from each other. The Right might have accepted another PDC candidate – Frei, perhaps, but the Chilean constitution prevented the re-election of an incumbent president – but never Tomic, and Tomic was the obvious man to run for the Christian Democrats. For decades he had been second only to Frei in the party, he was the only leading DC politician who was not directly discredited by the government's domestic failure (Tomic was Chile's ambassador to the United States), and he was the only one who could revitalize the reformist image of the party in the eyes of the voters. It is also clear that, had the 1970 election been a fight between one rightist and one leftist candidate, Allende's percentage of the votes would have increased markedly since a considerable share of the votes for Tomic would have been given to him.

As for Allende, member and founder of Chile's Socialist Party, his organized support came from the parties and movements making up the Popular Unity (Unidad Popular, UP), a coalition with the Communist and Socialist Parties as driving forces, but also including the Radical Party (PR) and MAPU, the leftist offshoot of the Christian Democrats, and two insignificant Social Democratic groups.

To general surprise, as Alessandri was considered to be the favorite, the election on 4 September gave the results shown in table 2.1.

Political background

Table 2.1   *Results of the 1970 presidential election*

	Number of votes	Percentage
Allende	1,070,334	36.3
Alessandri	1,031,159	34.9
Tomic	821,801	27.8
Blank and invalid votes	31,505	1.1
Total	2,954,977	100.0

From winning an election to taking office: September–October 1970

The small majority obtained by Allende did not automatically make him president. According to the Chilean constitution the National Congress[14] had to decide between the two leading candidates if no one received over 50 per cent of the votes. Normally a mere formality – in no case had the Chilean Congress refused to appoint the candidate with the largest percentage vote – the outcome of the second voting was this time quite uncertain, and the period between 4 September and 24 October, when congressional ratification was to take place, witnessed a sequence of dramatic events and right-wing maneuvers intended to prevent Allende from taking office.

Interesting as these events were they do not all interest us in this context. But because of their relevance for the future economic and political situation in Chile some of them cannot be completely neglected. What happened in September–October had a considerable influence both upon the new administration's choice of short-term economic policy and upon the political strategy adopted. Thus, we will briefly look at two important aspects of the post-election events: the attitude of the opposition to Allende and the financial panic that broke out immediately after the result of the election was known.[15]

The rightist plots

The Chilean Right – and here we must include President Frei and his followers – refused to recognize Allende's inconclusive victory. As a first effort to stop Allende the National Party tried to mobilize support from the PDC in order to obtain the Christian Democrats' congressional votes for the number two of the presidential candidates, Jorge Alessandri.

According to this 'Alessandri formula' – which was made public and is said to have counted on the government's and Frei's tacit approval – Alessandri would, once elected by Congress, resign and call for new elections, thus permitting Frei to run for the whole Right and confront Allende in a two-man race.

This plan failed, mainly thanks to the resolution of the Left – including, this time, Radomiro Tomic – and to the indecision of the Christian Democratic Right. The adherents of the *Unidad Popular*, and in particular the trade union movement, issued menacing statements declaring their firm decision to 'defend the victory' – if necessary, with arms – and Tomic and the whole DC Left repeatedly assured Allende of their full support in the coming congressional vote. Faced by the certainty of a split in the party and the possibility of a civil war, the leadership of the PDC decided to discard the 'Alessandri formula' and took up negotiations with the UP instead in order to obtain a constitutional amendment that would formally guarantee what the PDC called the 'survival of democracy'. After the UP's acceptance of the main ingredients of the Christian Democrats'.proposal, which in no way compromised the basic program of the UP but which nevertheless contained some inexpedient clauses (cf. ch. 3, note 8), the constitutional road was effectively blocked for the opposition, which had to resort to other means when trying to stop Allende.

The post-election economic crisis

The immediate reaction to the election result was financial panic: bank accounts were liquidated by worried Chileans planning to flee the country[16], the Central Bank's sales of dollars for 'tourist' trips abroad increased more than threefold in September as compared to preceding months[17], the dollar rate went up sharply on the black market, indicating capital flight, and the Santiago Stock Exchange index fell over 50 per cent in two weeks.[18] Soon the effects spread to other sectors as well. Building projects were cancelled and construction workers laid off; investments were postponed and retail sales of consumer durables fell off sharply. In the countryside the big landowners, for sabotage purposes or out of pure fear, interrupted the springtime sowing and began to slaughter cows, even reproductive cattle.

At the beginning the Frei government added to the panic rather than trying to check it. An important role in this context was played by a highly alarmistic radio and television speech by the Finance Minister, Andrès Zaldìvar, who depicted the state of the national economy as disastrous, putting the blame on the election result and adding much fuel to the crisis.[19] Also important were the activities of certain foreign interests operating in Chile[20] which elaborated a plan for economic sabotage. For example, the following recommendations were distributed to the North American companies in Chile:

1. Banks should not renew credits or should delay in doing so. 2. Companies should drag their feet in sending money, in making deliveries, in shipping spare parts, etc. 3. Savings and loan companies are in trouble. If pressure were applied they would have to shut their doors, thereby creating stronger pressure . . . 4. Companies in a position to do so should close their doors . . .[21]

But this plan failed, too. The American companies were, in general, not very cooperative,[22] and at the beginning of October it was clear that the difficult economic situation would not turn into a collapse, whatever is understood by collapse. Banking activity was returning to normal,[23] and although unemployment continued to rise the immediate threat of chaos seemed to be over. The hope that a 'swiftly deteriorating economy would touch off a wave of violence, resulting in a military coup'[24] was far from fulfilled, and the army was, according to the plotters, held back by the Commander-in-Chief, René Schneider, among others, who was reported as unwilling to 'budge an inch without Frei's okay'.[25] And Frei, 'playing the part of Hamlet', finally said no, after much vacillation.[26]

The first of the UP's battle was practically won. When, in a last attempt to provoke military intervention, groups from the extreme Right, headed by ex-General Roberto Viaux, initiated a terror campaign which culminated in the assassination of Schneider two days before the congressional vote, the effects were totally counter-productive. The deed was repudiated by an almost unanimous opinion, and the Right found itself more isolated than ever. On 24 October, Allende was elected president with votes for Unidad Popular and the whole PDC, and on 3 November he and the UP government formally took office.

The significance of the September–October events

In September something that hardly required proof was proved, namely that a Marxist can win a majority in a Latin American election. In November it was proved that a Marxist, if elected, can be permitted to take office, albeit not without certain difficulties. But what interests us here is the importance that the post-electoral events came to have for the economic and political development in Chile in the years that followed. There are four points that deserve to be made.

1. The economy that the UP inherited had not only been stagnating for four years, it was also in an acute state of depression and uncertainty. The main economic decision makers had little, if any, confidence in the new government. This circumstance had substantial influence upon the short-term economic project the UP was elaborating in the middle of the crisis.

2. The position taken by the Christian Democrats increased the UP's expectations of being able to establish a parliamentary alliance with the DC Left. (It should also be observed that the role played in the September–October plots by Frei and other leading rightists within the PDC was largely unknown in Chile before the publication of the *ITT documents* in 1972.)

3. Both the election result and the ensuing events – above all the official attitude of the PDC and the (temporary) isolation of the National Party – strengthened the moderate, 'pragmatic' line within the UP (i.e. Communists, supported by Radicals) at the expense of the more leftist sectors.

4. The extreme Right's extra-parliamentary machinations, which culminated in the assassination of Schneider, considerably strengthened the overall position of the Left. A large part of the Right was strongly discredited, and the split within the anti-UP forces had been accentuated. The initially shaky UP coalition, on the other hand, looked united, disciplined and resolute. It looked so mighty that the easily frightened *US News and World Report* could announce: 'Make no mistake about this: Chile is going Communist . . . What remains in opposition in Chile is little more than a divided Christian Democratic Party that has been calling for an end to capitalism for years. In that party, moderates are a minority. Says our man in South America: "A strong leftist tide is running in Chile".'[27]

Many Chileans were equally worried, and quite a few sold their houses – beautiful homes were sold for 1,000 US dollars or less during the last few months of 1970 – packed their bags and left the country. What was the character of the program that had frightened them so?

PROGRAM AND STRATEGY

A necessary starting point for an understanding of what happened in Chile after the election of Salvador Allende is the program of the Unidad

Popular, agreed upon in 1969 (before an agreement on whom to select as presidential candidate was reached) by all the political forces making up the UP. The importance of this program, *Programa Básico del Gobierno de la Unidad Popular*, must be stressed. There can be little doubt that both the government and the opposition took the program seriously, judging it not as an electoral platform later to be more or less forgotten but as a document containing central political and economic objectives that the UP was bent on reaching.

This program and the UP's attempts to implement it will also be a major subject of attention in this study.[28] Some emphasis must, then, be put on the Allende government's explicitly political aims. Traditional economic criteria would clearly be insufficient in the case of the UP, whose programmatic objectives were not confined to the more efficient administration of an existing society but consisted in the simultaneous destruction of an old social and economic order and the laying of the foundations for a new one.

In order to get a better understanding of what the UP wanted to achieve and why, we will first take a look at the UP's own analysis of the main economic and social ills that affected the Chilean society at the time the new government took over.

The UP diagnosis of the Chilean society

The *Basic Program* asserts: Chile is going through a deep crisis, manifested in social and economic stagnation, in widespread poverty and in all kinds of deprivations that workers, *campesinos* and other exploited classes are subject to, as well as in the growing difficulties that confront white collar workers, professionals, and businessmen with small- or medium-sized enterprises, and in the miserable employment opportunities open to women and youth.

What is it that has failed? What has failed in Chile is a system which does not correspond to today's requirements. Chile is a capitalist country, dependent upon imperialism and dominated by sectors of the bourgeoisie which are structurally tied to foreign capital and which cannot solve the country's fundamental problems, problems which derive precisely from the bourgeoisie's class privileges which will never be given up voluntarily.

Let us also look at a couple of summaries made by the key persons in the UP's economic team during the first two years, Amérigo Zorrilla (Communist, Finance Minister 1970–72) and Pedro Vuskovic (Independent, Minister of Economy 1970–72). In his first exposition in Congress

of the 'actual state of the Chilean economy'[29] Zorrilla describes the
economy as characterized by

three outstanding features which up to now have defined our economy: its
monopolistic character, the situation of dependence, and the big monopolies'
utilization of the State for their own benefit. In economic terms the main effects
of this system . . . can be summarized as follows:

1. An enormous inequality in the distribution of income . . .
2. Unemployment . . .
3. Underutilization of installed capacity . . .
4. Inflation . . .
5. Economic stagnation . . .

Vuskovic's summary[30] is similar:

In short, the stagnation, the inflation, the inequality, the unemployment and the
denationalization of the economy were the inevitable results of the type of
capitalist dependence that characterized the Chilean economy and society. The
State itself, with its tradition of heavy intervention in the national economy,
merely acted as an accomplice in the process of monopolization and dependence
inherent in the system.

How these conclusions were reached is of minor interest to us here.
What makes them important is the fact that they ought to be taken
seriously and in no way discarded as mere propagandistic statements,
since they did constitute the basis of the economic and political strategy
adopted by the UP.

Political objectives

We shall return on several occasions in the chapters that follow to the
specific components of the new government's program. This section is
intended as a brief overview only, indicating the character of the
transfer of political and economic power envisaged by the UP.

The decisive passage of the program reads: 'The united popular forces
seek as the central aim of their policy to replace the present economic
structure, to put an end to the power of national and foreign monopolistic capital and of latifundism in order to initiate the construction of
socialism.'

To dispel imperialism and the domestic oligarchy – the terms most
commonly used by the UP when defining the 'popular forces'' main
enemies – was regarded as imperative for both economic and political

reasons. First, it was indispensable for the establishment of 'popular power' (*poder popular*), which alone could guarantee the development of a genuine democracy in Chile. It was also looked upon as a necessary condition for economic development. The whole UP diagnosis of Chile's underdevelopment was based on the fundamental assumption – or, in Vuskovic's words, 'scientific conviction'[31] – that the structural defects of the Chilean economy, its 'deformations' which 'limited the development of the productive forces'[32], were inevitable consequences of the existing power structure.

That the full implementation of the program would signify a revolutionary change in the Chilean society was emphasized by all the UP parties. The intention was to achieve a profound transformation of political power, a transformation which was to take place simultaneously with a 'revolutionary change' in the economic structure. In Marxist terms, the changes in the economic 'base' and those in the 'superstructure' were to go hand in hand, supporting each other through increasing the 'popular forces'' control of both the dominant sectors of the economy and of the whole institutional superstructure not directly related to the economic base. Pedro Vuskovic explains the program's revolutionary implications in the following way:

[the program] defines as its fundamental aim the transformation of the system and the character of the State... it is a question of a program which can be defined not only as anti-imperialist, anti-oligarchic, and anti-feudal, but as outright anti-capitalist as well.

Thus, the program does not propose structural reforms directed towards a modification of the traditional functioning of the economy, but towards a qualitative transformation of the very nature of the economy; not in order to resolve the problems within the proper limits of the system but in order to substitute a different system.

We are, in short, dealing with a program which has a clear revolutionary, and not purely reformist, content.[33]

Strategy

Vuskovic continues,

This being our point of departure, it means that the economic policy is faced with problems which are of an essentially political, and not merely technical character... What the economic policy is confronted with is a problem of power, a problem of social forces, of correlation of forces, to which the economic policy has to subordinate itself in order to serve – and herein lies its principal objective – as an instrument to widen and consolidate the workers'[34] power positions.

The final point deserves to be emphasized – the subordination of economic policies to explicitly formulated political goals, as well as the explicit recognition of the class character of the policies. Salvador Allende's government never pretended to be a government standing above the classes, serving society as a whole. It openly presented itself as a participant in a class struggle, where power was to change hands through the overthrowing of the ruling classes' political and economic dominance.

But despite the UP's revolutionary ambitions the strategy outlined pointed to a gradual achievement of the objectives. 'The progressive construction of a new power structure' was one of the phrases used by Allende in his First Message to Congress, and in the economic field the gradual and simultaneous character of *la vía chilena hacia el socialismo* was also emphasized. The 'destructive' and 'constructive' phases were to run a parallel course:

Our first task is to do away with [this] restraining structure which only generates a deformed growth. But simultaneously it is necessary to build the new economy in such a way that it succeeds the old one without a loss in continuity, to build it so that we conserve as much as possible of the productive and technological capacity that we, despite the vicissitudes of our underdevelopment, have at our disposal.[35]

The institutional continuity was also stressed. We are far, far away from the classical Marxist–Leninist notion of the necessity to 'break up, smash' the old state machinery in order to initiate the construction of socialism. (The whole UP strategy had, of course, little to do with classical Marxist–Leninist notions about revolutionary theory and socialism.) The Chilean revolution was to take place in pacific and constitutional forms, without violating any of the political liberties which were recognized as 'achievements of the Chilean society as a whole'.[36] By contrast with the historical building of socialism in other countries, Allende argued, 'our revolutionary road' will be 'a pluralist road, anticipated by the Marxist classics but never hitherto realized'.[37]

This is not to say that the institutional framework would not be subjected to change, that all that was envisaged was a mere change of face within decision making bodies or that traditional legal norms would remain sacrosanct. It should be interpreted to mean that the institutional heritage should be modified within the (very wide) boundaries of the constitution. 'One has to plough with the oxen one has' was one of Allende's favorite proverbs, to which he added: 'We will change the constitution by constitutional means.' And in the *First Message* we read: 'Our legal system ought to be modified . . . it is not the principle of legality that we, the popular forces, criticize. It is a legal order reflecting an oppressive social order that we protest against . . . In the regime of transition to socialism, the juridical norms will respond to the requirement of a people striving to build a new society. But there will be legality.'[38]

But whether revolutionary changes are to take place gradually or abruptly and whether inside or outside constitutional boundaries, what is required is political power, and control of only the executive branch of the state is clearly insufficient for achieving the objectives set up by the UP. Allende's electoral victory had given him the *right* to govern, true, but the *power* to rule is, as would soon become evident to all Chile, a totally different matter. Of this the UP was quite aware from the very beginning. As indicated by Vuskovic when discussing the role of economic policy, the taking of office of the new government was conceived not as the termination of the struggle for power but as the initiation of a new, and far more difficult, stage. Or in the words of Luis Corvalán, secretary general of the Communist Party (written in November 1970):

The struggle for power is still unsettled in our country. The principal enemies of the poeple – imperialism and the landowning oligarchies – continue to conserve strong positions from which they must be displaced in order to guarantee the revolutionary development of Chile.[39]

The government was considered a tactical instrument only:

Our principal objectives are, obviously, to capture the entire power and to build socialism. These are our strategic objectives. The government is an instrument to utilize, a tactical instrument that we make use of in order to reach these objectives.[40]

What other instruments did the UP dispose of in this struggle? Essentially, the mass organizations[41] – above all the trade union movement, but also many of the originally PDC-controlled 'neighborhood organizations', as well as the UP's own Comités de la Unidad Popular (CUP). The latter Organizations had been founded mainly for electoral purposes but were supposed to be made permanent in order to be able to play a decisive role in the building up of a new power structure 'from below'. The optimists within the UP even regarded these CUPs, or 'red cells', as embryonic Chilean forms of soviet power.

The central idea was, in short, to utilize both the executive power – the government – and the 'popular power' arising out of various mass organizations against the 'fundamental enemies' who, according to the plans, would be unable to resist the double pressure exercised both from above and from below and who, consequently, would lose one power position after another to the working class and its allies.

In this struggle for power embracing all levels of society the industrial working class would be the 'driving force'[42], although certainly not without help. The program of the UP was written so as to satisfy wide sectors of the population, and among the potential allies of the working class we encounter not only *campesinos*, white-collar workers, students, intellectuals, etc., but also small businessmen who were said to be exploited by the big monopolies and whose objective interests should coincide with those of the vast majority of the population.[43] The government would, primarily through its economic policies, demonstrate to these groups that its intentions were to benefit not only the industrial workers but also all those sectors which could not be included among the enemies of the people.

Divergencies within the UP

So far we have treated the UP as if it were one homogeneous political force with a single interpretation of the program and with one and only one notion of political strategy. This is, however, a gross simplification. The UP's program was little more than a compromise designed to satisfy various sectors of the Left, and rivalry between the different parties was an everyday occurrence both before and after the election. Long standing and deeply rooted theoretical and ideological differences of opinion were impossible to cover up, despite ambitious efforts by the general arbiter of the UP, Salvador Allende.

Within the UP we can clearly discern one 'leftist' block, mainly represented by the PS majority – including the leadership of the party – and one 'moderate' or 'reformist' block, dominated by the PC in an informal alliance with the Radicals and, often but far from always, with the smaller and at least initially quite insignificant parties and movements forming part of the UP.[44] In order to avoid getting lost in details I will confine myself to a brief overview of the principal points of divergence between the basic lines of the two hegemonic forces within the government: the PS and the PC.

An old and important question for the Chilean Left had been to define who exactly should be included among the 'popular forces'. The traditional Communist line had always been to try to achieve the widest possible 'popular unity', and the party had been quite open to alliances with the so-called 'progressive sectors of the national bourgeoisie'. On several occasions during the 1960s the PC, despite undisguised oppostion from the Socialists, tried to integrate those sectors into a 'People's Front' (*Frente del Pueblo*) directed against 'imperialism, monopoly capital and feudalism', and various proposals were made to Radicals and Christian Democrats in order to seek political support for such an alliance.[45] The PS, on the other hand, categorically rejected any alliances with the 'national bourgeoisie' – whose very existence, let alone progressive character, was cast in doubt – and called for the formation of a 'Workers' Front' (*Frente de Trabajadores*) as opposed to the much wider 'People's Front' of the PC.[46] With respect to the bourgeois reformist parties, possible allies according to the Communists, the Socialist Congress in Chillán in 1967 repudiated any cooperation with the PDC and the PR which was not limited to reaching purely tactical objectives – parliamentary support for certain reform proposals which the traditional Right opposed, for example – and affirmed in one of the resolutions adopted that 'it is the decomposition, not the artificial survival, of the Radical and Christian Democratic Parties which is the strategic aim of the revolutionary Left'.[47]

These strategic conflicts, which were temporarily buried after the 1970 elections but which time and again came to the surface later on, corresponded to two different concepts of what in Marxist theory is called the 'principal contradiction' within a given society. The PC's opinion was that the principal contradiction in Chile continued to be between the 'people' on the one hand and 'imperialism and the domestic oligarchy' on the other, while the Socialists emphasized as the principal contradiction the one between the bourgeoisie and the proletariat, arguing that the whole bourgeoisie was both reactionary and pro-imperialist.[48]

Connected with these divergencies were two different time perspectives with respect to the establishment of socialism in Chile. The Communists envisaged the Chilean revolution as passing through two distinct phases, the first one being limited to the fulfillment of the 'bourgeois-democratic' goals (agrarian reform, nationalization of foreign and domestic monopolies, a general democratization of society, etc.). Once these tasks had been performed and consolidated, the strengthened working class, in close alliance with peasants and other progressive groups whose objective interests coincided with those of the working class, would be prepared to proceed to the second, socialist stage. A victory for a left wing coalition in Chile would, according to the Communists' analysis, merely signify the initiation of the first of these two stages; only for the sake of unity of the Left is the PC said to have accepted the inclusion of explicit references to socialistic objectives in the 1970 program, and the PC leaders in fact very rarely mentioned the word 'socialism' in their propaganda. In general they preferred to interpret the UP program as 'anti-monopolistic' rather than 'anti-capitalistic' – a distinction with far-reaching implications for the choice of economic and political strategy.

This 'longer view' on the construction of socialism was not shared by the PS. Referring to the discussion within the UP held immediately after Allende's electoral triumph, the Central Committee of the PS declared in an internal party document:[49] 'The difference between our opinion and that of the rest was that we Socialists demanded that the initiation of *socialism should be a task of this government and not only a historical perspective*' (emphasis in original).

The insistence of the PS on the rapid realization of outright socialist objectives can be explained both by its more 'radical' positions in general and by its far more sceptical view of the possibility of realizing the 'anti-imperialist' and 'anti-oligarchic' tasks without running the risk of a serious confrontation with the whole bourgeoisie. The two-stage revolution was discarded as highly unrealistic (and, in fact, undesirable). The opposition would never permit an armistice letting the Left consolidate the conquests of the 'first stage'. Once initiated, the PS argued, the revolutionary process would generate a struggle for power which would necessarily involve not only those sectors identified as oligarchic but the whole non-socialist opposition as well, and the outcome of this struggle could only be victory or defeat, socialism or counter-revolution.

The Revolutionary Left inside and outside the Unidad Popular never did believe in a 'Chilean road to socialism'. The implications of differences of opinion as serious as those prevalent within the UP are obvious. Not only did internal conflicts make the government work pretty badly from an administrative point of view, with incessant frictions and concomitant confusion at all political and administrative levels,[50] they also, and this is far more important, impeded the implementation of a consistent economic and political strategy. While the Left remained in opposition its theoretical discussion about 'principal contradictions', 'class alliances', etc., might to some people have appeared hair-splitting without much practical significance, but with the UP in government, the relevance of these questions for the strategy to follow became, as will be confirmed on several occasions later on, of utmost and quite concrete importance.

CHAPTER 3

Theoretical prospects of the 'Chilean road'

GENERAL CONSIDERATION

The lack of experience with attempted constitutional, 'parliamentary' transitions to socialism makes the situation in Chile under Allende pretty well unique, and most aspects of the 'Chilean road' have to be analyzed without much help from historical analogies. The 'popular fronts' of the 1930s are, for example, rather inadequate as precedents since their aims were mainly defensive – to turn back the tide of fascism – and the many examples of social democratic governments in Western Europe and elsewhere do not help us much, either. For whether we call Dr Allende's government 'socialist' or not – and many people within the UP itself in fact hesitated to call it a socialist government – it is undeniable that its ends and means were appreciably more radical than those of traditional left-wing 'fronts' or social democratic governments. And the UP's Basic Program contained, despite all its ambiguities and compromises, basic elements which clearly distinguished it from current Latin American reformism.

Partly because of the scarcity of examples the Marxist theory of the 'parliamentary road to socialism' is quite abstract – if such a theory can be said to exist at all. Although Marx, Engels and Lenin did not completely discard the possibility of a constitutional transfer of power to a working-class government and a successive transition to socialism, their limited optimism with respect to this option has continued to be shared by later Marxists, who have done little to formulate concretely the relevant problems with which a constitutionally elected socialist government would be confronted.[1] This lack of concretization has unfortunately come to characterize most theoretical contributions from those Communist parties (which today constitute the great majority of Communist parties, at least in parliamentarily ruled countries) that have opted for a non-insurrectionary road to socialism.

But before proceeding to the Chilean case with all its peculiarities one Marxist theorist deserves to be quoted. This is Oscar Lange, who thirty-

41

five years ago drew attention to a number of general problems connected with socialist transformation of a society. 'An economic system based on private enterprise and private ownership of the means of production,' Lange wrote, 'can work only as long as the security of private property and of income derived from property and from enterprise is maintained. The very existence of a government bent on introducing socialism is a constant threat to this security. Therefore, the capitalist economy cannot function under a socialist government unless the government is socialist in name only.' Once the capitalists are caught by this easily comprehensible insecurity investments and efficient management are in danger, 'and no government supervision or administrative measures can cope effectively with this passive resistance and sabotage of the owners and managers.'[2] Lange's recipe is the following:

A socialist government really intent upon socialism has to decide to carry out its socialization program at one stroke, or to give it up altogether. The very coming into power of such a government must cause a financial panic and economic collapse. Therefore the socialist government must either guarantee the immunity of private property and private enterprise in order to enable the capitalist economy to function normally, in doing which it gives up its socialist aims, or it must go through resolutely with its socialization program at maximum speed ... Socialism is not an economic policy for the timid.

On the other hand, as a complement to its resolute policy of speedy socialization, the socialist government has to declare in an unmistakable way that all property and enterprise not explicitly included in the socialization measures is going to remain in private hands, and to guarantee its absolute security ...

To avoid the growth of an atmosphere of panic in this sector of private property and enterprise the socialist government may have to prove the seriousness of its intentions by some immediate deeds in favor of the small entrepreneurs and small property holders.[3]

But government power is not enough:

To be successful, the socialist government must put itself at the head of a great mass movement ... in the absence of such a mass movement, there is little a socialist government in office can achieve.[4]

THE CHILEAN CASE

The problems pointed out by Lange, as well as the possible road to overcome them, were clearly present in the minds of most UP leaders. They had witnessed how the moneyed classes panicked immediately after the elections, and they were well aware of the imminent danger of sabotage and passive resistance on the part of the new government's adversaries. Their initial socialization plans also coincide in vital respects with the bold strategy recommended by Lange; they feared that nothing short of a rapidly gained control over the 'commanding heights' of the economy could assure a satisfactory degree of economic tranquility, and over and over again they declared their willingness to delimit the state's domain in the economy in such a way that all small and medium-sized producers and property holders could feel absolutely secure against expropriation.

They also emphasized the need for support from a mass movement in order to carry through the program, although there existed various opinions within the UP – and, certainly, between the UP leadership and the Chilean workers – with respect to the division of labor between the government and the mass organizations.

But what were the prospects for a leftist government to realize its program in Chile? We have earlier seen how the UP envisaged the process from a political point of view, and the rest of this chapter will be devoted to an overview of a few aspects of relevance for an understanding of the theoretical prospects for the new government. Emphasis is first placed on more formal matters such as the division of power between the various branches of the state apparatus – a brief overview which will be of some help for an understanding of the Allende government's 'administrative freedom of action' – and thereafter I will try to indicate the relative strength of the UP and the opposition in terms of social and political forces in Chile by the time the Unidad Popular initiated its task.

Legal and institutional aspects

The constitution of Chile which Allende inherited[5] was based on the classical Montesquieuian division of power between three independent bodies: the executive power (the president, to whom all ministers were exclusively responsible), the legislative power (the national congress divided into two chambers), and the judiciary, represented by its highest organ, the supreme court. To these powers, easily recognizable in any parliamentary republic, we should add two independent institutions lacking clear correspondencies in most other countries: the *Contraloría General de la República*, whose main function was to see to it that the executive acted in accordance with the constitution, and the *Tribunal*

Constitucional, which was set up to supervise the parliament but whose tasks mainly consisted in trying to solve the conflicts that arose between the executive and the congressional majority over how the constitution ought to be interpreted.[6]

There is little unique in these parts of the constitution, although it should be stressed that the independent character of the authorities making up state power was appreciably more pronounced in Chile than is usually the case.[7] But if we proceed to look more closely at the specific faculties attributed to each body significant singularities appear, the foremost of these being the very ample powers with which the president was equipped – powers so ample that the Chilean constitution was sometimes said to establish a system of 'legal Caesarism'.

Immediately after taking office a Chilean president gained absolute control, both centrally and regionally, of the administration of the country. He appointed ministers and high-ranking officers[8] – he was, of course, *generalísimo* of the armed forces. He appointed governors (*intendentes*) with whom the executive power within all the different provinces was vested, and he also appointed all high- and middle-ranking officials within the entire public administration, including state-owned enterprises. In total several thousand posts were filled directly by the president and his advisers, and as long as all these people avoided being convicted for crimes – crimes in general or 'violations of the constitution' – the president, and he alone, could remove them from office.

In economic matters the constitution also provided the president with a remarkable amount of latitude. The executive had, for example, the right to establish the size of all remunerations within the public sector, as well as industrial and agricultural minimum wages in the private sector. In practice all wages and salaries in Chile have tended to follow the presidential norms, although the trade unions were free to ask for more and the employers often tried to pay less.

Now, in addition to the clear recognition of a presidential regime in the constitution the legal and institutional framework which the UP took over also favored the executive power. Not only did there exist an incredibly large number of valid laws (over 20,000, it was often said) which the president was legally free to use, the traditionally heavy state interference in the national economy had also resulted in a host of decrees with the force of law to regulate both the public and the private sectors of the economy which could be adapted so as to suit the purposes of a leftist government. A government body, DIRINCO (Dirección Nacional de Industria y Comercio) was in charge of the whole price control system and had the power to set the prices of all goods of 'prime necessity' – a concept interpreted generously enough to cover virtually anything salable. In a country with a 'normal' inflation of some 20–40 per cent this price control system could clearly serve as a useful instrument for a government like Allende's acting in a hostile business environment and in constant need of bargaining power. CORFO and CORA – the Industrial Development Corporation and the Agrarian Reform Corporation, respectively – as well as a great number of other public bodies directly dependent upon the government, could intervene in vital industrial and agricultural matters, and the laws and decrees regulating their activities were flexible enough to permit them to exercise both direct and indirect control over private interests. To this we should add that public credit institutes for decades had played a dominant role in the financing of private investment. In 1970, the state financed over 70 per cent of all investment made in Chile.

The list of state bodies created by earlier governments and given a wide range of economic faculties could be made very long. But having already demonstrated the heavy involvement of the state in economic life in Chile and the great variety of means that the executive power had at its disposal to control the functioning of the economy, we can stop the enumeration here and go over to the question: what limitations were there on the extensive powers with which the president was equipped?

First we note that the Congress had absolute authority with regard to taxation. The president had, of course, an initiative right in taxation matters, but the Congress alone decided. It was free to raise and lower tax rates on its own, without the executive power's interference. Secondly, the Congress had to approve the executive branch's budget proposals, and it could, within certain limits, modify any public expenditure included in the bill.[9] Thirdly, the supervisory power of the Congress was extended since a congressional majority could dismiss any minister or *intendente* if he were convicted – and here the Congress acted as both prosecutor and judge – of 'infraction of the constitution'. With a simple majority the Congress could remove any displeasing minister or *intendente* from his duty, and with two-thirds of the congressional seats even the president, if found guilty, could be impeached and forced to resign. Fourthly, and what is most important when it comes to the UP's chances of realizing its reform program, the Congress alone was entitled to legislate.

The latter point merits a short digression. For a government content with the mere administration of the country the influence of the Congress was fairly easy to circumscribe. The powers attributed to the president were ample enough to make it possible for him to impose his will in most current matters without having to consult parliament. But for a government like Allende's, bent on achieving fundamental economic and social changes, the situation was different. New legislation could not be passed without congressional support, and the full implementation of the UP program would clearly be rendered difficult within the boundaries of the old legal framework. Although the president could veto all legislative projects accepted by Congress as long as he could count on at least one-third of the seats in the Senate, he could pass no new legislation without having the majorities of both chambers of Congress supporting him, majorities which could not possibly be gained before the March 1973 parliamentary elections.[10]

There was one option open to a president wanting to get round the legislative power of the parliament: to call for a plebiscite. With an absolute majority in a plebiscite any constitutional reform presented by the executive could be carried through, irrespective of congressional opinion. This important means was clearly envisaged in the program of the UP, which in a crucial passage stated that the prevailing bicameral system should be abolished and a 'People's Assembly' (Asamblea del Pueblo) substituted for it. Knowing that the parliamentary majority would refuse to commit political suicide, the UP planned to submit this reform proposal to the Chilean people to obtain the verdict in a plebiscite. The UP failed, however, to capture the legislative power; nothing happened that could break the deadlock. The UP remained a minority in Congress, and only in a limited number of cases were the president's bills accepted. Allende did not call for a plebiscite to override congressional opposition and he had, indeed, to plow with the oxen provided him by earlier governments and parliaments. And this he unquestionably did with a certain amount of legal ingenuity. Some of the tens of thousands of valid laws and decrees that the UP inherited turned out to be quite useful to the new government, a circumstance which repeatedly occasioned confrontations with the Supreme Court and the *Contraloría General*, organs whose interpretations of existing laws only rarely coincided with those of the legal experts of the UP and which were outstanding as sources of diehard resistance to the Allende government.

The correlation of forces

The legal and institutional setting in Chile – including the important role played by the state as the regulator of economic life – provided, as we have seen, the executive branch of the state apparatus with a host of instruments which the UP was free to apply, but it also contained serious obstacles to the government's socialist ambitions. The parliament, the judiciary and the *Contraloría General* were from the very beginning anti-UP[11] (although it took some time for the PDC to make its position absolutely clear), and the same can naturally be said about the domestic economic establishment in alliance with powerful foreign interests. Because of its ideological and political impact the mass media constituted an especially serious impediment to the UP. The parties which were later to form the anti-UP coalition *Confederación Democrática* controlled, by 1970, two of the three main TV-stations, 95 per cent of Chile's radio stations (in total, about 150), 90 per cent of the newspaper circulation and close to 100 per cent of all weekly magazines.[12]

Furthermore, the great majority of officers in the armed forces and national police were decidedly against the Unidad Popular, although for a long time many of them managed to maintain a façade of neutrality.

The position of the Catholic Church – whose ideological influence is less pronounced in Chile than in most other Latin countries – was somewhat ambiguous. A large number of individual priests either combatted or supported the UP, of course – and the former were more numerous than the latter – but the relations between the institution as such and the Allende government could, at least during the first two years, best be described as characterized by almost cordial neutrality.

What could the UP count upon, then? Having been elected with little more than one-third of the votes and with all the important institutions being either hostile or conditionally neutral, the Allende government had apparently engaged itself in an extremely uneven struggle. But this picture of the correlation of forces is no doubt misleading; the UP was, in fact, much stronger than it looked 'on paper'.

The popular support for Allende was, to begin with, politically much more significant than its numerical strength would indicate. The bare 36.3 per cent obtained in 1970 included the best organized and most politically active sectors of the Chilean population (if a handful of big landowners and industrialists is disregarded), namely the industrial and mining workers whose economic importance and role in Chile's political life are difficult to overrate. With very few exceptions[13] this 'classical proletariat' was enthusiastically pro-UP, and at every critical juncture – and there were several – Allende could count upon resolute and organized backing from the urban industrial workers.

In general elections, however, support from the industrial working class – numerically small and, as we have seen earlier[14], with a historical tendency to decline rather than increase as a share of the economically active population – was far from sufficient. If the poorly organized and politically rather passive group of craftsmen is excluded, all blue-collar workers employed in manufacturing, construction and mining amounted to no more than about half a million in 1970, or about one-sixth of the labor force and some ten per cent of the whole population aged between fifteen and sixty-five. Of these less than half, or about 200,000 – or, to make an extreme comparison, some two per cent of the whole Chilean population – were organized in trade unions.

The above point is important. The class structure that the UP inherited was, from an electoral point of view, extremely disadvantageous for the Left. For we can now see how the very small share of modern industrial and mining workers in the Chilean work force was reflected at the political level. The well organized, radical and politically active groups supporting the big working-class parties were easily outnumbered by the mass of people employed in small-scale business or in the service sectors, people who were far more difficult to organize and whose political consciousness was likely to be individualistic and rightist oriented rather than socialist – this quite irrespective of the fact that they, from a narrow economic point of view, often suffered more from the existing system (but had less to gain from the UP's program, too) than many of the comparatively well-paid miners and factory workers in large-scale industry.

A concrete example will serve to indicate the disproportion that existed between political influence and numerical weight. While the 20,000 miners of the Gran Minería copper pits constituted less than one per cent of the whole labor force and were but a small fraction of, say, Chile's 200,000 domestic servants[15], the miners' political activities were constantly in the newspapers' headlines while the opinions of the unorganized and politically weak domestic servants were completely ignored.

Chile's underlying economic structure also served to weaken the solidarity between different groups of urban and rural poor. The economy's high degree of heterogeneity resulted in huge disparities in productivity – and in wages and profits – both between and within the different sectors, and its inegalitarian character was not only a question of inequality between the 'very rich' and the 'very poor'. There were also very pronounced differences in economic and social conditions between, say, blue- and white-collar workers, copper and coal miners, workers in modern industry and in crafts, between rural and urban workers, taxi-drivers and domestic servants, between domestic servants and unemployed *pobladores*, between office clerks and hawkers, etc. To carry out an economic project acceptable to all these groups was virtually impossible. The objective conditions did not favor 'popular unity', and we will later see that the UP's adverseries understood how to take advantage of the contradictions that inevitably arose.

A few words should also be said about the correlation of forces within the non-industrial sectors of the Chilean population. The *campesino* organizations were predominantly anti-Allendist in 1970, but a shift was clearly under way and as early as 1971 the UP got a clear majority in the farm workers' trade unions. However, for reasons we will return to, most of the direct beneficiaries of the land reform – members of the reformed cooperatives – tended to side with the Christian Democrats.

The organized support that the UP could count on from the middle strata of white-collar workers, small and medium-sized property holders, etc. was quite limited. Within the public sector several large trade unions had traditionally been dominated by the Left, while privately employed salary earners were in general both poorly organized and predominantly anti-UP. Support from small-scale enterprise and self-employed workers could, at best, be expected to be conditional and unreliable. No real effort had been made by the Left to integrate these large and often very impoverished sectors into political organizations or trade unions, and the phrases dedicated to them in the UP program were hardly convincing.

If we are to summarize this overview of social forces in Chile one conclusion is obvious: among the directly productive workers the dominance of the UP was overwhelming, and to the solid core of supporters among the urban and rural proletariat we can add important sectors of organized white-collar workers. Even if the professionals' unions – often but not always controlled by the rightist opposition – were included, the UP could count upon a comfortable majority among all Chile's organized wage and salary earners. In the June 1972 elections to the Central Union of Workers (CUT), to which practically all organized workers, *campesinos*, white-collar employees, etc. belonged, the UP parties received more than 70 per cent of all votes, as against 25.5 per cent for the PDC (the Right did not even present candidates).

The opposition, on the other hand, had its strongholds among heterogeneous and – at least initially – politically rather passive groups. In addition to the obvious backing from the upper and upper-middle classes it could count on the majority of self-employed workers, certain layers

49

of the peasantry, a large part of the workers and employees within the services sector and, last but not least, it could count on the Chilean women, especially the housewives whose conservative leanings constituted an incessant problem for the Chilean Left.[16]

In elections the opposition was powerful, but in the daily economic and political struggle the organizational strength and social composition of the adherents of the Left gave the UP an extraordinary force.

The other factor favoring the UP was the specific political conjuncture before and after the 1970 elections. Both the election campaign and the mass mobilization in defense of the victory generated an enormous impetus which the Left could rely upon. The initiative was in the hands of the 'popular forces'. After the prolonged crisis of the late 1960s the September–October events left behind a divided, demoralized and discredited Right and a strengthened UP which, despite all its internal divergencies, had two things at its disposal which the rightist opposition lacked: enthusiasm and a common political program. If the acute economic problems could be coped with, the new government was pretty sure to get a good start, notwithstanding the absence of governmental preparations. The depth of the surprise caused by the September election is shown by the fact that the UP had not even composed a shadow cabinet beforehand. If the split within the opposition were not bridged – and this could not possibly happen without provoking a split within the Christian Democratic Party – an initial political hegemony of the UP would be almost guaranteed.

As for the international situation, the position of the UP also looked rather promising in 1970. This is not the place to try to analyze the overall correlation of forces in a global perspective, but it should be pointed out that southern Latin America was characterized by a general leftist offensive. Bolivia under General Torres was rapidly moving towards a pre-revolutionary – or, as we can say today with hindsight, pre-counter-revolutionary – situation, and in Peru the stand of the Velasco government was openly pro-UP and anti-US. The military dictatorship in Argentina and the repressive Pacheco regime in Uruguay both found themelves in a stage of outright decomposition and represented no immediate threat to the Allende government's position. The Brazilian generals had consolidated their power, and had converted their country into an aggressive, sub-imperialist power on the continent, but it was nevertheless counteracting tendencies that prevailed in the southern cone of Latin America.

But let us now return to Chile and summarize the domestic political panorama at the time the Unidad Popular initiated its task. By November 1970 the UP government had, as we have seen, a clear advantage from a tactical point of view, an advantage which it had to convert into strategic advances in order to be able to realize its program. Unless rapidly overcome, the UP's institutional minority position – in particular the lack of control of most of the vital institutions of the state apparatus – would sooner or later act as a powerful brake on the socialist ambitions of the new government, which had, furthermore, to try to find means with which to defend the economy against expected resistance and pressure from strong domestic and foreign business interests.

Although the chapters that follow will be devoted mainly to economic matters they will, I hope, permit us to understand how and why the Unidad Popular failed to convert its good position at the outset into lasting victories.

CHAPTER 4

The short-term economic program

While the broad economic and political objectives of the UP were outlined in the electoral program, the short-term, or conjunctural, economic policy was not. Immediately after the elections, however, an economic team was constituted, which in the midst of the September–October crisis elaborated a plan[1] for the new government's first economic steps, steps which were fundamentally designed to achieve a rapid reactivation of the economy. The purpose of this chapter is to discuss this conjunctural part of the economic program of the UP – its objectives, means and principal results.

For expository reasons it is, unfortunately, necessary to study this short-term economic program separately, outside the general context, although its intimate links with the other aspects of the program ought to be kept in mind. When using the expression 'short-term policy' I do not mean to say that the implementation of the various components of the UP's economic project followed strictly chronological lines. Quite the contrary: all the three basic ingredients of the economic program – reactivation of the economy and income redistribution, acceleration of the agrarian reform and expansion of the state area of the economy – were to take place simultaneously, supporting each other and supporting the fundamental objective of the UP, namely the 'popular forces' taking of power in society as a whole. In the words of the *Basic Orientations*[2]: 'One cannot imagine a first stage of merely conventional means as an initial step towards achieving economic "recovery" followed by a second stage when the basic programmatic objectives ought to be initiated. No – from the very beginning it is, both from an economic and political point of view, imperative to undertake both things simultaneously.'

Thus, the division of labor between the various aspects of the economic program of the UP was not primarily of a chronological nature, and neither is the disposition of the chapters in this study. A good excuse for using the term 'short-run' or 'conjunctural' policy is, however, that the UP economists always did so, well aware of the fact that the distinction between this part of economic policy and the others was a question of ends and means rather than of months and years.

OBJECTIVES

The two main, and mutually interdependent, objectives of the short-term program were to achieve 1. a rapid recovery of the economy and 2. a more egalitarian distribution of income. As explained by Pedro Vuskovic:

> The short-run economic policy can, in very general terms, be characterized as a policy of economic reactivation based upon an income redistribution.

> The rapid recovery was presented as a task of extraordinary priority – not only because it was easier to carry through a redistributive policy in an expanding economy, but also because of the fact that the economy, when the People's Government took office, found itself in a very profound crisis, a product of the prolonged campaign of political terror that preceded the September 1970 elections and to which, once the election result was known, was added a campaign ... of economic and financial terror.[3]

Both the policy of reactivation and of income redistribution had, of course, not merely economic but also political aims. In the UP's 'march towards power' it was imperative to widen the popular support of the regime, and a considerable dose of 'populist' policies was deemed necessary. The UP judged that if future elections were to be won the government could not possibly – even if it had wanted to, which it did not – impose any material sacrifices on the majority of the people, and it was undoubtedly this political restriction that Allende had in mind when he stated that 'the political model towards socialism that my government is applying requires that the socio-economic revolution take place simultaneously with an uninterrupted economic expansion'.[4]

MEANS

Income policy

The pillar of the reactivation program was the income policy, and immediately after taking office the new government took up negotiations with the Central Workers' Union (CUT) in order to establish criteria for private and public remunerations in 1971. The following basic principles were agreed.:[5]

The short-term economic program

1. To restore, for all workers and employees earning up to twenty *sueldos vitales*, the level of real income on 1 January 1970 – that is, to give everyone but the very highest paid full compensation for the rise of consumer prices during 1970 (which turned out to be 34.9 per cent).

2. To give an appreciably higher readjustment to the lowest paid workers.

3. To initiate a process of standardization and levelling of all social benefits such as pensions and family allowances.

Apart from the obvious aspect of social justice the policy of income redistribution was also justified for economic reasons. Giving money to the poor, it was argued, would have a relatively large impact on the absorption of unemployment since the demand for goods of 'popular consumption', whose production was more labor-intensive than that of the consumer durables bought by the upper and upper-middle classes, was likely to increase most. (This positive employment effect should not be taken for granted in the short run. The low-income groups spent a sizeable share of their extra earnings on imported foodstuffs.)

It should, however, be pointed out that the redistributive program of 1971 was not primarily aimed at changing the distribution of income between different groups of wage and salary earners – although the very poor were given preferential treatment – but rather at increasing labor's overall share of national income. It was the receivers of profits and rents rather than the well-paid professionals who were to pay the bill.

In monetary terms the outcome of the first year's incomes policy far exceeded the norms set up in the CUT-government agreement, which only indicated the lower limits of the 1971 remunerations. When all local negotiations had been concluded in July, average income per employee had increased by 54.9 per cent, as against the 40–45 per cent envisaged by the government.[6] The 54.9 per cent was distributed almost equally between wage and salary earners – 55.4 and 54.3 per cent, respectively – but with a considerable dispersion between different sectors, the average increase per employee varying between 41.3 per cent (public utilities) and 72.1 per cent (mining).[7] In both the private and public sectors the legal minimum wage was raised from 12 to 20 escudos a day, or by 66.6 per cent, and the basic salary for employees, the *sueldo vital*, went up more than 35 per cent, reaching an average of just over 800 escudos a month.[8]

In any normal economy these massive increases in purchasing power would probably be judged sufficiently drastic to produce a demand-induced reactivation of the economy, especially since they were not accompanied by tax increases which could have absorbed part of the liquidity.[9] The UP economists also hoped that the rise in labor costs should work in the same direction, i.e. stimulate production. Since the price control system was to be extended and its implementation made far more rigid,[10] the industrialists were to be faced with the necessity of responding by raising production levels to compensate for the decline in profit margins. But the government did not want to rely upon the response from private business only, and the incomes policy was accompanied by a remarkable expansion of public spending.

Public expenditure

Despite the parliamentary opposition's efforts to cut down both the income and expenditure sides of the UP's first budget, 1971 became a year of vigorous increases in public spending. At the end of the year fiscal expenditure alone had increased over 70 per cent in nominal terms, or from 19 to 33 billion escudos between 1970 and 1971. The budget was in deficit, of course. Of the 33 thousand million, 10 were financed with credits from the Central Bank, as against 1.8 the year before. Total public expenditure – including spending by public institutes and state-owned enterprises of various kinds[11] – increased even faster, from 39.1 to 69.7 billion, or by almost 80 per cent in current prices.[12]

Although the expansion affected the whole sector, priority was given to projects which both promised a rapid absorption of manpower and were designed to satisfy urgent social needs such as housing, education, health and sanitary services. Unemployment among construction workers being especially high (27.0 per cent in Santiago in December 1970), the residential construction program was perhaps the most ambitious one of all. During 1971, 73,000 new housing units were initiated by the public sector, a figure which can be compared with the 23,700 units that were started in 1970 by the public and private sectors together.[13] A huge number of urban infra-structual programs were also undertaken – the budget of the Ministry of Housing and Urbanism increased more than 150 per cent over 1970,[14] and especially during the first half of 1971 a wave of 'mobilization programs' swept over the Chilean *poblaciones*. Sustained by popular enthusiasm, Central Bank credits and technical assistance from the Ministry, various 'construction brigades', 'water brigades', etc. were formed by the *pobladores*, who themselves assumed the main responsbility for the actual carrying out of the badly needed improvements of housing and sanitary conditions in

the urban slums. In the countryside, various infra-structural works — ·
above all irrigation and reforestation projects — were initiated in order
to absorb part of the high unemployment and underemployment among
farm workers and, of course, to raise the productive capacity of the
Chilean land.

But there is little point in going into details. What has been said above
can serve as examples only, illustrating the magnitude of the public
expenditure program and its close integration with socio-political
objectives. Some of the results of this policy will be studied later on.
Let us first consider briefly those instruments which were to complement the short-term program and assure its success.

Money and credit

Monetary policy has never played a very sophisticated role in Chile.
The Central Bank has satisfied the private and public sectors' demand
for money and has been a generous contributor to the financing of
public expenditures, while the main function of the commercial banks —
including the state-owned Banco del Estado — has been to provide the
private sector with loans on very favorable terms. The real rate of
interest has traditionally been negative, and discount policy has consequently had a very small effect upon the demand for credit. With
demand always being larger than supply a system of informal rationing
has had to do the job of distributing the available credit.

With the Unidad Popular in government the scope for traditional
monetary policy was even more limited, and the UP did, in fact, pay
very little attention to monetary issues. Official statements only indicated that monetary policy was to be 'closely integrated' with the government's general program, its main function being, in the words of the
President of the Central Bank to be 'an instrument for its [the program's] realization' or, somewhat more concretely, to 'help mobilize
all the productive resources in the country and to orient these towards
activities to which the government has given priority'.[15] In the future
planning of the economy credit policy was to play an important role, and
a gradual nationalization of all commercial banks was initiated so as to
make it possible for the government to exercise direct control of an even
larger share of Chile's investments.[16] No specific anti-inflationary task
was attributed to monetary policy. Since it was the UP's contention
that the 'inflationary process . . . is generated by the economic structure',
it was considered that monetary policy could best fulfil its price stabil-

ization role by facilitating the carrying through of the basic political and economic program of the UP, designed to do away with the existing, inflation-creating structure.[17]

In the short run, which is what interests us here, monetary policy was aimed at contributing to the success of the general reactivation program. Credits had to be granted to the public sector in order to finance its expansion, and private investments were stimulated through a fairly rapid increase in the supply of commercial credits. For a start even consumers' credits were expanded, but as the stimulation of consumption by other means soon began to appear threatingly easy to achieve this type of credit was gradually cut down, finally to disappear almost completely.

Interest rates were lowered, especially on loans for priority projects. The standard bank interest rate was lowered from 24 to 15 per cent and the maximum contractual rate from 24 to 18 per cent, rates that were kept stable all through 1971, and on certain favored categories of loans the rate of interest was brought down to 12 and even 9 per cent.

The public sector's share of total bank credit rose (see table 4.1) from less than one-third to almost 60 per cent of the total amount of credit, and the treasury alone increased its indebtedness tenfold in 1971.

This vigorous credit expansion was naturally accompanied by a rapid increase in the general liquidity of the economy. By the end of December 1971 the proportion of money in the hands of the private sector to GDP had jumped to 16.8 per cent, as compared with 10.9 per cent in 1970.[18] Notes and coin in circulation increased from 5,256 to 11,556 million escudos betwee 31 December 1970 and 31 December 1971, and the total supply of money more than doubled in one year.[19]

In the distribution of commercial credit priority was given to state-owned industries, low-cost residential construction, the reformed area

Table 4.1   *Total amount of credit granted by the banking system, December 1970–December 1971 (millions of escudos)*

End of	The public sector			The private sector	Total
	Treasury	Other	Total		
December 1970	916	1,152	2,069	6,777	8,846
July 1971	6,487	2,634	9,121	8,512	17,633
December 1971	9,301	6,814	16,115	10,785	26,900

SOURCE: Banco Central, *Boletín Mensual* no. 537, November 1972, p. 1362.

of agriculture, to export-promoting activities and to small and medium-sized private enterprises. The heavy concentration of credit – including the regional concentration – was censured severely by the UP economists, and both for economic and political reasons a more balanced distribution was to emerge. Thus, although the sectoral distribution of credit remained more or less unchanged as compared with 1970, there was a marked shift away from private 'monopolies' towards the public sector and towards smaller economic units within the different sectors. But if we are to summarize the monetary policy of the Allende government's first year we can no doubt conclude that, as in the case of the incomes policy, the general expansionary aspect clearly dominated over the redistributive aspect, and we can also conclude that tremendous inflationary pressures were bound to arise in an economy where average wages and salaries rose by 54.9 per cent, total public expenditures by 80 per cent and bank credits by more than 200 per cent in one year.

Price and supply policy

In the 'new economy' price stabilization was to play an important role, although this part of economic policy was certainly subordinated to the basic programmatic objectives. Like most other Chilean governments the UP put far more emphasis on the struggle against inflation while in opposition than while in power.[20]

Since fiscal policy, monetary policy and incomes policy were all used as 'Keynesian' instruments to achieve a rapid economic expansion, the UP had to resort to other means when trying to stabilize the price level. What the government did was, first, to start applying the old price control system in a much more rigorous way than had been customary in Chile and, second, to hope that the reactivation program would result in large increases in production which could satisfy part of the drastically inflated demand for commodities. The UP had assured the workers that the gains in purchasing power obtained in the 1971 wage settlements would be maintained and would not be eaten up by violent price increases on goods of prime necessity, and the industrialists were, in turn, promised 'fair' utilities if they compensated for the lesser rate of return per produced unit with higher levels of output. The new and higher wage costs would not be allowed to be shifted over to the consumers. With the 'excessive, monopolistic profit margins' being a 'basic factor behind the inflation', the price regulation aimed at letting the profits 'absorb ... most of the wage increases', and the latter could 'only in very special cases, where it was manifestly necessary', be used as arguments for price rises.[21]

To make the price control system more effective organized support from consumers was judged indispensable. Hundreds, later thousands, of so-called Price and Supply Committees (JAPs, *Juntas de Abastecimiento y Precios*) were created, mainly by housewives, all over the country in order to keep an eye on the merchants and check that they stuck to official prices and did not hoard any goods of prime necessity. In those districts were the JAPs worked well – that is, in working-class districts where the Left was strong – a good share of all commodities was distributed under the direct supervision of the JAPs, which in a few cases managed to establish cordial relations with the local merchants.

But without a substantially larger supply of goods to distribute the work of the price control system and the JAPs would clearly encounter insurmountable obstacles. Some of the government's economic projects – such as the acceleration of the agrarian reform and the long-range industrialization program – were not expected to give any immediate results, but others were. The whole reactivation program was, of course, designed to stimulate production, and the 'battle of production' was given highest possible priority in the UP's propaganda.[22] *Vis-à-vis* the industrialists the government relied upon the carrot as well as the stick; the capitalists who hesitated to take advantage of the excellent markets they were promised would nevertheless feel obliged to raise output in order to avoid trouble. If sabotage or resistance occurred the state had at its disposal a host of legal sanctions, ranging from mild persuasion and economic pressure to the establishment of 'production contingents' or even outright expropriation.

The new government's anti-inflationary task was also facilitated, at least initially, by the particular economic situation that prevailed in 1970. During the last Frei years sales had been even more depressed than production, and large stocks of consumer goods had been accumulated. Depression and high copper prices had also made possible a considerable hoarding of foreign exchange which the former administration could hand over to Allende, and the foreign trade and exchange rate policy became, in fact, the pillars of the UP's supply policy. Imports of foodstuffs thus increased very rapidly, despite the fact that the agricultural year 1970/71, mainly thanks to excellent weather conditions, gave a surprisingly good harvest. To keep prices down the bank exchange rate (i.e. the rate used for foreign trade transactions[23]) was kept unaltered at a rate of 12.21 escudos to the dollar from August 1970 to the end of

Table 4.2   *Bank exchange rates established in December 1971 (imports)*

Classification	Escudos per dollar
Foodstuffs and fuels	12.21
Raw materials	15.80
Machinery, equipment and spare parts	19.00
Consumer goods other than foodstuffs	25.00

December 1971, when a differentiated devaluation affecting all imports but those of foodstuffs and fuels was undertaken (see table 4.2).

To avoid imports of non-priority consumer goods – generally labelled 'luxuries' – the already existing system of non-tariff restrictions was tightened up. In certain cases a previous deposit of up to several times the value of the imported commodity was required, for example, and the direct state control of imports was also increased. By the end of 1971 the public sector accounted for over 50 per cent of all imports.

We are now able to make a summary of this brief overview of ends and means of the UP's short-term economic program. In order to re-activate the depressed economy and absorb the high unemployment, raise living standards and increase the popular support of the government the UP launched a drastically expansionary program based on an overall increase and slight redistribution of wages and salaries, massive increases in public expenditure and a substantial expansion of credit. To counteract inflationary tendencies and protect the purchasing power of the working class the expansionary policy was accompanied by rigorous price controls supervised by vigilant consumers' organizations and supported by imports at favorable exchange rates.

In the rest of this chapter we will study the results of this policy during 1971.

ECONOMIC DEVELOPMENTS IN 1971

We have earlier seen how political developments before and after the 1970 election strengthened the Unidad Popular, how the comparatively united Left emerged as the undisputed major political force in Chile. Tactically the situation was excellent, but the strategical weaknesses of the UP were equally evident.

The same could be said about the specific economic conjuncture. From a short-term point of view, Allende arrived at the right moment. The economy was depressed, with large amounts of idle resources to be mobilized, and only massive and organized resistance from business circles could have prevented the reactivation program from being successful. But the long-term prospects were, of course, far gloomier.

When taking office, the new government could count on:

1. *Idle capacity.* Capacity utilization rates in 1970 averaged, according to ODEPLAN estimates, 63 per cent in the capital goods and consumer durables sector, 77.6 per cent in the traditional mass consumption goods industry, and 85.5 per cent in the intermediate goods industry, the overall average in manufacturing being 75.3 per cent.[24] In other sectors, such as transportation, commerce, excess capacity was also high.

2. *Idle manpower.* Unemployment figures were in 1970 among the highest ever recorded since reliable data was first collected in the mid-fifties. In December 1970 the rate of open unemployment reached 8.3 per cent in Santiago and 9.9 and 17.0 per cent in Concepción-Talcahuano and Lota-Coronel, respectively.[25]

3. *Large stocks of consumer goods.* The size of these are difficult to estimate, but they were, as mentioned above, undoubtedly large. Especially during the first half of 1971 sales of consumer goods rose much faster than production.

4. *Large reserves of foreign exchange.* In 1970 the Central Bank's dollar reserves reached an all-time peak. At the end of December they amounted to 333 million dollars, or equivalent to over thee months' imports of goods and services.[26]

To this we should add another 'asset' from which the UP expected a lot but the utilization of which was not exactly at the government's free disposal, namely the huge profits obtained by private business. In 1970, under Eduardo Frei, distributed profits as a share of national income exceeded the sum of all wages of Chile's blue-collar workers.[27]

The private sector's behavior

A key problem was to what extent the government could mobilize the economy's idle resources and force the rentier class to accept the material sacrifices imposed upon it. If the crisis atmosphere could be dissipated and a certain cooperation obtained from private decision makers, the economic program designed by the UP looked promising from a short-term point of view. If not, it was doomed to failure, and nothing short of a drastic nationalization offensive – with unpredictable economic and political sequels – or an unmistakable retreat from the UP's basic programmatic objectives could lead to the re-establishment of a necessary minimum of economic order.

How did the private sector react? Most of the small and medium-sized industrialists, artisans, merchants, peasants, etc. benefited strikingly from the economic policies of the UP, and in 1971 no organized opposition, and certainly no economic sabotage, arose from these groups. But the higher up one gets, the more the homogeneity of reactions tends to disappear. There were, for example, many cases of deliberate loss of production, cutting down of staff by means of sudden sackings, deliberate bankruptcy and even self-inflicted sabotage. Many of the big landowners slaughtered their cattle for sale before and immediately after Allende assumed office, and among the longer industrialists reactions varied from 'business as usual' to passive or active resistance. The latter was undoubtedly the case with the textile magnate who put a bomb in his own factory and crossed the border illegally, while leaving behind huge debts and charges of fraud and tax evasion. Some of the foreign companies in Chile cut down production or stopped it completely, and several cases of outright sabotage – for which the foreign companies were made responsible by the new Chilean administration – were detected in plants that were nationalized.

In general the cases of sabotage were few, however. Far more common during the first months was an expectant, wait-and-see attitude and in one important respect this expectant policy was maintained during the whole year; private investment fell considerably, especially in large-scale industry.[28] But to the great relief of the government, the reactivation policy began to give positive results early in 1971. The coercive apparatus certainly contributed. In not a few cases where production was paralyzed the workers resolutely occupied the factory and asked the government to 'intervene' or to 'requisition' the company in question – legal possibilities which were of great help to the government and which, in fact, constituted the most commonly used mechanisms for the transfer of private enterprise to state control.[29] Milder forms of coercion were the agreements reached between government and private industries: the so-called 'production pacts' had a fairly voluntary character, with the state and private business promising to provide technical and financial assistance and to increase production, respectively; while others – for example, the unilateral establishing of 'production contingents' which directly, under the threat of expropriation, forced the companies to raise production levels – were used by the government to try to make private enterprise utilize the existing excess capacity. In line with the general policy of the Unidad Popular the workers' own organizations were also to play an important role in the supervision of private business: so-called Comités de Vigilancia, whose main task was to check the owners' administration, were formed in all important manufacturing industries. A large number of 'interventions' and 'requisitions', as well as other milder forms of sanctions, were direct results of the workers' own reports on irregularities committed.[30]

The combination of economic incentives and outright threats turned out to be successful. As seen in table 4.3, the industrial recovery, later followed by an almost unprecedented expansion, can be roughly dated to March 1971.

Industrial employment also showed a pronounced tendency to recover as from the spring (that is, Chilean fall) of 1971.

Thus, having verified that the most critical obstacle to the success of the short-term program – the response from private industry – was gradually being overcome, we can go over to a survey of the main achievements in terms of output, employment, and prices during 1971.

MAJOR SECTORS OF ACTIVITY

According to still incomplete data gross domestic product increased 8.6 per cent in 1971,[31] and all major sectors of activity showed moderate or high rates of growth (table 4.5).

With regard to the distribution of use of total output, consumption increased while investment declined. Private and public consumption rose by 12.9 and 4.6 per cent, respectively, and investment fell off as shown in table 4.6.

Expressed as share of total product this signified a decline in the rate of gross capital formation from 15.7 to 13.3 per cent of GDP. The public sector's share rose appreciably; public investments increased slightly in real terms, while private investments fell off abruptly.

Agriculture

During the agricultural year 1970/71 Chile had favorable weather.[32] The area under cultivation remained virtually constant (1,262,400 hectares as compared with 1,251,500 in 1969/70 and an annual average of 1,243,500 in 1966–70[33]), but output from crop-farming rose by 8.6 and that of livestock products by 1.8 per cent, the latter thanks to substantial increases in poultry and milk production.

63

Table 4.3 *Percentage changes in industrial production (volume), January–December 1971 as against corresponding months in 1970*

Jan.	Feb.	March	April	May	June	July	August	Sept.	Oct.	Nov.	Dec.
−2.0	1.2	6.9	1.3	17.1	9.9	7.8	18.1	27.4	12.1	30.7	31.3

Total change 1971/70: 14.7

SOURCE: Based on data from the National Institute of Statistics (Instituto Nacional de Estadística, INE), currently published in Banco Central, *Boletín Mensual.*

64

Major sectors of activity

Table 4.4 *Industrial employment in Greater Santiago 1970 and 1971 (thousands of persons) and unemployment in manufacturing (percentages)*

	1970				1971			
	March	June	Sept.	Dec.	March	June	Sept.	Dec.
Employ-ment	234.1	265.5	271.1	254.7	253.5	271.2	283.6	295.2
Unemploy-ment	6.8	6.4	5.3	6.7	8.2	4.7	3.5	2.7

SOURCE: Instituto de Economía, *Ocupación y Desocupación en Gran Santiago.*

Table 4.5 *GDP at factor cost, 1970 and 1971 (millions of escudos at 1970 prices)*

Sector	1970		1971		% increase	
Agriculture	6,084		6,419		5.5	
Fishing	285		321		12.6	
Mining	10,076		10,368		2.8	
Manufacturing	25,430		28,609		12.5	
Construction	3,792		4,152		9.5	
Subtotal: goods		45,667		49,860		9.2
Electricity, gas and water	1,645		1,887		14.7	
Transport and communica-tions	4,305		4,533		5.3	
Subtotal: basic services		5,950		6,420		7.9
Commerce	18,742		20,204		7.9	
Banking and finance	4,131		4,742		14.8	
Government	5,382·		5,694		5.8	
Miscellaneous services	10,694		11,550		8.0	
Subtotal: non-basic services		40,577		43,851		8.0
Total	92,194		100,140		8.6	

SOURCE: Based on data from ODEPLAN, taken from Millas, *Third Exposition*, p. 55.

Thus, in the midst of an acceleration of far-reaching agrarian reform and with uncertainty ruling all over the countryside, the harvest of 1971 nevertheless turned out to be very good, second only to that of 1968 in the history of Chile.

Table 4.6 *Gross domestic investment, 1970 and 1971 (millions of escudos at 1970 prices)*

	1970	1971	% change
Construction	7,600	8,550	12.5
Imported machinery and equipment	5,184	4,303	−16.8
Miscellaneous	1,673	481	−71.3
Total	14,457	13,334	−7.3

SOURCE: ODEPLAN, *Informe Económico Anual 1971*, p. 19.

Table 4.7 *Index of agricultural production 1970/71 (1969/70 = 100)*

Cereals	104.9	
Pulses	111.1	
Potatoes	122.2	
Wines	131.1	
Main industrial crops	90.9	
Fruits	105.1	
Vegetables	104.2	
Crop-farming		108.6
Meat	94.5	
Poultry	113.9	
Milk and milk products	108.3	
Wool	82.5	
Livestock		101.8
Total agricultural production	105.5	

SOURCE: Instituto de Economía, *La Economía Chilena en 1972*, p. 480.

Mining

In 1971 all vital mineral resources were nationalized. To the circumstances surrounding these nationalizations and to their international repercussions we will return in chapter 6. What interests us here is how production and prices developed.

Major sectors of activity

Copper

Had it not been for the recent incorporation of two new mines, Andina and Exótica, into the Gran Minería, output in large-scale copper mining would have declined considerably. Production in the three old mines reached its lowest level since 1961, but because of the new mines total output reached an all-time peak.

With regard to prices, the new government was less fortunate. The copper bonanza of the late 1960s had come to an end, and against the 2.3 per cent increase in production between 1970 and 1971 stood a 24 per cent decline in Chile's export prices.

Other minerals

Next to copper, iron and nitrates are Chile's most important minerals, especially in the export trade, which absorbs the bulk of output. Production and exports developed as shown in table 4.9:

Manufacturing

The UP's reactivation program was primarily expected to stimulate manufacturing industry. Fulfilling and even exceeding the government's most optimistic expectations, the rate of industrial expansion in 1971

Table 4.8   *Copper production 1971 as compared with 1970 (thousands of metric tons)*

Mine	1970		1971		% change
Chuquicamata	263		250		−4.9
El Teniente	177		147		−17.0
El Salvador	93		85		−8.6
Subtotal: 'old' mines		533		482	−5.5
Exótica	2		35		
Andina	6		54		
Subtotal: all Gran Minería		541		571	−5.5
Medium and small-scale mines	151		137		−10.2
Total copper mining	692		708		2.3

SOURCE: Corporación de Cobre (CODELCO).

Table 4.9   *Production (thousands of metric tons) and exports (millions of dollars) of iron and nitrate products, 1970 and 1971*

	Production			Exports		
	1970	1971	% change	1970	1971	% change
Iron	11,265	11,225	−0.4	71.0	67.7	−4.9
Nitrate, iodine and sulphate	671	845	26.0	25.1	36.1	43.1

SOURCE: ODEPLAN, *Informe Económico Anual 1971*, pp. 122ff, and Allende, *Second Message*, pp. 337ff.

became the highest reached in more than a decade, and the stagnating trend of the late Frei years was temporarily broken.

Although the industrial expansion that took place was general, the variation in growth rate between different industries, and between different plants within each individual industry, was considerable. To explain these differences would require a separate analysis with detailed information about all those factors that conditioned the 1971 industrial growth: the effects of the rise in purchasing power on demand for different commodities and the effects upon supply and demand of the (often quite arbitrary) price policy of the government, the various degrees of idle capacity at the beginning of the year, the different industries' and individual firms' access to credit and to imported raw materials, the distribution of labor conflicts (which as a whole experienced a 50 per cent decline, but which nevertheless affected a few big industries whose production as a result fell short of even the 1970 levels), the degree of co-operation on the part of the owners, etc. But for our present purposes we can content ourselves with what has been said above and conclude that the UP's reactivation program, with all its different ingredients, gave strikingly positive results in the manufacturing sector during 1971.

Construction

According to preliminary estimates the construction sector as a whole grew by 10.7 per cent.

Low-cost residential construction was given highest priority, and the initial plans envisaged an extraordinary effort to 'build away' part of the notorious housing shortage. The public sector alone initiated the construction of over 70,000 housing units in 1971, as against about

Table 4.10   *Index of manufacturing production (volume) 1970 and 1971*
(1968 = 100)

Personal consumption goods	1970	1971	% change
Food	99.6	107.7	8.1
Beverages	91.1	114.9	26.1
Tobacco	97.7	123.1	25.5
Textiles	96.0	110.1	14.7
Clothing and footwear	104.8	118.9	13.4
Furniture	113.4	109.1	−3.8
Printing and publishing	109.5	173.8	58.7
Miscellaneous	81.0	108.6	34.1
Intermediate goods			
Wood	108.1	131.7	21.8
Paper and paper products	88.3	91.8	3.9
Leather and leather products	103.9	119.7	15.2
Rubber and rubber products	111.0	135.5	22.2
Chemical products	120.9	144.0	19.1
Petroleum and coal products	105.4	128.6	22.0
Non-metallic minerals	102.9	120.9	17.5
Basic metals	108.0	116.7	8.0
Consumer durables and capital goods			
Metal products	98.6	109.1	10.6
Electrical machinery and equipment	99.5	113.3	13.8
Non-electrical machinery and equipment	94.2	126.3	34.1
Transport equipment	127.0	111.1	−12.5
General index	104.0	119.3	14.6

SOURCE: National Institute of Statistics (INE).

Table 4.11   *Growth in the construction sector*

	% change 1971/70
Residential construction	16.1
Non-residential construction	7.2
Public works	10.0
Repairs	−0.4
Total	10.7

SOURCE: ODEPLAN, *Informe Económico Anual 1971*, p. 151.

6,000 in 1970 and 20,000 as an average for 1967–70 (see table 4.13),
and the public Housing Corporation (Corporación de la Vivienda,
CORVI) – responsible for the 'slum removal' building in Chile's
poblaciones – greatly increased its activity.[34]

Many of these projects were never finished. Towards the end of 1971
it was clear that the housing program of the government had been far
too ambitious for Chile's resources. Bottlenecks began to appear – financial bottlenecks and, above all, lack of materials (the shortage of
cement became acute, for example) and of transportaion facilities. Production schedules were prolonged, and as late as in November 1972 only
28,600 of all housing units initiated by the public sector during 1971
and 1972 had been completed.[35] Still more than during earlier administrations, certainly, but far below original expectations.

Among non-residential projects in 1971 the increases in the construction of hospitals (50,000 square meters completed as against 28,000 in
1970) and of schools (226,000 square meters in 1971, 79,000 square
meters in 1970) deserve to be mentioned, together with the great pride
of Chilean architects and construction workers, the impressive building
of over 40,000 square meters where the UNCTAD III conference was
held in April 1972. It was not decided until mid-1971 that Santiago
should become the seat of the conference, and the sudden necessity of
concentrating on the completion of this building during the latter half
of the year naturally helped to delay the full realization of other parts
of the construction program.

Employment

We have earlier dated the industrial recovery at around March 1971,
and this date is confirmed by data on the employment situation, which,
at least in Santiago, began to improve in March. In the other two
regions from which reliable data are available the occupational expansion was slower and less pronounced; both the market mechanisms
and the state bureaucracy operated with a considerable lag in the
provinces.

According to ODEPLAN's rough estimates[36] the average number of
employed exceeded in 1971 that of 1970 by some 146,000 people, of
which 89,000 were new entrants to the labor force and some 57,000
formerly unemployed who had now managed to get a job. The sectors
which showed the largest percentage increases in employment were
construction (11.7 per cent), public utilities (7.6 percent), manufacturing

Major sectors of activity

Table 4.12   *Residential construction 1971 as compared with 1970 and annual average 1967–70 (number of housing units initiated)*

	Average 1967–70	1970	1971	% change 1971/1967–70
Public sector	20,347	5,914	73,009	259
Private sector	19,830	17,792	12,000	−39
Total	40,117	23,706	85,009	111

SOURCE: Ministerio de la Vivienda y Urbanismo, *Política Habitacional del Gobierno Popular*, pp. 22 and 45.

Table 4.13   *Rate of open unemployment in Greater Santiago, Concepción–Talcahuano and Lota–Coronel 1970–71 (percentages of labor force)*

	Santiago			
	March	June	September	December
1970	6.8	7.0	6.4	8.3
1971	8.2	5.2	4.8	3.8
	Concepción–Talcahuano		Lota–Coronel	
	April	October	April	October
1970	10.2	9.9	15.1	17.0
1971	9.7	8.4	15.6	12.8

SOURCE: Instituto de Economía, *Ocupación y Desocupación*, current issues.

(7.1 per cent), and transport and services (both 5.1 per cent). The trend towards services of preceding years was temporarily broken.

Prices

To most people's surprise – and, certainly, contrary to the political opposition's sombre prophecies – the rate of Chile's endemic inflation diminished appreciably in 1971. The consumer price index of the National Institute of Statistics rose by no more than 22.1 per cent between December 1970 and December 1971, as against 34.9 per cent the year before.

Wholesale prices rose even less (21.4 per cent), with imported

71

Table 4.14 *Absorption of new employment by sector 1966–70 and 1971 (percentages)*

Sector	1966–70	1971
Agriculture	6.8	8.4
Mining	1.9	0.9
Manufacturing	11.7	28.0
Construction	×	14.5
Public utilities	–	0.6
Transportation	8.7	6.3
Commerce	33.4	13.2
Other services	37.5	28.1

NOTE: × denotes negative value, – insignificant value.
SOURCE: ODEPLAN, *Informe Económico Anual 1971*, p. 23.

Table 4.15 *Consumer price increases December 1970–December 1971*

	Weight in total	% increase
Foodstuffs	41.7	28.1
Housing	22.2	15.8
Clothing	21.3	25.2
Miscellaneous	14.8	14.0
General index	100.0	22.1

SOURCE: INE.

products – owing to the exchange rate policy – and manufactures lying below the average and domestic agricultural products considerably above.

The government no doubt managed to squeeze profit margins in 1971. This, in combination with the drastic increase in nominal wages, caused a remarkable rise in consumption standards for wage and salary earners, whose real incomes can be estimated to have increased by almost 30 per cent between December 1970 and December 1971[37] and whose share in total income rose from 53.7 to 58.6 per cent in one year.[38]

Major sectors of activity

The external sector

Of the Central Bank's large reserves of foreign exchange in 1970 less than one-tenth was left by the end of 1971.[39] Official estimates of the balance of payments development in 1971 indicate a drastic deterioration, pointing to an overall deficit before compensatory financing of over 400 million dollars.

Exports

The heavy decline in export earnings was due to the fall in copper prices, which the slight increase in volume failed to compensate for.

Thus, if the high prices of copper in 1970 had prevailed during 1971, Chile's export earnings would have exceeded the actual level by more than 200 million dollars. Other export products developed satisfactorily. Minerals other than copper increased by some three per cent in value, from 115 to 119 million dollars, and industrial products from 115 to 122 million, while exports of agricultural products suffered a slight decline from 32 to 29 million dollars.

Imports

In 1971 import prices also developed unfavorably to Chile. According to Pedro Vuskovic these higher prices signified a loss to Chile of about 110 million dollars over 1970.[40] Together with the decline in average export prices this would mean a deterioration of Chile's terms of trade in the range of 25 per cent in one year.

But lacking detailed data on the development of import and export prices we can stick to aggregate figures in value terms only, keeping in mind that the overall volume of imports might actually have been kept more or less constant between 1970 and 1971. However, it is clear that the composition of imports changed appreciably, with intermediate goods and consumer goods – especially of agricultural origin – increasing their shares while imports of capital goods and services suffered a decline both in absolute and relative terms. The fact that the UP's economic policy was oriented towards consumption rather than accumulation was clearly reflected in Chile's balance of trade.

With respect to imports another circumstance deserves to be mentioned – the change in national origin of Chilean imports. As a consequence of the political reorientation initiated by the UP the United

Table 4.16 *Chile's balance of payments 1970 and 1971 (millions of dollars)*

	1970	1971	% change
Exports of goods and services	1,271.8	1,066.1	−16.2
Goods	1,128.8	964.7	−14.5
Services	143.0	101.4	−29.0
Imports of goods and services	1,201.9	1,311.7	+8.4
Goods	1,020.0	1,165.6	+12.5
Services	181.9	146.1	−19.7
Non-monetary gold sales	1.5	1.0	
Balance of trade	71.4	−244.6	
Net foreign investment income	−128.8	−89.8	
Balance of current account	−57.4	−334.4	
Capital account	148.5	−99.7	
Total before compensatory movements	91.1	−434.1	

SOURCE: Millas, *Third Exposition*, p. 60, and Banco Central.

Major sectors of activity

Table 4.17 *Copper production and exports 1970 and 1971*

Year	Production (metric tons)	Exports (metric tons)	Average export price (cents per pound)	Export earnings (millions of dollars)
1970	692,000	668,000	64.2	868
1971	708,000	704,000	48.5	695

SOURCE: Based on Instituto de Economía, *La Economía Chilena en 1972*, pp. 400–1.

Table 4.18 *Imports by category in 1970 and 1971 (millions of dollars)*

	1970		1971		% change	
Goods	1,020.0		1,165.6		12.5	
Consumer goods[a]		61.0		100.5		39.3
Raw materials and intermediate goods[a]		484.0		554.3		14.5
Foodstuffs and agricultural products		165.0		310.9		86.6
Machinery and equipment		310.0		200.0		−35.5
Services	181.9		146.1		−19.7	
Total	1,201.9		1,311.7		8.4	

[a]Excluding foodstuffs and agricultural products.
SOURCE: Banco Central and ICIRA, 'Diagnosis'.

States ceded ground to the rest of the world as supplier of goods to Chile. (see Table 4.19)

Other items in the balance of payments

No systematic information on the development of Chile's non-commercial foreign transactions in 1971 was ever released. It is clear, however, that the political changes introduced in Chile had a heavy impact upon autonomous capital movements. Traditionally strongly positive, Chile's capital account showed a deficit of approximately 100 million dollars in 1971.[41]

The period of the United States' favoring of Chile as the continent's largest *per capita* receiver of American aid and credits had come to an

Table 4.19   Origin of Chilean imports 1970 and 1971
(percentages)

	1970	1971
United States	37.2	17.0
Latin America (excluding Cuba)	20.3	31.8
Other market economies	42.0	47.3
Countries with planned economies	0.5	3.9

SOURCE: Millas, *Third Exposition*, p. 58.

abrupt end. Both the Agency for International Development and the Export–Import Bank rejected all Chilean requests for credit during 1971 (and 1972), and so did the Inter-American Development Bank and the World Bank. Credit lines that American commercial banks had traditionally offered Chile for current import requirements were also gradually being cut down. While in November 1970 Chile could call on short-term credits from US banks of approximately 220 million dollars the corresponding figures were to fall to 88 and 25 million in November 1971 and January 1972, respectively.[42] The entry of private capital for investment purposes virtually disappeared as well.

This 'invisible blockade', as the UP called it, had both political and commercial causes. The UP government soon found itself involved in a – not unexpected – constant dispute with the United States on various economic matters, especially after the nationalization of the Gran Minería of copper (which, it should be noted, signified a considerable direct relief for Chile's balance of payments since profit remittances ceased after July 1971), and the US government issued a large number of statements urging various financial organizations under its direct or indirect control not to grant Chile any new credits until due compensation for expropriated American property were paid.[43] But strictly commercial considerations also contributed: Chile was becoming a bad risk, especially for North American institutions which probably feared that an eventual breakdown of US–Chilean relations would make it difficult to recuperate loans to Chile.

The 'invisible blockade' did not signify that Chile's access to foreign loans was cut off, however. The Soviet bloc provided Chile with credits which, together with funds made available from several Western European and Latin American countries, compensated for the virtual closing down of American financial assistance. The UP continued on the same road as earlier Chilean administrations: accepting whatever foreign credit was available. When the balance of payments situation became critical in 1972 Chile could reach a fairly favorable agreement on the renegotiation of her foreign debt, which threatened to absorb over 400 million dollars of Chile's shrinking export earnings in that year alone.[44]

To summarize, we can conclude that Chile's foreign exchange situation deteriorated alarmingly in 1971. According to Pedro Vuskovic it had even become 'the principal restriction on the further realization of the government's program'.[45] In part this impairment of the external position was the direct result of the UP's own economic policy (for example, the demand-induced increase in low-priced agricultural products), in part it was the indirect consequence of the efforts to implement a program clashing with powerful foreign economic interests (with subsequent effects on both the private investment balance and on the availability of North American financial assistance), and, finally, it was the consequence of factors completely beyond the control of the Chilean government, such as the unfortunate change in Chile's terms of trade. Without the relief that credits from non-American sources signified, an acute balance of payments crisis would have become reality early in 1972.

YEAR ONE: AN EVALUATION

From a short-term point of view the success of the 1971 policy was spectacular. Never since 1952 had the Chilean economy grown so fast in one single year. Real wages rose considerably, and personal consumption expanded by 12.9 per cent over 1970. For most of the Chilean people, and especially for the very lowest paid and for those unemployed who got new jobs in 1971, the first year of UP rule brought striking benefits, and several 'social indicators' (for example, the rate of infant mortality which appears to have fallen over ten per cent in one year[46]) indicate that the gains reached the most modest and underprivileged sectors of the population.

But when making an evaluation of Salvador Allende's first year in office we cannot stop in December 1971. The UP's drastic short-term program had heavy – and largely negative – repercussions upon later political and economic developments. It proved, in fact, to be most difficult to make the planned transition from a policy based on an overall increase in consumption and a quite indiscriminate effort to mobilize idle resources to a more sophisticated development policy based on capital accumulation and economic planning. In part the increase in output and consumption in 1971 took place at the expense of possibilities of future growth, and various external and internal restrictions were bound to arise sooner or later as foreign exchange reserves were approaching zero and the existence of idle capacity and skilled manpower was gradually being exhausted. Investment fell off markedly,[47] despite the efforts by the public sector. By the end of the year various kinds of bottlenecks were already beginning to appear, and future rapid growth could clearly not continue to be based on the philosophy of letting capital accumulation lag far behind consumption increases.

To this we should add the monetary explosion, which soon threatened to confront the Chilean economy with unprecedented inflation with unpredictable economic and political consequences.

In short, in only one year the economic panorama had changed completely. In January 1972 it was no longer a question of trying to cure an acute depression, but of trying to manage an economy which was beginning to exceed all its bounds.

A few words should finally be said about major political events. Since the government's economic policies were subordinated to its explicitly formulated political objectives, we cannot make an evaluation of 1971 without referring to the political advances that, at least initially, were made by the Unidad Popular.

The magnitude of these advances is indicated by the extraordinary increase in public support for the Left as expressed in the municipal elections in April 1971, when the groups and parties which at that time made up the UP managed to get slightly over 50 per cent of all valid votes, and against 49.1 per cent for the opposition. The government, elected in 1970 by little more than one-third of the voters, had ceased to represent a minority of Chileans, and the two big Marxist parties – the PC and the PS – alone got over forty per cent of the votes, thus reducing further the electoral weight of the Social Democratic forces within the UP. As hoped and expected by the UP, a large number of people who had supported Radomiro Tomic in the 1970 presidential election had been won over by the UP, and most of these by the explicitly Marxist parties.

How much of this spectacular electoral victory should be attributed to the government's expansionist economic policy is difficult to tell. The reactivation program had only recently begun to give tangible results, although it is obvious that the wage increase already granted gave the consumers a feeling of prosperity that created a favorable climate for the government. But most of the explanation of the election result probably lies in the UP's success in maintaining the overall political initiative on every front (for example the initiation of the most popular program of bringing the country's basic mineral resources under Chilean control, the acceleration of the agrarian reform, the government's nationalism, supported by a resolute and very ably handled foreign policy) and in the still divided opposition's failure to present any viable political alternative.

During the months immediately preceding and following April 1971 the electoral strength of the UP probably reached its peak. After April 1971, when the UP had proved to be a national majority, there seemed to be a good chance of the Left winning a plebiscite on the question of dissolving parliament, thoroughly dominated by the opposition, and asking the citizens to elect new representatives to the 'People's Assembly' which they intended to substitute for Congress.

No effort was made to gain the legislative power this way, however. It was no secret in Chile that the Socialist Party insisted on calling for a plebiscite, while the Communists, Radicals, and Allende personally rejected the Socialist proposal, feeling that a plebiscite would immediately force the opposition to unite and hoping that the political gains of the UP could be consolidated during the period to come. Presumably they also hoped that the long expected split within the Christian Democratic Party would materialize and the electoral position of the Left would thereby improve further.

Later, it was officially admitted by many leading UP people that this decision to postpone the calling for a plebiscite on the People's Assembly issue had been a serious mistake.[48]

Both the unification of the opposition and the DC split took place fairly soon. In May the rightist, 'Frei-ist' faction took over the control of the leadership of the PDC at a party congress in Cartagena, and in June the Christian Democrats and the National Party agreed upon a common candidate in a complementary election in Valparaíso to fill a vacant seat in the Chamber of Deputies. To the great disillusionment of the UP the candidate from the united Right defeated the Socialist who ran for the Left; the margin was small, but large enough to rule out the question of a plebiscite for the moment.

Another political episode, for which neither the UP nor the opposition had any responsibility whatsoever, also came to favor the Right. Frei's former Minister of the Interior, Edmundo Pérez Zújovic, was assassinated by a group of leftist extremists, and the event was easily converted into useful propaganda for the opposition, which for long had been conducting a stubborn but so far not too convincing campaign against the government's supposedly soft treatment of all kinds of 'dangerous extremists'.

As could be expected, internal discord was growing within the Christian Democrats as the party more and more openly allied itself with the traditional Right. After the Valparaíso election it was no longer a question of *whether* a split would occur, but of *when* and in what proportions. In July these questions were answered when nine dissident DC deputies and two senators and a number of influential members – not including Tomic, however – declared it impossible to change the party 'from within' and decided to form a new movement, the Christian Left (Izquierda Cristiana, IC), which immediately joined the UP. At the same time the UP suffered a serious setback. A group of Radicals, including five senators and nine deputies, accused the Radical Party of having turned 'Marxist', left the PR and formed a middle-of-the-road party, the Radical Left Party (*Partido de Izquierda Radical*, PIR) which first gave the government its (conditional) support but which finally arrived at the same position as the Radical Democrats (DR), the offshot of the PR from 1969, on the far Right. When the PIR and the DR early in 1973 fused into one party the two groups had become both very small and utterly reactionary.

To conclude, 1971 was a year of definitions. After July 1971 no more party splits took place, and the political forces were lining up in two antagonistic blocs, with only the small PIR disturbing the picture during a vacillating period when it could not decide whom to support. The UP no doubt strengthened its general position, despite the fact that the headway made during the first six months or so was not followed by still greater victories but rather by a prolonged stalemate. The 'march towards power' had got off to a seemingly good start, but the leadership of the Unidad Popular failed to take advantage of the situation.

All the Allende goverment's major obstacles remained to be overcome. The opposition's parliamentary majority was intact, along with its control of most central institutions. The judiciary, the Contraloría General, the army, most branches of the state bureaucracy and the mass media industry were thoroughly dominated by bourgeois interests. These power bastions were valuable assets in the war of attrition that followed, and the rightist opposition knew how to make use of them to make the 'Chilean road to socialism' a blind alley.

CHAPTER 5

1972 and 1973: inflation and stagnation

The distinction made earlier, in the analysis of 1971, between the UP's short-term or conjunctural economic policy on the one hand and its program of structural reforms on the other was somewhat artificial, and is even more so when applied to the years that followed. But an effort to maintain it will nevertheless be made in the remainder of this study. In this chapter we will thus extend the analysis of 'traditional' economic policies and of the behavior of incomes, money, prices, production levels, etc. to 1972 and 1973, while chapters 6 and 7 will be devoted to the political economy of the UP's nationalization and agrarian reform programs.

The interdependence of all the above-mentioned aspects of economic policy is obvious, as is the interdependence of 'economic' and 'political' factors, and the lines of causation become more and more difficult to trace the further we proceed in time. While it was, for example, still quite legitimate to regard the economic boom of 1971 as occasioned mainly by the government's short-term reactivation program, it is much more difficult to divide the responsibility for the economic performance later on between the effects of (*a*) the UP's initial, exaggeratedly 'Keynesian' manner of stimulating demand, (*b*) the program of structural transformations and (*c*) the overall political situation. All these factors and several others were certainly influential – and influenced one another – and to do full justice to the dialectics of the Chilean process under Allende a better synchronized analysis than the one presented below would no doubt be required.

It should however be stressed that the intensification of class struggles and the further polarization that characterized Chile during the latter half of the UP administration gave political factors in the most narrow sense of the word a more decisive impact upon the behavior of the economy than had been the case in 1971. Without wanting to emphasize the distinction between economics and politics, or to suggest a one-way causal relationship between the two, I will therefore indicate the differences between 1971 and 1972–3 by making a change in the disposition of this

81

chapter with respect to the preceding one: in what follows the political panorama will be presented before I turn to 'strictly economic' developments.

MAJOR POLITICAL EVENTS

After reaching its high-water mark some six months after Allende took office the political strength of the UP gradually began to deteriorate, and by 1972 all the parties of the Chilean Left admitted that the 'popular forces' had been losing ground. It was not primarily a question of a decline in electoral support for the government – in terms of votes the UP apparently lost very little from late 1971 onwards[1] – but rather of a general inability to cope with the economic and political problems that arose and to counteract the increasingly violent attacks launched by the rightist opposition. The latter, by now unified around the common objective of ousting Allende but maintaining certain tactical and strategic differences as to how to do it and what should come after, had taken over the initiative.

Political events in neighboring countries also developed unfavorably for the Unidad Popular and for the South American Left in general. In August 1971 the progressive Bolivian government headed by General Torres was overthrown by a strongly pro-US, pro-Brazilian and anti-Marxist military junta. In Uruguay the forces of the extreme Right gradually consolidated a terror regime. Parliament was closed in June 1973; the trade union movement and most political parties were outlawed and a rightist military dictatorship was established.

But let us first look at some of the methods used in the Chilean bourgeoisie's counter-offensive and then turn to the increasingly defensive tactics adopted by the leadership of the Unidad Popular.

In Congress the opposition's rather passive resistance of 1971 evolved into more agressive lines of action. The PDC and the PN, acting in concert and with the help of their petty allies among the ex-Radicals, continued to block all bills – even the most harmless ones – presented by the government, but they also tried to enforce completely new legislation: for example a couple of 'constitutional reforms' to impede the extension of the state's control of economic activity and the further carrying through of the agrarian reform were thus passed by the congressional majority during 1972. Prolonged but resultless conversations between the UP – which was anxious to reach agreements with hoped-for 'progressive sectors' of the Christian Democratic Party – and the PDC traditionally followed before Allende decided to veto the opposition's projects.

The administration's current economic policies were also obstructed. When, for example, the UP wanted to raise taxes in order to reduce somewhat the budgetary deficits, the opposition's prompt answer was to lower taxes instead. The Chilean constitution's specification of the division of power in economic matters between the President who was to control the expenditure side of the budget and the parliament whose responsibility it was to grant income made such maneuvers possible, though rendering stabilization policies impossible.

Impeachment of ministers and *intendentes* (provincial governors) also became increasingly common. In 1971 only two such cases took place; in 1972 four and in 1973 ten ministers and *intendentes* were suspended from office after censure motions passed by the congressional majority.[2] 'Failure to protect private property and personal rights' was the standard formulation used. The opposition tried, in short, to change the 'rules of the game' in Chile's political life by eroding presidential power in an attempt to convert Chile into a country run by the Congress.[3]

The judiciary too was active in openly defying the administration's authority. We will in subsequent chapters have occasion to deal with the struggles of the Supreme Court and the Contraloría General against the nationalization program. Suffice it here to say merely that the Allende government, and the whole Chilean Left, came to regard the decisions of the rightist-controlled Supreme Court as strongly politically motivated, and this political bias was felt as a very serious handicap for the UP.[4]

The general strategy of the legislative and judiciary powers was, in short, to try to impose their will against that of the executive in order to curtail the wide range of faculties with which the Chilean constitution equipped Salvador Allende. In their efforts to make governing as difficult as possible the judges and the rightist senators and deputies had the wholehearted support from all the opposition's mass media – which were both quantitatively and qualitatively far superior to those of the Left – and, of course, from their political parties and organizations. From 1972 on the entire DC leadership – though certainly not all Christian Democratic members, let alone voters – participated very actively in the general policy of obstruction. It is symptomatic that it was a Christian Democratic senator (Juan de Dios Cármona) who, in April 1972, was the first to launch publicly an appeal for 'civil disobedience', later to become so common, as a method to weaken the government.[5]

This and similar appeals fell on fertile ground, and instead of advancing towards the overriding objective of taking power in society as a whole the UP had to face the fact that the authority of the government was becoming undermined. When the armed forces and *carabineros* eventually began to change their neutral attitude in order openly to join the anti-UP forces the Allende government lost all chance of using state repression against the various forms of civil disobedience, sabotage, fascist terrorism and street fighting instigated by the whole of the Chilean Right.

These circumstances would never have produced such fatal results if, firstly, the alternative organs of power 'from below' (*poder popular*) had been allowed to develop into true organs of *power* and, secondly, if private business had continued its 1971 policy of near cooperation in the economic field.

The latter point leads us over to another, very important and effective, part of the counter-offensive launched against the Allende regime: economic opposition and sabotage.

The strategy behind the whole 'Chilean road' was based on the underlying assumption that it was possible to divide the bourgeoisie into two separate and well-defined parts: one monopolistic sector, which should be fought and expropriated, and one non-monopolistic sector which in no way should feel threatened by the UP but which instead should and could be won over to the side of the 'popular forces' (or at least 'neutralized', to use an expression often used by the Chilean Left). But this theoretically clear-cut distinction, which appeared to make some sense at the beginning of the Allende administration, turned out to be more and more illusory as the Right to an increasing extent managed to mobilize the whole of private business, monopoly capitalists and petty traders alike, to fight the 'Marxist threat'.

The expected and not too pronounced 'investment strike' of 1971 was complemented with less passive forms of resistance. Speculation, black marketeering and minor economic dislocation serving both pecuniary and political ends flourished – the UP's own economic policies certainly encouraged such phenomena – but far more serious were the sometimes very prolonged waves of boycotts, lockouts, strikes and sabotage that affected the Chilean economy from late 1972. As early as in October of that year, when the first of these massive and well coordinated actions by big business, wide sectors of the petty-bourgeoisie and conservative professional's unions[6] took place, the political objectives were clear. In their attempts to bring about complete and indefinite cessation of all vital economic activities – the common slogan during the 'October crisis' was 'Paralyze Chile!' – the rightists, including the PDC leadership, were trying to force Allende to resign and/or the military to intervene.[7]

These and similar events will be touched upon now and then in the chapters that follow, and I will also – and this is of major interest for an explanation of the Unidad Popular's failure – try to analyze *why* the economic and political strategy of the UP had to clash with the interests of not only the 'oligarchy' but of the working class's hoped-for allies within the petty-bourgeoisie as well. For it is crucial to stress that the fierce opposition to the Allende government that the class of medium and small-scale industrialists, merchants, etc. engaged in had some objective grounds and was not merely the result of clever manipulation by the Chilean Right. In spite of the role that was played by intrigues, plots, propagandist lies and criminal sabotage and violence – and all this was very much present in the rightist offensive – it would be super-ficial indeed to blame the failure of the 'Chilean road to socialism' on such factors only. The conflicts and contradictions that arose were, as will be shown later, inherent in the very socio-economic structure of Chile and in the overall strategy followed by the UP.

Before we turn to economic policies and events a few words should finally be said about the attitudes adopted by the UP and about the divergencies within the Chilean Left that became increasingly sharp from mid-1972 onwards.

The one thing that all the different leftist parties agreed upon was that the political panorama looked less favorable to the UP than in 1971. But when it came to the question of how to confront the critical situation unanimity ended. The Communists, supported by Radicals and, more often than not, by Allende personally, advocated a defensive 'consolida-tion-of-gains' policy based on concessions to the rightist opposition, while the UP Left – and, certainly, the MIR – emphasized the socialist con-tent of the struggle, opposed the conciliatory line of the PC and called for a vigorous mobilization of the masses and for a working-class offensive based on revolutionary objectives.

The arguments sustaining these two lines, which clearly reflected the unresolved strategic differences that had long existed between the PC and the PS,[8] deserve to be presented directly by participants in the in-ternal UP debate. Let us first listen to Orlando Millas (Senator, PC) when in an important article from mid-1972[9] he exposes his own party's positions:

The characteristic feature of the situation today is that the correlation of forces has deteriorated for the working class and for the government as a result of political and economic mistakes which we could briefly describe as *transgressions of the UP program* ... It would be unfortunate to continue to increase the number of enemies, and what should be done is quite the opposite, namely to *make concessions* or at least neutralize certain sectors and social groups. [Emphasis added.]

In synthesis, the PC argued that things had gone *too far*, that the time had come not for a new offensive but for a period of consolidation of the gains already obtained. Emphasis was put on discipline – no more factory occupations or land seizures, for example – and on economistic slogans such as the 'battle of production'.[10] The word 'socialism' was seldom mentioned by the Communists, and never in connection with the UP's immediate tasks.

An opposite view was given in an interview by Oscar Garretón, MAPU's new secretary general, in which he argues that '[in our opinion] the socialist tasks are the most important ones today. This implies a critical position towards those within or outside the UP who assert that the process which our country is going through is a gradual process which can suddenly be arrested in order to postpone the socialist objectives to a later stage ... As far as we understand the UP program these [socialist] objectives are in fact expressed in the program'.[11]

In a document[12] elaborated by the political commission of the Socialist Party the position of the PC is equally refuted: 'A correct analysis leads to the conclusion that the present process is a revolutionary process ... and that it has already advanced so far that we should not try to defend ourselves by consolidating it halfway, but should accelerate it further.'

And, finally, the position of Carlos Altamirano, secretary general of the PS: 'The actual class struggle is irreconcilable, that is, there is no place for either conciliation or coexistence. It will come to an end only when one of the classes assumes complete power.'[13]

It was, by and large, the position of the PC which imposed itself within the government. The victory for the 'consolidationist' line is illustrated by the cabinet reshuffle that took place in June 1972, when Orlando Millas was made Minister of Finance and a technocratic representative of the rightist faction of the PS, Carlos Matus, became Minister of Economy. The main symbol of an aggressive policy against private business, Pedro Vuskovic, was sacrificed by Allende at the PC's insistence, while negotiations over the size of the state area of the economy were taken up with a sector of the Christian Democratic leadership.

The new economic situation

Outside the ministries, political events took a different turn and, as often happens when antagonisms intensify in society as a whole, the masses became much more revolutionary than their leaders.[14] Some of the socio-economic reasons behind this development will be analyzed later on, in particular when we come to the implementation of the nationalization program and the agrarian reform, but exactly how the workers' radicalization expressed itself, and how the different mass organizations and autonomous organs of 'parallel power' developed, will only very occasionally be touched upon in subsequent chapters. What is important in the present context is to emphasize that the salient feature of the Chilean political scene as from 1972 was precisely the polarization that took place, the working class's own revolutionary mobilization and the fact that the UP leadership more and more began to tail behind the mass movement instead of conducting it.

With this brief overview of political positions and developments in mind it will, I hope, be easier to understand both the reasons for and the effects of what will be the main topic of the rest of this essay: the *economics* of the political economy of the latter half of the Allende administration.

THE NEW ECONOMIC SITUATION AND THE LACK OF NEW POLICIES

As early as 1 May 1971, President Allende warned that difficulties lay ahead. 'The purchasing power now at your disposal', Allende told the mass of workers listening to his speech, 'has given rise to a sales boom never experienced before in Chile's history, but you must remember that it is necessary to restore certain things. In fifteen days or in two months our stocks will be depleted ... Chile is not accustomed to rationing, and we do not want such a system to be introduced. Therefore, comrades, we have to produce ...'[15]

Despite good-sized increases in output in 1971 the 'battle of consumption' had turned out to be much easier to win than the 'battle of production'. The recession of the late Frei years had been cured; now the problem that arose was how to find remedies for the overdose of stimulants and for the explosive inflationary pressures that had been created.

To confront the new circumstances more drastic measures than appealing to the workers' consciences by asking them to produce more were called for. But whatever these drastic measures might have consisted of they were not implemented, and with the political situation

87

growing increasingly critical the government's always very limited freedom of action was further and further reduced. The first of the economic battles that was irrevocably lost was the battle against inflation.

The revival of inflation

After a brief period of relative stability of prices in 1971, when consumer prices rose by only 22.1 per cent, the pace of price increases began to accelerate at an unprecedented speed.

It should be stressed that the official index given in tables 5.1 and 5.2 became increasingly unrealistic[16] as shortages and black markets mushroomed. By 1972 Chile experienced a situation of both galloping inflation and widespread scarcities. Through price regulations the government continued to try to keep prices of 'popular consumption' goods low while letting 'luxuries' become relatively expensive,[17] but a larger and larger share of trade within the private sector escaped the eyes of the price inspectors and JAPs.

With the political costs of shortages and black markets being high and rising, the government felt that a modification of the price policy of 1971 had to be made. In August–September an effort was thus made to normalize the distribution of consumer goods, and particularly of foodstuffs, by permitting large price increases. The formula 'stabilization on a higher level' launched by the Millas–Matus economic team proved inoperative, however. The UP economists had calculated for a drastic, once-and-for-all movement towards equilibrium between demand and supply for a wide range of commodities, but the queues and black markets failed to disappear.[18] The 'higher level' was no doubt reached, but not the 'stabilization' part of the project. Prices continued to rise.

The inflationary pressures were too strong to permit manipulations with price controls. Behind the 1972–3 inflation lay an explosive increase in the quantity of money in circulation in Chile. During 1971 the price spiral could still be partly suppressed, owing to idle capacity, curtailment of profit margins, cheap imports and, last but not least, to the existence of large stocks of commodities which could absorb part of the inflated demand for goods. In 1972 these roads were all becoming blocked, and after a certain lag even official prices caught up with the massive injections of money into the economy. In 1972 and 1973 both series accelerated upwards in an almost parallel way.

Table 5.1 *INE's consumer price index, percentage increases.*
Selected twelve-month periods

Period	Rate of increase (%)
January 1971–January 1972	24.8
July 1971–July 1972	45.9
January 1972–January 1973	180.3
July 1972–July 1973	323.2
January 1973–January 1974	800 (?)[a]

[a]The junta's estimate. See explanation in ch. 5, n. 16.

Table 5.2 *INE's consumer price index 1972–3 (1969 = 100).*
General index and monthly variations (percentages)

Month	General index	Monthly variations	Change during preceding 12 months
December 1969	100	—	—
January 1972	170.8	6.5	24.8
February 1972	181.9	3.7	32.0
March 1972	186.9	2.7	34.0
April 1972	197.5	5.7	38.1
May 1972	205.9	4.3	40.0
June 1972	210.2	2.1	40.1
July 1972	219.5	4.4	45.9
August 1972	269.4	22.7	77.2
September 1972	329.3	22.2	114.3
October 1972	379.4	15.2	142.9
November 1972	400.7	5.6	149.9
December 1972	434.1	8.3	163.4
January 1973	478.8	10.3	180.3
February 1973	498.7	4.1	174.1
March 1973	528.6	6.2	183.3
April 1973	582.5	10.2	195.5
May 1973	695.6	19.4	238.5
June 1973	804.1	15.6	283.4
July 1973	927.1	15.3	323.6
August–September 1973	n.a.	n.a.	n.a.

SOURCE: Instituto Nacional de Estadísticas (INE). As from March 1973 the figures – always based on the INE index – have been taken from *El Mercurio*.

Table 5.3   *Quantity of money and consumer price index, percentage increases. Selected twelve-month periods*

End of:	Quantity of money	Consumer prices
December 1970–December 1971	114	22
December 1971–December 1972	172	163
April 1972–April 1973	219	196
July 1972–July 1973	292	324

SOURCE: Based on Banco Central, *Boletín Mensual*, various issues, and table 5.2 above.

But why did the supply of money increase so fast? The fact is that the UP's reactivation program, once initiated, became impossible to check for both economic and political reasons. Tough stabilization policies were out of the question, since the good times *should* continue. We recall Dr Allende's words about 'continuing expansion' being a necessary condition for the viability of the 'Chilean road to socialism'.[19] Wages should not be cut down, material sacrifices should not have to be imposed upon the Chilean people. Taxes should be raised for the high-income groups, true, but this could not be done against the will of the Congress (which flatly rejected all tax increase bills). And the UP argued that the public sector had to continue to expand, which allowed the budgetary deficit to increase from 10 to 26 thousand million escudos between 1971 and 1972.[20]

Let us now see how the government's intentions and efforts to cope with the new situation were reflected in its incomes policy – a policy which was both a cause and a symptom of the rapidly approaching monetary crisis.

The UP's first year brought, as we have seen, great economic benefits for Chile's wage and salary earners. The new government also promised that the real income gains obtained in 1971 should be maintained in subsequent years. In the general CUT–government agreement it was thus established that from 1972 onwards almost all income groups were to receive full compensation for the inflation. That is, wage readjustments at the beginning of each year should be based upon, and should not fall short of, the preceding year's rise in the cost of living. The UP's formula was that the purchasing power of 1971 should be neither increased nor reduced in real terms, but that living standards of the great majority of the population should nevertheless continue to rise through improvements in various public services such as education, health, etc.[21]

Because of galloping inflation it was found necessary to adjust wages more often than once a year. The price rises hit the weakest groups hardest, and not only arbitrary injustices but total chaos in the whole wage structure threatened unless an overall settlement was reached. Conversations with the trade unions were begun in mid-1972, and on 1 October a general wage rise compensating for the inflation of the first nine months of the year was agreed on. At one stroke all but the very highest wages and salaries increased by 99.8 per cent.

By and large, the UP thus continued to rely upon non-discriminatory criteria – almost everybody should be compensated. Why? Let us stop for a moment and look at the UP's way of arguing.

The income policy of 1971 was based primarily on the principle of overall expansion rather than redistribution. Quite consciously, the UP decided to favor not only the poor majority (which in percentage terms did receive a little more than average) but the comparatively well-to-do middle classes as well. The underlying philosophy was explained in the following way by Orlando Millas, then Minister of Finance, in an interview in October 1972[22]:

Interviewer: Do you believe that is is possible to carry through the actual economic policies without hurting the interests of certain sectors of the middle strata (*capas medias*) like professionals, technicians, and middle and high officials within the state bureaucracy?

Millas: This is of course not only absolutely possible but also indispensable... I think that it is evident that everything that the People's Government has done has resulted in higher living standards and better possibilities for the above-mentioned middle sectors. And we will continue with these policies since all revolutionary processes get strengthened precisely through the alliance between the working class and the middle strata.

The UP's strategy was, as Carlos Altamirano put it early in 1973, based on the belief 'that *all* Chileans, with the exception of a handful of monopolists and *latifundistas*, could increase their well-being.' By now Altamirano dissociated himself completely from this illusion (which the UP Left never really believed in): 'Reality,' he continued, 'has clearly demonstrated that this conception was false.'[23] Not only did the exaggerated generosity towards the middle strata aggravate the economic difficulties (inflation, shortages, etc.), the UP Left argued, but the idea that one could 'bribe' these sectors to support a socialist government had also proved to be erroneous.[24]

1972 and 1973: inflation and stagnation

The debate around these questions was always very heated within the UP, but the 'official' line tended to be the one advocated by the PC and its allies. By March/April 1973, when a new general wage settlement was to take place, the UP seemed to agree that a change was called for, however, and this time the government and the CUT decided to differentiate income readjustments. While all incomes inferior to five *sueldos vitales* were raised with a common percentage of 60.8 per cent, corresponding to the inflation between 1 October and 31 March, all groups in higher income brackets received no proportional increase but a lump sum equivalent to 60.8 per cent of five *sueldos vitales*, or some 6,100 escudos per months.

The March/April agreement was received with indignation by the rightist parties, which established their own criteria in Congress, refused to pass the UP's proposals and agreed upon a non-discriminatory readjustment with full proportional compensation for the past five months' inflation to rich and poor alike. Allende successfully vetoed this readjustment, arguing that the legislative branch had no power whatsoever to determine wages.[25]

In October 1973 a new general rise was to take place. The snowball put in motion immediately after Allende's electoral victory grew and grew. Wage rises of the order of 200 per cent would have been required to compensate for the inflation between March and October 1973.

The situation was already absurd in 1972, but no political force in Chile was interested in recognizing its absurdity. Wage and salary earners suffered badly from the inflation and the economically and politically most powerful groups – copper miners, professionals, technicians, skilled workers – were bent on fighting for their own interests, well aware of the fact that the Allende government neither could nor wanted to repress them by force. Wage-drift necessarily accelerated. In order to forestall strikes and discontent, protect the weak and keep its old and oft-repeated promises the UP government thus felt obligated to grant general readjustments at shorter and shorter intervals. The political Right finally became much more interested in precipitating the overthrow of the government than in protecting the industrial bourgeoisie's immediate profits. The opposition parties constantly urged Chileans to demand higher wages and salaries, and through their organizations and mass media they instigated and fomented any labor conflict within reach. It was also typical of the situation that early in 1973, when the congressional opposition decided to try to change the administration's wage proposals, it passed a program which was more and not less generous than that of the UP.

The new economic situation

In this the opposition failed, but the deadlock between the executive and legislative powers nevertheless directly aggravated the situation. Although the Congress had no influence over wages it did control taxes, and this control was used to make certain that the government's wage bills passed Congress with more and more inadequate financing. In October 1972 the UP estimated public expenditures to increase by some twenty thousand million escudos as a result of the wage readjustment, and according to the administration's original project twelve and a half of those twenty would be financed through tax increases, leaving an expected deficit of eight thousand million escudos to be printed by the Central Bank. The bill was sabotaged, however; in Congress it was modified to such an extent that only 4,840 million escudos out of the proposed 12,540 million remained with adequate financing.[26] The government's plan to make taxes more progressive was determinedly rejected, and a 'simplified' system of income taxation which in practice favored the wealthy was passed.[27]

In March/April 1973 the situation was repeated. Allende warned: 'There will be a plebescite. We will veto the program if the Congress insists on letting the wage readjustment bill pass without adequate financing.'[28] But nothing unusual happened. The congressional majority refused to revise upwards and reduced a couple of property taxes instead, and Allende's words about calling for a plebescite were buried in silence.

We thus see that, although the wage trap in which the Allende government was caught was originally set by the UP itself and by the general situation in late 1970, the opposition saw to it that later political developments placed solutions out of reach. No political force in Chile could − or wanted to − halt the wage race, and the attitude adopted by the opposition-controlled parliament rendered increased taxation of the wealthy impossible. The situation called for drastic measures, but by now the government lacked the political strength to take drastic measures of any kind against anyone.

And the annihilation of the value of the escudo continued. A sophisticated analysis of the Chilean inflation in 1972 and 1973 would of course require the taking into account of a large number of mutually reinforcing promoters of inflation neglected above: the government's credit, exchange rate, public expenditure and price control policies, the bottlenecks that arose, the losses incurred in state-owned enterprises and in the reformed sector of agriculture, the flourishing stockpiling, speculation and spreading of rumors, etc. All of these factors were influential and ought to be studied. Most of them will be studied in the chapters that follow, but no effort will be made to integrate them into a systematic analysis of the inflation. An account of the Allende government's and the Congress's income and tax policies has been given and it is, I hope, sufficiently telling – as long as we remember that the inflation that developed was both a cause and an effect of the huge nominal income rises granted in 1971–3.

SHORTAGES SPREAD

Late in 1971, on one of the first days of December, a novel political manifestation took place in Santiago: down the fashionable shopping street Providencia thousands and thousands of mostly well-fed and well-dressed Santiago housewives were marching and screaming and banging on pots to express their protests against the 'scarcity of food' imposed upon them by the UP.[29] The economic reasons for the women's complaints were not very convincing – beef was really the only foodstuff in short supply – but this 'march of the empty pots' was an unmistakable omen of what was to come. It was followed by innumerable similar and apparently more easily justifiable actions.

Both in Chile and abroad the shortage of foodstuffs came to symbolize the economic problems that arose under Allende. In a sense this picture is highly misleading. Long queues did occur outside the grocery stores, but the overall supply of foodstuffs *increased* remarkably fast, at least during the UP's first two years. Food became short not because there was less available than before but because it was so cheap that the great majority of the Chilean people could now afford to eat much better than ever before, a circumstance which disturbed many upper-class Chileans, who were used to eating beef seven days a week.[30]

This will be examined in more detail in chapter 7, which deals with the agrarian reform and the overall availability of foodstuffs during 1970–73. What I wish to stress at this juncture is, first, that as from December 1971 queues and shortages did begin to appear and the general economic situation began to deteriorate and, second, that although much will be said about scarcities in what follows we should always keep in mind that the shortages of consumer goods that arose were more the result of high nominal wages and price controls than of a diminishing supply of commodities.

But let us temporarily leave all monetary issues aside and look at what is, together with inflation, the most important feature of the Chilean economic panorama after 1971: the rapid growth of various restrictions and bottlenecks which turned the previous expansion into stagnation and, eventually, into decline.

The limits of idle capacity

When initiating the short-term reactivation program the UP could count upon a good-sized margin of excess capacity in manufacturing. Implicit the government's way of reasoning was the belief that this idle capacity was at the free disposal of the economy in much the same way as were inventories and foreign exchange holdings, and optimism with respect to continued industrial expansion was widespread.

The average rate of idle capacity in 1970 was calculated to be approximately 25 per cent.[31] During the successful year of 1971 there was an increase of manufacturing output of some 14 per cent. If we take into account the (very modest) net investment that took place we can suppose that perhaps 13 to 15 per cent – our estimates are very rough – of the initial idle capacity was left by January 1972.

But although demand remained adequate, to say the least, the rate of industrial growth stagnated. A bare 2.8 per cent increase was recorded in 1972, to be followed the next year by an outright decline. As in so many other cases when 'Keynesian' policies have been pursued in underdeveloped countries problems originating from the supply side very soon checked the speed once the wheels had been set in motion.

To talk about excess capacity in average terms is very illusory in a poorly articulated economy with supply rigidities. The margins of, say, twenty-five per cent in 1971 and fifteen in 1972 that existed in Chilean manufacturing turned out to be meaningless averages as the amount of idle capacity 'at disposal' varied widely between different sectors, and bottlenecks appearing in one industry often affected others as well. Excess capacity thus became exhausted 'from below'; all of it could not be utilized. This is particularly clear if we recall that ODEPLAN's estimates of the pre-UP situation indicated that capacity utilization rates were highest precisely in the intermediate goods industries, where less than 15 per cent of excess capacity was registered in 1970. In many vital individual industries the margins were even narrower, of course.

It should also be pointed out that excess capacity estimates are based on the assumption of normal supply of raw materials, fuels, electricity, spare parts, skilled workers, etc. But in Chile one or several of these crucial elements began to be lacking here and there as early as the beginning of 1972. Problems with imports of spare parts and alloys created great difficulties in the huge Pacific Steel Company (CAP), for example, and the shortage of cement and building materials in general became acute at an early stage. The repercussions on the rest of the economy of these and other scarcities were considerable.

To identify exactly where and why these bottlenecks originally appeared is difficult indeed, but it is important to stress that once in existence these bottlenecks tended to spread, and spread fast. The government tried to catch up with the help of emergency imports and all kinds of improvisations, but its control of the economy was very limited and both for economic and political reasons it became increasingly cumbersome to cope with the new problems.

Among the many different factors responsible for the emergence of what we could call an almost generalized bottleneck economy one in particular deserves to be pointed out: the poor quality of Chile's infrastructural facilities and above all her road transportation system where, to make things worse, the rightist political opposition had one of its most strategic strongholds.

Infrastructural bottlenecks

Even a superficial glance at an economic map of Chile reveals the vulnerability of the economy and its dependence on a smooth working transportation system. In the north: a vast desert, apparently worthless but containing mineral resources providing most of the country's export earnings. Greater Santiago: over one-third of the whole population, with more than half of the total purchasing power, crowded on a small piece of land some 80 miles away from the closest port (Valparaiso) and without important natural resources in the vicinity. South of Santiago, down to Puerto Montt: the narrow 600-mile long Central Valley, the fertile soils of which supply the rest of the country with cereals, meat, vegetables and wines. Further south: a cold, rainy and mountainous archipelago inhabited by a scattering of fishermen and sheepfarmers and, far down on the Tierra del Fuego some 2,500 miles south of Arica, by a handful of petroleum settlers.

The transportation system serving this awkward geography is far from adequate. Trains are few and time-consuming. It takes, for example, three full days to go by train from Arica to Santiago, and on the single-track and somewhat decayed railroad between Santiago and Valparaiso very little freight can be carried. In all directions both goods and passenger traffic is heavily dependent on trucks and buses.

The lack of port facilities is another weak link. Chile's coast line is immense, but good natural ports are scarce and docking and discharging capacity in the main ports very limited.

The Allende government could hardly be blamed for this legacy of the past. The UP was perfectly well aware of the situation: Chile's deplorable infrastructure was repeatedly criticized, and in the government's investment plans transportation was always emphasized as a priority sector. A large number of ambitious projects was undertaken. But gestation periods were long and certain vital imports (vehicles, spares, tires, machinery, etc.) became difficult to obtain, and serious bottlenecks began to arise.

In the port of Valparaíso one could at times see over five large vessels carrying imports lying at anchor waiting to be discharged, and once unloaded the cargo could pass weeks in Valparaíso waiting for road or railway transportation to Santiago or elsewhere. Industries often had to slow down for lack of fuels or raw materials (margins in the form of inventories had already become very small by early 1972). In the agrarian districts in the south fertilizers from the north or from abroad often arrived late, and after harvest large quantities of potatoes and vegetables could perish for lack of carriage. Shortage of warehousing and refrigeration arrangements meant that cheap and nutritious fish, of vital importance for the Allende government's battle against the protein deficiency afflicting a high proportion of the Chilean people, would reach consumers half rotten. The list of infrastructural bottlenecks giving rise to interruptions of production or other forms of losses could be made very long.

The capacity of Chile's passenger transportation system also became insufficient. Tickets on buses and trains soon became short, mainly as a result of the UP's price policy. To travel in Allende's Chile was indeed inexpensive, and to obtain tickets correspondingly difficult. Within the capital the demand for fares increased tremendously; employment was high, and many a worker could now for the first time afford to take the bus to the factory. Part of the local transportation system almost broke down, and traffic congestion in greater Santiago reached new heights of absurdity.[32]

The national airline company LAN-Chile also benefited by the demand boom. With the 32.9 per cent expansion of passenger traffic reached in 1971[33] almost all idle capacity was absorbed, and as from 1972 flights were booked up for weeks, eventually months, in advance.

In short, all kinds of travelling increased, and the low-income groups, who could not afford much travelling before, benefited in particular. At the same time, of course, the policy of cheap fares and tickets brought some inconveniences. The costs of waiting and/or of changing one's plans multiplied, as it was sometimes impossible to move from one place in Chile to another at short notice (a situation of which all kinds of speculators and reserved ticket dealers were quick to take advantage).

So far we have only dealt with the economic reasons for the bottle-necks that arose in the field of transportation. The chain of causation was simple: the generally deficient infrastructure that existed in Chile proved incapable of satisfying the extra demand for transportation services to which the 1971–2 overall economic expansion and the government's price policy gave rise. On the supply side problems also set in, mainly as a consequence of the scarcity of certain vital imports.

But everything cannot be explained with reference to economics alone. Political factors contributed, too, and we should not leave the transportation sector without mentioning a circumstance to which we will have occasion to return: the attacks from the Right.

The crucial importance of distribution and of road transportation in particular did not escape the attention of the Chilean bourgeoisie, and the *gremios*[34] controlling most of the country's truck and bus traffic were converted into key organizations in the preparations for the overthrow of Allende. The *gremio de los camioneros* (Truck Owners' Association), a mafia-type organization headed by León Vilarin and receiving generous financial assistance from abroad,[35] was particularly active. It played, for example, a very leading role in what came to be known as the 'October crisis', the general lockout launched in October 1972 by almost all Chile's employers' associations. Through this lock-out, initiated by the truck owners and followed in rapid succession by the *gremios* of merchants, bus owners, professionals, etc., almost all road transportation – and many other activities as well – was virtually halted for over three weeks. Minor strikes and lockouts were common, and the conflicts, which were officially presented as protests against low freight charges, lack of petrol and tires, unfair competition from state-owned enterprises, etc., added considerably to the serious distribution problems that affected Chile. Less conspicuous forms of sabotage, such as the provoca-tion of artificial shortages of spare parts and tires through stockpiling, were other methods used by the *gremio* of truck owners in its struggle against the government.

At the end of next chapter we will look more closely at the efforts by the UP to tackle the problems arising in the field of distribution. But it should be emphasized here that the government completely failed to break the private sector's dominance in both road transportation and in whole-sale and retail trade, and that it was precisely in these sectors that the political opposition concentrated its economic sabotage. Although it is impossible to assess in quantitative terms the role that these activities played in the creation of bottlenecks and general scarcities they did become a decisive factor from October 1972 onwards.

The external sector

The UP often blamed shortages and other economic difficulties on re-strictions originating abroad, and asserted that the low price of copper and the 'invisible blockade' rendered it impossible to obtain the necessary imports. Part of the argument was true: Chile did have bad luck with copper prices, which in 1972 fell even below the poor average for 1971 (while import prices continued to rise), and the United States did obstruct both new lending and the sales of certain vital products to Chile. But total imports nevertheless expanded. The great difference in comparison with previous years was that under Allende the general increase in purchasing power, the government's ambitious nutrition and development projects and the gross overvaluation of the escudo made foreign exchange appear far more scarce than it really was.

Chile's economic difficulties cannot be said to have been caused by a reduced supply of imports for the simple reason that no such reduction took place. But it is also clear that once the number of bottlenecks had begun to increase the foreign trade situation gained strategic impor-tance. Bottlenecks arising from a lack of certain crucial imports were rapidly transmitted to other parts of the economy, and it therefore often looked as if the limited supply of imported goods was the Chilean economy's major constraint.

Between 1970 and 1971 total goods imports grew some 13 per cent in current prices (dollars), with consumer and intermediate goods – espe-cially those of agricultural origin – rising fast, while imports of capital goods declined.[36] In 1972 the general upward trend was reinforced. Agricultural products continued to increase in both absolute and relative terms and capital goods – in particular those related to the transporta-tion sector – recovered.

The differentiated exchange rates became more and more unrealistic. In June 1973 there were four different dollar prices for commodity imports ranging from 20 escudos to the dollar (foodstuffs and fuels) to 240 (luxury goods), the weighted average being around 40 escudos to the dollar.[37] While consumer prices had increased over five times between

Table 5.4 *Chile's imports of goods 1971 and 1972 (millions of dollars) and changes 1971/72*

Category	1971	1972	Change	% Change
Agricultural products	310.9	468.2	157.3	50.1
Other consumer goods	100.5	74.2	−26.3	−26.3
Raw materials and intermediate goods[a]	554.3	577.5	23.2	4.2
Capital goods	200.0	341.8	141.8	70.9
of which				
machinery and equipment	139.0	158.5	19.5	14.0
transport materials, vehicles	57.9	173.3	115.4	199.1
reproductive animals	3.0	10.0	7.0	233.3
Total	1,165.6	1,145.7	296.1	25.4

[a] Excluding all products of agricultural origin. For a discussion of price changes, see ch. 7.

SOURCE: Banco Central, Departamento de Estudios.

November 1970 and June 1973, the official devaluation of the escudo lagged far behind. On the brokers' market the dollar stood at 420 in mid-1973; on the black market one dollar was worth some 1,500–2,000 escudos.

The system of neither plan nor market that characterized the economy during the latter half of the UP administration makes it difficult to estimate the effect the government's exchange rate policy could have had on the volume and composition of foreign trade. The state controlled all legal external transactions, and a system of import planning – or import budgeting, as it was called – gradually emerged. The structure of Chile's import trade should consequently mirror directly the UP's own priorities to a larger and larger extent, and with the escudos being overvalued for all kinds of transactions the variations in the rates of exchange had little or no influence upon what was imported and by whom (although they certainly did distort domestic relative prices).

The government preferred to foster exports through cheap credit rather than by means of preferential exchange rates. In spite of the fact that export-creating activities were ranked third by Allende among those sectors to which special priority should be given,[38] the escudos that the exporters received for each dollar's worth of sales were too few to stimulate Chilean producers wanting to sell abroad. Recurrent adjustments of these exchange rates (there were several, and the whole system became increasingly complex) were made, and in the case of agricultural and industrial exports the devaluations were appreciably more drastic than those affecting the import trade, but the emergence of black or gray domestic markets, especially for foodstuffs, usually made it very bad business to engage in exporting.[39]

For mineral exports the exchange rates established were entirely unfavorable – 20 escudos to the dollar after the August 1972 devaluation, 45 after June 1973. We can safely assume that the elasticity of supply lay very close to zero in the nationalized large-scale mining industries, but the exchange rate policy must have greatly discouraged many of the private small and medium-sized producers. The (relatively mild) fluctuations in world market prices that Chile's mineral exports experienced in 1972 were, on the other hand, virtually wiped out by the Central Bank's large exchange rate modifications and by domestic inflation.

Chilean exports performed very poorly in 1972. Problems in copper mining and in agriculture will be dealt with in subsequent chapters; suffice it here to mention that whatever were the reasons – production

Table 5.5 Chile's exports of goods 1971 and 1972 (millions of dollars) and changes 1972/71

Category	1971	1972	Change	% Change
Mineral products	813.2	734.5	−78.7	−9.6
Copper	701.8	657.0	−44.2	−6.3
Iron	67.7	44.5	−23.2	−34.4
Nitrate and iodine	35.2	24.5	−10.7	−30.4
Miscellaneous	8.5	7.9	−0.6	−7.1
Agricultural products	29.4	19.3	−10.1	−34.3
Manufactures	122.1	83.4	−38.7	−31.7
Total	964.7	836.2	−128.5	−13.3

SOURCE: Banco Central, Departamento de Estudios

bottlenecks, the domestic price level and the lack of price incentives to exporters, etc. – all major export trade items fell below 1971 levels which themselves were not very high.

Table 5.6 summarizes the development of Chile's balance of trade in the years 1970 to 1972.

In 1973 the picture of growing deficits worsened. The import boom of the preceding years was no longer allowed to continue, and the volume of imports during the first eight months appears to have been kept more or less constant with respect to 1972, with only a slight increase in value terms. The scattered date hitherto released are both provisional and incomplete, but what matters in the general economic context is not the exact figures but rather the crucial circumstance that the stagnation of imports now coincided with a considerable *decline* in domestic industrial and agricultural production. The total supply of home-produced plus imported goods still remained above the pre-UP levels, but with bottlenecks becoming increasingly generalized the foreign trade restriction exacerbated the shortages that had developed.

At the same time as imports stagnated export earnings started to rise. The hoped-for miracle that alone could somewhat alleviate Chile's balance of payments crisis finally occurred as copper prices rose rapidly on the world market. Early in January 1973 the price of copper was still what it had been all through 1971 and 1972, or slightly below 50 cents per pound, but in March it had already exceeded 70 cents, in July it passed 90 and in August it temporarily reached over 100 cents per pound. The slight decline following this all-time record level caused the average price of 1973 to stay at 76.6 cents, well over fifty per cent above the 1972 average.[40]

The foreign trade gap could not possibly be closed with the help of improved copper prices alone. With normal volumes of copper sales a

Table 5.6 *Chilean imports and exports of goods 1970–72 (millions of dollars)*

	1970	1971	1972
Exports	1,128.8	964.7	836.2
Imports	1,020.0	1,165.6	1,461.7
Balance	+108.8	−200.9	−625.5

SOURCE: Table 5.4 and table 5.5.

103

price rise of some 25–30 cents per pound signifies an improvement of Chile's balance of payments in the range of 350–400 million dollars; the 1972 deficit exceeded 600 millions, and in 1973 import prices continued to rise while Chile's industrial and agricultural exports continued to decline. The 1973 deficit in the balance of trade probably did not fall short of 400 million dollars, and to this we should add some 30–50 millions as a minimum for the deficit on invisibles (tourism, royalties, profit remittances, etc.).

How were these import surpluses financed? In 1971 the stock of foreign exchange had been sufficiently large to cover the whole current account deficit and even to reduce the debt load slightly; after 1971 this was no longer possible. Chile had to postpone the servicing of most of her giant foreign debt. In interest and amortizations 400 million dollars were due in 1972 and another 496 in 1973,[41] or about half of these two years' total export earnings.

After a series of negotiations during February to April 1972 most of Chile's creditor nations – the so-called Paris Club – accepted the fact that the Allende government had neither the intention nor the capability of fulfilling payment obligations. Chile's initial bid in the Paris Club talks was a three-year total moratorium, and what was granted was a 70 per cent moratorium on payments due in 1972 and six years of grace for the balance. The agreement was received with relief by the UP and carried, as far as we know, no political compromises. 'We went to Paris to negotiate our foreign debt and not our political program,' Allende emphasized,[42] and the efforts made by some of the members of the Paris Club – the United States and a few others – to enforce upon Chile a 'stand by' agreement which would have given the International Monetary Fund decisive control over Allende's economic policies were rejected.

Both during and after the Paris Club agreement Chile took up bilateral negotiations with her creditor nations and with private American and European banks. More or less advantages settlements were reached,[43] and in 1972 Chile serviced her foreign debt according to the schedule only with certain international organizations, such as the World Bank. Altogether Chile escaped with paying approximately 100 million dollars.[44]

With the US government no understanding was reached, however. The Chilean debt to the United States amounted to some 1,720 million dollars, of which 185 were credits from private banks and the remainder from public agencies like the Agency for International Development (AID) and the Export–Import Bank (EXIM-BANK).[45] After the US–Chilean conversations over the interpretation of the Paris Club settlement had broken down completely, Chile decided to suspend unilaterally all debt servicing to American public institutions.[46]

Chile's debt went virtually unserviced in 1973. Talks with the Paris Club over a new renegotiation were to be held in May, but they were postponed time after time and in the meantime all Chilean debt payments were suspended. By September 1973 the conversations were still of a 'preliminary' character.

But in spite of the relief brought by the renegotiation and the unilateral suspension of interest and amortization payments, additional credits were needed to pay for current imports. Systematic information about these new credits and about the size of various private capital movements was never made public, but in spite of the poor quality of the data a few points deserve to be considered.

It is clear that the overall volume of credits granted to Chile remained very high, as it had been throughout the 1960s. Almost all of the huge 1972 and 1973 balance of trade deficits must have been covered by new lending. The Chinese motto of 'relying on one's own forces' was no more applicable to the UP's strategy than it had been to that of the two previous Chilean governments.

The main difference with respect to the Alessandri and Frei periods was that the composition of creditor nations changed appreciably under Allende. The 'invisible blockade' resulted in the ending of financial dependency on the United States: from having represented 78.4 per cent of the value of all short-term credits in November 1970, two years later the share of the United States had fallen to 6.6 per cent.[47] Long-term loans from US public agencies and from the big international credit institutions were, with the exception of two large IMF-credits,[48] either drastically reduced (the Inter-American Development Bank, EXIM-BANK) or cut down to zero (AID, The World Bank).

Other lenders therefore had to step in, and it was not only, or even primarily, the Eastern European countries and China which helped the Allende government to overcome Chile's acute balance of payments problems. The UP's application of Pedro Vuskovic's formula of 'taking advantage of the contradictions that exist within the capitalist world'[49] was apparently successful. The UP did manage to replace the credits the United States refused to grant with loans from a wide variety of Western countries: Argentina, France, Spain, Mexico, Brazil, Japan, Sweden, Holland, West Germany, Finland – the list could be made even longer.

The UP was no doubt right when arguing that the world had changed since the days of the Cuban revolution, when Fidel Castro's regime soon found itself economically isolated from practically the whole capitalist world. Our conclusion from this overview of the development of Chile's external sector must however be that those who outside or inside the Unidad Popular asserted that the United States' 'invisible blockade' played the dominant role in the creation of the economic difficulties that confronted Chile under Allende were exaggerating the impact of the critical balance of payments situation. The latter no doubt became a serious restriction in 1972 and 1973 (above all as a result of unfavorable shifts in the terms of trade). Shortages of badly needed spare parts and equipment arose from lack of imports, and these shortages, often affecting key industries, gave rise to bottlenecks which were, in turn, easily transmitted to other sectors of the economy. Most of these problems must, however, be blamed on factors other than the US financial blockade. The overall volume of credits – and imports – rose markedly, and if the amount and commodity composition of Chilean imports nevertheless turned out to be inadequate it was because of the domestic economic situation which made Chile's import requirements virtually insatiable.

STAGNATION AND DECLINE OF OUTPUT

Thus far very little has been said about how production actually developed in 1972 and 1973. But we have seen the problems arise: the inflation, first, and the monetary chaos, and then we noted how Chile's potential for future growth along 1971 lines was gradually exhausted as idle capacity in manufacturing began to disappear, as infrastructural bottlenecks arose and, finally, as restrictions originating from the external sector made themselves felt. By 1972 the policy of 'first consumption, then accumulation' – a policy which political circumstances rather than strictly economic considerations had 'forced' upon the UP – was, in short, reaching its limits. Worse still: no alternative policy was within sight.

The statictics available for the latter half of the Allende government are both meager and provisional but they should be sufficiently clear-cut to give empirical support to the title of this section: stagnation and decline.

Before we turn to the figures a reservation must be made. Although it is perfectly clear that the economic difficulties that arose were to a large extent conditioned by the limitations of the UP's short-term economic policy proper – the aftermath of the 1971 boom, one could say – it must also be kept in mind that the overall political situation, with rightist lockouts and sabotage and, albeit with lesser immediate economic repercussions, militant strikes and occupations on the part of the workers, also influenced events substantially, especially from October 1972 onwards. The fact that both agricultural and industrial production began to fall precipitately should definitely not be interpreted as a necessary consequence of the economic restrictions that have been described above. Chile's productive capacity was and is poor and rigid, but under normal political conditions – and a process of radical social change and intensification of class struggles is in no way characterized by normalcy – it would have withstood the strains much better than it actually did in 1972 and 1973. If I were to make an extremely schematic assessment of the responsibility for the economic crisis of the last UP year I would suggest the following simple formula: while *stagnation* of output was what could be expected from a 'strictly economic' point of view, the *decline* that eventually took place must be attributed to political factors alone.

Major sectors of activity

Data for the mineral and agricultural sectors – where problems were of a somewhat more special character and only partially related to the general economic situation – will be given in subsequent chapters.[50] It is sufficient in the present context to simply state that the agriculture sector and the Gran Minería of copper showed a fair performance in 1972, with production levels slightly above those of 1971. In 1973 copper production appears to have declined a little and agricultural output seems to have dropped substantially. In mining, other than copper, 1972 and 1973 were, on the whole, poor years, with decline registered in both.

As for construction, serious difficulties had already appeared in 1972 when transportation problems and shortages of building materials became acute. The public sector's ambitious residential construction programs were severely curtailed, and many projects already initiated had to be postponed.[51]

The value of basic services increased, according to preliminary estimates,[52] by 3.7 per cent in 1972, with large increases in electricity, gas and water and modest rises in transport and communications.

Let us finally look at manufacturing, the most interesting sector in the present context. In 1972 the aggregate volume of physical production rose by 2.8 per cent, with the sectoral distributions shown in table 5.7.

Table 5.7 *Index of physical industrial production 1972 (1968 = 100)*

Category	1972	% change 1972/71
Light consumer goods	113.5	0.8
Consumer durables	119.6	1.8
Transport equipment	120.3	7.5
Intermediate and capital goods (for use in manufacturing)	137.4	5.4
Intermediate and capital goods (for use in construction)	131.0	10.5
Miscellaneous	120.1	−1.1
General index	122.6	2.8

SOURCE: INE, taken from Banco Central, *Boletín Mensual* no. 542, April 1973, p. 353.

In the month-to-month development of industrial production the whole transition from recovery and expansion to stagnation and decline can be followed.

Finally it should be said that one important economic variable did not show any sign of stagnation, namely employment. Not even in 1973 does the occupational situation seem to have deteriorated – still another symptom of the fundamental differences that existed between the economic crisis of the Allende period and the more or less chronic recessions of earlier administrations (to say nothing of the disastrous decline in employment and real wages introduced by the Pinochet regime).

In the three areas from which reliable data on the employment situation were collected at regular intervals – Greater Santiago, Concepción-Talcahuano and Lota-Corenel – the rates of overt unemployment decreased under Allende as shown in table 5.9.

A note on living standards

The dismal picture given above of the economic situation during the last year of Unidad Popular would be highly misleading if it were not supplemented by a brief comment on the development of the standard of living of the majority of the Chilean people. The reason why I confine myself to a brief comment in this context is not that I regard this aspect as of little importance, but because it is dealt with on several other occasions

Table 5.8 *Monthly comparison of total volume of industrial production, January 1970 – September 1973, INE's general index (1968 = 100)*

Month	1971	Change 1971/70 (index points)	1972	Change 1972/71 (index points)	1973	Change 1973/72 (index points)
January	92.9	-2.1	111.4	18.5	108.8	-2.6
February	81.4	1.1	97.1	15.7	98.5	1.4
March	113.1	7.4	127.6	14.5	131.3	3.7
April	109.4	1.4	125.4	16.0	115.2	-10.2
May	119.2	17.4	126.5	7.3	n.a.	(-11.0)[a]
June	121.8	10.9	127.4	5.6	n.a.	(-14.6)[a]
July	124.7	9.0	128.3	3.6	n.a.	(-10.7)[a]
August	129.3	19.0	130.6	1.3	n.a.	(-12.0)[a]
September	130.6	30.3	119.1	-11.5		
October	129.3	22.5	118.4	-10.9		
November	138.6	32.6	126.1	-13.5		
December	141.3	33.7	132.6	-8.7		
January–December	119.3	15.3	122.6	3.3		

[a] These figures – all taken from *El Mercurio* – are based on the index made up by the Chilean Association of Manufacturers (SOFOFA) and are not directly comparable to the general INE index, although they no doubt reflect rather accurately the overall tendency of the last few months of the UP administration.

SOURCE: 1971–2: Banco Central, *Boletín Mensual*, current issues. January–April 1973: *Panorama Económico* no. 279, August 1973. May–August 1973: *El Mercurio* (International edn) 20–27 January 1974.

Table 5.9 *Rates of overt unemployment 1970–73 (percentages of labor force)*

Area	1970 (annual average)	1971 (annual average)	1972 (annual average)	March	1973 April	June
Greater Santiago	7.1	5.5	3.8	3.8		3.1
Concepción–Talcahuano	10.1	9.0	5.9		3.4	
Lota–Coronel	16.0	14.2	11.1		9.3	

SOURCE: Instituto de Economía, *Ocupación y Desocupación*, current issues. The 1973 figures are taken from *Panorama Economico's* statistical abstracts, the primary source always being the polls made by the Economic Institute. See also ch. 4, p. 71.

in this essay. We have just seen, for example, that employment remained very high even in 1973, and we also already know that both imports and domestic production of most consumer goods increased appreciably during the UP years (in addition to becoming more evenly distributed). The situation with respect to the most vital aspect of all when judging the development of the material well-being of the Chilean people, the availability and distribution of foodstuffs, will be dealt with separately in chapter 7.

But it should be said that the very ambitious program of social reforms that the Allende government undertook will be almost completely neglected in what follows. Many of the social schemes that were introduced – food for school children, the free delivery of half a litre of milk a day to all children under the age of sixteen, the medical, educational and social security reforms, etc. – resulted in hitherto unheard-of improvements in living conditions for the working class and for low-income groups in general. The rapid expansion of all kinds of social services was in part motivated by redistributive objectives. The UP's failure to achieve a sufficiently pronounced redistribution of income by means of ordinary incomes and tax policies was to a certain extent compensated for through 'exaggerated' increases in the public sector's provision of certain basic goods and services.

Many of the above programs – especially those related to the distribution of free or cheap food – came to constitute a form of rationing, and made further inroads in the supply of marketed commodities. They were, consequently, most unpopular among the well-to-do Chileans, whose politicians and newspapers never ceased to attack or at least make fun of free milk to children and school breakfasts. In many a modest Chilean family, however, the Allende years will be remembered as the time when the first school was built in the home village or *población* or when the poorly fed children of the family suddenly began to receive medical attention and half a litre of milk a day.

CHAPTER 6

The formation of the social area
of the economy

We have seen earlier that the Unidad Popular defined itself not only as anti-imperialist and anti-monopolistic but as anti-capitalist as well, although the emphasis that the UP put on the latter 'anti' was distinctly less pronounced than that put on the former two. The nationalization program was, then, above all designed to attack important foreign interests operating in Chile and those domestic enterprises which were defined as having a monopolistic character, while the overwhelming majority of medium and small-scale firms were supposed to remain in private hands, although subjected to various forms of public supervision.

The decisive passage in the UP program dealing with the state area (or 'social area', as it used to be called) reads as follows:

The process of transforming our economy will begin with a policy intended to create a dominant state area made up of enterprises already owned by the state plus those which are to be expropriated. As an initial step we will nationalize those basic riches – large-scale mining of copper, iron, nitrates, and others – which are now controlled by foreign capital and by domestic monopolies. This sector of nationalized activities will thus include the following activities:

1. large-scale mining of copper, nitrate, iodine, iron and coal;
2. the financial system of the country, in particular the private banks and insurance companies;
3. foreign trade;
4. large-scale enterprises and monopolies in the field of distribution;
5. strategic industrial monopolies;
6. in general those activities which condition the economic and social development of the country, such as the production and distribution of electrical energy, transportation by rail, air, and sea; communications; the production, refining and distribution of petroleum and its derivatives, including liquid gas; the iron and coal industry; cement, petrochemicals and heavy chemicals, cellulose, and paper.

All these expropriations will always be carried out with full regard for the interests of the small shareholders.

The formation of the social area of the economy

All the 'commanding heights' of the economy were thus explicitly included in what was to become the state area of the economy, and if we add to this the planned elimination of all Chile's *latifundios* it is clear that the program was designed to do away completely with the whole dominant sector of private business. The vagueness of some of the phrases used – 'as an initial step', 'those activities which condition the economic and social development of the country', etc. – also indicates, that the nationalization of the directly specified sectors could be interpreted as a minimum only.

The UP program also stated that a 'mixed area' combining both public and private, domestic or foreign,[1] capital should be created so as to make possible the direct control of activities not explicitly included in the social area. Thus, although the UP emphatically declared that the great majority of business establishments would remain in private hands there is little doubt that this majority of small and medium-sized firms were to be deprived of all chance of competing with the public sector in 'strategic' activities. The full carrying through of the UP's sweeping nationalization program could signify the virtual deathblow to Chile's most powerful domestic and foreign economic interests. The necessity of expropriating only a limited number of companies in order to control the economy was, of course, a corallary to the UP's thesis of the Chilean economy's extremely high degree of concentration. According to ODEPLAN, the National Planning Office, the nationalization of a few key firms in key sectors would permit the State to increase its share in the generation of GDP from some 10 per cent in 1970 to about 40 per cent in 1976.[2]

The distinction between 'monopolies', which should be fought and expropriated, and medium and small-scale entrepreneurs, who, in theory, were allies of the working class in their common anti-monopolistic struggle, turned out to be quite difficult to make and even more difficult to put into practice. There was perhaps no other political issue which so clearly reflected the differences that existed within the Chilean Left and the contradictions inherent in the UP's program. The Allende government's attempt to pursue a consistent policy in its nationalization project was soon shown to be illusory. For the so-called 'anti-monopolistic' strategy was unsatisfactory both from a social and an economic point of view, and as it was bound to clash with the interests of both the bourgeoisie and the working class it was politically impractical as well. But more on this below, when we analyze the politically important implications of the UP's efforts to create a strong state sector of the economy.

Despite violent resistance from those monopolistic interests which were to be expropriated, the UP program got off to a good start. In two years all major mineral resource interests and commercial banks had been taken over by the state, and the private sector's dominance in several other sectors was being broken. But before turning to the main purpose of this chapter – to study the advances and difficulties in the construction of the social area of the economy – the UP's main arguments for the nationalization policy have to be presented.

PRINCIPAL OBJECTIVES

Like all who claim to be Marxists, the UP leaders asserted that the abolition of private property in the principal means of production was a necessary – though certainly not sufficient – condition for the construction of a socialist society, and the UP's 'social area' was conceived as 'the embryo of the future socialist economy'.[3]

A far-reaching policy of nationalization was also considered indispensable from the point of view of economic and political power. The central aim of the UP was to 'put an end to the power of national and foreign monopolistic capital and *latifundism* in order to begin the construction of socialism'. The expropriation of private business and the construction of a state area would, in the words of Amérigo Zorrilla, not only bring economic benefits but would also 'represent the initiation of the destruction of the material base of support for the country's most reactionary sectors'.[4] It was hoped that the expropriation of property held by the 'monopolistic, reactionary sectors' would gradually undermine the political strength of the Right, thereby facilitating the 'popular forces'' march toward power. In the same way it was held that the taking over of the principal foreign interests doing business in Chile would deprive the domestic oligarchy of many of its most powerful allies.

The justification of a large state area of the economy was often presented – at least by Communists and Radicals – in pragmatic rather than ideological terms. The old economic structure was rejected as being responsible for the Chilean people's misery,[5] and the UP's analysis of the ills of society led to the obvious conclusion that it was imperative to transform the economic structure radically in order to solve the economic and social problems of the country. 'Economic independence' was emphasized as a necessary condition for development, and through the establishment of a dominant state sector the surplus generated by the monopolies would be used to further the development of the economy instead of being transferred abroad or dissipated through luxury consumption. The fradulent and speculative character of big business was also repudiated time after time. Through the nationalization of monopolistic enterprises huge surpluses which had earlier 'disappeared' in the form of capital flight, tax evasion, unproductive, speculative investment, etc. were to be recuperated for development needs.

The old pattern of industrialization was, furthermore, to be broken. 'From now on, the driving force of development will be based on "popular consumption" and not on exports and import substitution".[6] This and similar phrases indicate the new direction the economy was to take. The sectors, regions and social classes left behind or left out by the old capitalist system were to be favored in the 'new economy'.

In this 'new economy' the state-owned sector was to become large and centralized enough to be 'dominant' and permit firm public control of the economy. Planning was to substitute market forces in all investment decisions of strategic importance, and it would not be the kind of 'indicative planning' that every government since the 1930s had had in their programs. 'The central planning agencies will be at the highest administrative levels, and their democratically determined decisions will have an executive character.'[7] In the words of Allende: 'We are and will always be supporters of a centralized economy, and the enterprises will have to fulfill the production plans made up by the government.'[8] Or, to end this section on the why's and how's of the social area of the economy, as formulated in Allende's First Message:

Our government intends to make it [the public sector] quantitatively even more important than it has been up to now, but also qualitatively different.

The establishment of the area of social ownership does not signify the creation of a system of state capitalism, but the beginning of a truly socialist structure. The social area will be managed jointly by the workers and by representatives of the state ... The general criterion to define the socially owned area is the necessity of conceiving it as one single integrated unity, capable of generating all its potentials ... This implies the immediate establishment of a planning system with real power to allocate economic surplus to the different sectors of production ... It is our determination to see that no investment project not included in the centrally established plan is executed. In that way we will put an end to improvisation and, in accordance with the program of the Popular Unity, initiate the organization of socialist planning.

But socialist planning will not be a topic discussed in this chapter. Under the conditions that prevailed in Allende's Chile little progress was made in the 'constructive' phase of the nationalization program, i.e.

in the organization of the state area as an integrated whole, capable of generating its own surplus and directed in accordance with an overall economic plan. The serious economic and political difficulties that soon confronted the government also impeded effectively the 'putting an end to all improvisation', and most of the chapter that follows will be devoted to problems connected with the formation rather than the actual functioning of the state area of the economy.

BASIC MINERAL RESOURCES

Copper

All through its history (i.e. ever since the sixteenth century) the Chilean export trade has been intimately linked to the extraction of minerals. Most of the riches Chile's deserts and mountains have supplied to the world market have one after another ceased to generate private fortunes, tax incomes and export earnings. But copper has not: during the last fifty years copper has accounted for one-third or more of Chile's total sales abroad. A share which, thanks to prices rather than production levels, has shown a pronounced tendency to rise over time. In 1950 it reached 50.5 per cent, in 1960 68.4 per cent, and in 1970 76.9 per cent.[9] The bulk (some 85–90 per cent in the early 1960s) of total copper output originated from the US owned Gran Minería, which thus alone controlled over half of Chile's export earnings.

To this large and increasing share of Chile's foreign trade corresponded a small and declining share of tax incomes and employment, however. After having gained importance as the country's main source of tax income in the interwar period – especially during the 'Popular Front' administrations, which relied heavily on copper taxes – the leading position of the Gran Minería gradually diminished.

In terms of employment, large-scale copper mining became increasingly insignificant. The absolute number of workers declined by 16 per cent between 1931 and 1959[10], and in 1960 total employment amounted to no more than some 17,000 people.

Together with the giants of the Gran Minería there operated a large number of small and medium-sized Chilean owned mines with production techniques and labor productivity levels completely different from those in large-scale mining. Although these minor mines employed more people than the Gran Minería[11] they produced no more than some ten per cent of total output.

Thus, within the copper sector we encounter contrasts similar to those

Basic mineral resources

Table 6.1   *Direct taxes from the
Gran Minería of copper as a share
of total tax revenues (percentages)*

Period	Share
1930–34	3.0
1935–39	14.0
1940–49	21.0
1950–59	16.9
1960–64	9.3

SOURCE: 1930–39: Mamalakis in
Mamalakis & Reynolds, *Essays on the
Chilean Economy*, 1965, p. 55; 1940–
49 and 1950–59: Instituto de Economía, *La Economía de Chile en el
Período 1950–63*, 1963, vol. 2, table
195; 1960–64: ODEPLAN, *Antecedentes*, p. 389.

Table 6.2   *Employment in Gran Minería 1960*

Workers	Employees	Staff employees[a]	Total	Employment in Gran Minería as percentage of total labor force
12,548	3,474	1,062	17,084	0.7

[a] 'Staff employees' comprised managers and professionals – many of whom
were foreigners – who were remunerated according to the so-called 'gold roll',
receiving their payment in dollars.
SOURCE: Mamalakis & Reynolds, *Essays*, p. 392; and Instituto de Economía,
La Economía de Chile en el Período 1950–63, vol. 2, table 20, p. 13.

found within agriculture (*latifundios–minifundios*) and manufacturing
industry (modern industry–artisanry), but even more accentuated: a
few large units producing the bulk of output but employing a comparatively small number of all workers occupied within the sector.

Foreign dominance and copper

In the first few decades of the present century the three large mines, then
known as the Gran Minería, Chuquicamata, Potrerillos[12] and El Teniente,
were established by two North American companies. Profits were high

and Chilean control over the operations nil, but the foreign investors were, by and large, left in peace by all subsequent Chilean governments. Not even the 'Popular Front' during its early, most radical period ever suggested measures against the Gran Minería that went beyond increased taxation. This compliancy towards foreign capital stood in sharp contrast with the situation that prevailed at the end of the nineteenth century, when widespread discontent with the British nitrate investors' ways of disposing of Chile's prime export product made the 'nitrate question' the most burning political issue of that time, provoking both a civil war and the fall of a president.[13]

Several factors contributed in creating a Chilean attitude toward foreign control of the Gran Minería best characterized as one of tolerance or resignation. The American managers' superiority in terms of 'know-how' and technological skill was generally recognized as an indisputable fact, and the circumstance that the large copper mines had not been taken over by foreigners but belonged to them from the very beginning of their operations also helped to subdue public resentment. To this we should add the rather indifferent political attitudes adopted by the workers themselves, attitudes which differed greatly from those of the combative, anti-imperialist nitrate miners. The living standards of the various categories of miners were also very unequal. While the nitrate workers constituted one of the very poorest groups in Chile, dying young and, while living, starving, the miners of the Gran Minería of copper enjoyed wages considerably higher than those of other Chilean workers.

Conflicts arose, however, and beginning with the commencement of the 'great copper debate' in the early fifties an increasingly active and broader opinion resulted in a serious questioning of the harmony of interests between Chile and the foreign copper companies – a development which culminated in the unanimous support given by the Chilean Parliament to the Allende government's nationalization bill presented in 1971.

In the first phase of the debate, lasting up to the 'Chileanization' versus 'nationalization' controversy introduced during the election campaign of 1964, the copper companies' price policy constituted the main target for the Chilean attacks. The prices paid for Chile's copper were consistently inferior to those obtained in the world market, the reason for this being found in the peculiar arrangement according to which prices were set by the government of the United States – until the mid-fifties the main buyer of Chile's copper – through negotiations with the large copper producers in the United States and abroad. The difference between these regulated prices and market prices became spectacularly large during World War II and the Korean War. Between 1941 and 1945 Chile's copper was sold at a fixed price of 12 cents per pound when world market prices averaged 17.35 cents,[14] and in 1951 and 1952 the price was raised to first 24.5, then to 27.5 cents while the price on the free, international market was over 40 and by the end of 1952 over 50 cents per pound.

The official arguments from the government of the United States were of both an economic and a political character. Prices ought to be 'stabilized', it was argued, and cheap sales of Chilean copper constituted, furthermore, Chile's contribution to the 'fight for democracy' in the 'free' world.

The freezing of prices during the Korean War caused a storm of indignation in Chile, and a delegation was sent to Washington early in 1951 to negotiate directly with the American government. Results were meager: the 'Washington agreement' conceded the right to Chilean authorities to dispose of 20 per cent of the sales from Gran Minería in any market they found convenient (with the exception of socialist countries, to which sales were explicitly forbidden), but they were forced to accept the US price regulations for the remaining 80 per cent.

Both within and outside the Chilean Parliament a growing opinion demanded the 'Chileanization' of the copper sales. Even members of the governing Radical Party, responsible for the copper policy since 1938, criticized severely the American price decrees. As, for example, the Radical Deputy Humberto Enríquez put it:

We know that while 80 per cent of our copper is sold at 27.5 cents per pound or 600 dollars per ton, the price at the world market is 1,200 dollars per ton. . . . This difference represents more than 180 million dollars or, translated into our currency, some 180,000,000,000 pesos per year. This is what we are presenting to the United States as a gift. This is our contribution to the cause of democracy.[15]

Despite various Chilean efforts to gain control over the export sales of copper – especially in 1952–4 when the Central Bank of Chile bought the copper from the American companies at the regulated price and re-sold it in the world market[16] – the price anomalies continued to appear every time international prices went up substantially. In 1965, for example, prices on the London Metals Exchange stood at 58.6 cents per pound, while Chile's copper was sold for 30.1 cents.[17] One year later the United States forced the Frei government to sell 90,000 tons of copper as a contribution to the American strategic reserves – which were diminishing rapidly due to the war in South East Asia – at a price of 36 cents, when the London price was almost 70.[18] Only in 1968 did Chile manage to reach an agreement which made it possible to sell all copper at London Metals Exchange prices.

Not only the price and marketing policy of the copper companies was subjected to criticism, however, although this policy in particular constituted the most humiliating aspect of the foreign investors' control over Chile's copper (and, many argued, over leading Chilean politicians). The lack of expansion of capacity and output was also hard to justify from a Chilean point of view. Despite gradually rising prices and profits, net reinvestment in Chile was kept low or negative, and while repatriated profits climbed upwards,[19] production stagnated. Thus, it was not until the 1960s that Gran Minería output reached World War II levels.

Chile, possessing some 30 per cent of all known reserves of copper and offering her investors three of the most easily exploited mines in the world, was lagging behind in the rapidly expanding world market. As a consequence of the American companies' growing unwillingness to increase mineral extraction within the country the decline in market share of refined copper was especially pronounced.

In the early 1960s the poor rate of expansion became the main theme in the copper controversy. Increased Chilean control over the sales was not enough, many people argued. To come to grips with the stagnation of production it would be necessary to 'nationalize' or to 'Chileanize' investment and production decisions as well. Owing to Eduardo Frei's

Table 6.3   *Production of copper in Gran Minería (annual averages)*

Period	1,000 metric tons	Index (1940–44 = 100)
1940–44	441	100
1945–49	398	90.2
1950–54	345	78.2
1955–59	437	99.1
1960–64	501	113.6

SOURCE: Max Nolff, 'Los Problemas Básicos del Cobre', in Martner (ed.), *El Pensamiento Económico*, table 3, p. 186. If the shift in the composition of output (see below) were taken into account, the index for 1955–9 and 1960–64 would have to be adjusted downwards considerably.

Basic mineral resources

Table 6.4 *Chile's share of world production of copper (percentages)*

Year	Copper minerals	Melted copper	Refined copper
1947	19.1	17.9	10.5
1950	14.4	13.7	9.4
1955	13.9	13.1	6.3
1960	12.6	11.8	4.5
1964	13.1	12.8	4.8

SOURCE: ECLA, *Algunos Aspectos de la Industria de Cobre en América Latina*, 1968, p. 35. In 1950, 41.5 per cent of Gran Minería's copper was refined within Chile; in 1961, this share had fallen to 12.2 per cent. For further details, see Mario Vera Valenzuela, *La Política Económica del Cobre en Chile*, 1962, pp. 32–4 and Appendices 1 and 2.

victory in the 1964 election the 'Chileanization' program got the first chance to be tested – a circumstance which undoubtedly contributed to the popularity of the nationalization formula.

Frei's 'Chileanization' of the Gran Minería

The Gran Minería of copper, defined as mines with an annual production exceeding 75,000 metric tons, consisted of three mines, Chuquicamata, El Salvador, and El Teniente, owned by two American companies, Anaconda and Kennecott, through their Chilean subsidiaries. The situation prior to the 'Chileanization' is shown in table 6.5.

As presented by the Christian Democrats the broad objectives of the Chileanization program were to raise investment and output, to increase Chilean control over decision making and to increase the integration

Table 6.5 *The Gran Minería prior to Chileanization*

	Chuquicamata	El Salvador	El Teniente
Owner	Anaconda	Anaconda	Kennecott
Name of subsidiary	Chile Exploration Co.	Andes Mining Co.	Braden Co.
Year when exploitation began	1911	1959	1913
Output in 1964, 1,000 metric tons	288.2	76.7	163.2

of the Gran Minería into the national economy, the latter mainly through the creation of more industries based on the further processing of copper minerals within the country.

Immediately after taking office the Frei government began conversations with Anaconda and Kennecott in order to settle the future relations between the foreign firms and the Chilean state. In brief, the content and consequences of the agreement reached were as follows.[20]

El Teniente

The first mine to be affected by the 'Chileanization' was Kennecott's El Teniente. Even prior to 1964 the American owners had been in contact with the Chilean government and suggested an arrangement that would transfer a 51 per cent ownership interest in Braden Copper Company to the Chilean state. From Kennecott's point of view it was considered necessary to ally oneself with domestic capital in order to secure the company's future in Chile, and the state offered the best prospects for both political and economic reasons.[21]

The Kennecott proposal, willingly adopted by the new Chilean government, was soon a concluded deal, and in 1967 Chile began to purchase her 51 per cent share. For purposes of compensation Braden was valued at 160 million dollars, and Chile's share thus amounted to 81.6 million, which was to be paid to Kennecott in three annual installments bearing an interest charge of $4\frac{1}{2}$ per cent.

The price paid came as a shock to the Chileans. Braden's book value in 1967 was no more than 72.5 million dollars, or less than the sum paid by Chile for only half the shares. Although it was generally agreed that Braden's book value was an underestimation in view of the company's high profits, it was considered quite remarkable that the value of the fifty-year-old and poorly maintained mine had been inflated to 160 million dollars. Even a fairly optimistic calculation of the flow of future profits would have given a real value for Braden far below the 160 million assessment of the Frei government.[22]

The deal included other conditions which were no less favorable to Kennecott. Taxation on profits was heavily reduced so as to stimulate increased production, and despite the fact that Chile now owned a majority interest her total revenue from pre-tax profits declined. If the *Nuevo Trato* of 1955 had remained valid Chile would have received a higher percentage than was actually received after 'Chileanization'. Possessing 49 per cent of the shares, Kennecott's net profits not only increased in absolute terms, but also as a percentage of gross profits (see table 6.6).

Chile's participation in decision making fared little better. The minority partner was guaranteed the exclusive right to administer the new, mixed enterprise, to appoint executives, etc. for a minimum period of twelve years.

In return for these benefits Kennecott had to promise to invest. According to the 'Chileanization' agreement some 230 million dollars were to be invested during a span of four years so as to make possible an increase of output from some 160,000 to 280,000 tons of copper.

When it came to the financing of this expansion plan Kennecott escaped without having to raise a single dollar in fresh capital. Its only contribution was a credit of about 90 million dollars (that is, the sum, including interest, received by the Chilean state) which Kennecott granted the new mixed company *Companía de Cobre El Teniente*. The rest was supplied by the US Export–Import Bank (119 million) and the Chilean state. Thus, while the Frei–Kennecott agreement failed to 'Chileanize' both the profits and the administration of the company it did 'Chileanize' a large part of the capital costs as well as the responsibility for the repayment of credits from outside sources.

The results of the 'expansion plan' turned out to be meager. In 1970, the last year in which El Teniente was under the exclusive administrative control of Kennecott/Braden, production amounted to 176,600 metric tons, while the plans made up four years earlier indicated 213,400 tons (see table 6.8). This further confirms the verdict of Keith Griffin, expressed before the outcome of the 'expansion plan' was known: 'The agreement with Kennecott appears to be a disaster from Chile's point of view.'[23]

Table 6.6 *Taxation of Gran Minería according to the legislation of 1955, 1967 and 1969*. Percentage of profits accruing to the Chilean state as taxes and, after 1967 (El Teniente) and 1969 (Chuquicamata), dividends

Law of	El Teniente	Chuquicamata	El Salvador
1955	78.13	71.5	60.5
1967	72.56	58.4	50.0
1969	—	76.7[a]	75.7[a]

[a] Not including a special 'overprice tax' which varied according to the price level of copper.

SOURCE: ODEPLAN, *Antecedents*, pp. 136–7.

Table 6.7   *Output from Gran Minería*
1964–70 (thousands of metric tons)

Year	Output	Year	Output
1964	528	1968	519
1965	496	1969	540
1966	538	1970	535
1967	537		

SOURCE: ODEPLAN, *Antecedentes*, p. 128.

Table 6.8   *Output projected for 1970 according to the expansion plans and actual production in 1970 (thousands of metric tons)*

Mine	Output projected	Actual output	Plan fulfillment (%)
Chuquicamata	317.8	263.0	82.7
El Salvador	95.3	93.0	97.6
El Teniente	213.4	176.6	82.8
Exótica	22.7	1.9	8.4
Total	749.2	534.5	71.3

SOURCE: Banco Central de Chile, *Boletín Mensual*, May 1972, p. 626 (actual production); and *Panorama Económico* no. 246, July 1969, p. 20 (planned production).

Chuquicamata, El Salvador, and Exótica

Anaconda, owner of Chuquicamata and El Salvador, first refused to be 'Chileanized'. It only let the Chilean state acquire a 25 per cent interest in the future exploitation of a new mine, Exótica, which was to start producing in 1970. Anaconda did, however, sign an agreement with the Chilean state in 1966 in which the company promised to increase production in the three mines it controlled by some 210,000 tons in five years. As compensation, taxes were drastically reduced (see table 6.6 above). The capital needed for the new investments was to be raised in part by the Chilean state, in part by foreign banks and other credit institutions.

The copper debate continued, however, and reaction from the government's political opponents varied from astonishment to fury. The results of the copper policy were visible to all: in the beginning of 1969 Chile still controlled none of the mines of Gran Minería, and while production stagnated both copper prices and Chilean costs climbed upwards rapidly.

Kennecott's and Anaconda's profits rose drastically, too; the annual average of net profits remitted abroad from the Gran Minería increased from 48.8 to 119.8 million dollars between 1960–66 and 1967–9.[24]

In June 1969 the government unexpectedly announced that a new agreement had been reached: Anaconda had agreed to sell a 51 per cent controlling interest in Chuquicamata and El Salvador. Compensation was set at 175 million dollars, to be paid in twelve years and bearing an interest charge of six per cent. The deal also included a paragraph giving the Chilean state the right to buy remaining shares in Anaconda during a period lasting from 1973 to 1982.

But just what the long run results of the 'Chileanization' of the Gran Minería might have been is now difficult to tell. The gradual nationalization of Chuquicamata and El Salvador was never carried into effect, and the various expansion plans never got a chance to be completed under the control of the former owners. Our information about what did take place in 1967–70 is however clear-cut enough to support the conclusion that the Christian Democrats' 'Chileanization' program was a very poor deal for Chile.

THE UNIDAD POPULAR'S COPPER NATIONALIZATION

The Gran Minería comprised, as we have seen, three 'old' mines – Chuquicamata, El Salvador and El Teniente – and two minor ones which had only recently started operations, namely Andina and Exótica. The situation with respect to ownership and control in 1970 was as follows: the Chilean state owned 51 per cent of the share capital in the 'old' mines, with Anaconda (Chuquicamata, El Salvador) controlling the remaining 49 per cent, and 25 per cent in the two new mines, where Anaconda (Exótica) and Cerro Corporation (Andina) held the rest. In all the five mines administrative control lay in the hands of the foreign associates.

The complete nationalization of the whole Gran Minería was on both Allende's and Tomic's electoral programs and was also supported by the overwhelming majority of the Chilean people. The UP had, then, little to fear in terms of domestic opposition, within or outside Congress. The rightist parties could hardly afford to make objections, and had they tried to stop the planned take-over Allende would only have had to call for a plebiscite and let the people decide. (The fact that Allende chose to present the nationalization project as a constitutional amendment and not as an ordinary law served to intimidate the congressional opposition, since this procedure provided Allende with the possibility of a plebiscite in the event the Congress refusing to pass the bill.) This latter expedient never became necessary, but the constitutional reform by means of which the Gran Minería of copper was expropriated was, in fact, the only major reform the UP was able to effect through new legislation. In no other issue of importance did Allende get the congressional majority's support.

The constitutional reform and its sequels

On 11 July, 1971 the UP's proposal was ratified unanimously by both chambers of the National Congress, and four days later the Chilean state took possession of the Gran Minería. The state was, to begin with, made sole owner of all mineral deposits within the country's border. The constitutional amendment thus declared null and void all previous contracts granting private interests, domestic or foreign, the right to ownership of Chilean mineral resources; a clause mainly affecting Kennecott, which claimed to own not only the installations in the mine it exploited but all copper ore within the whole region as well.

The concept of nationalization was, moreover, introduced into the Chilean constitution for the first time, although its validity was exclusively confined to the copper mines of the Gran Minería.

Thirdly, and herein lay the great originality of the copper bill, the right to make various forms of deductions from the amount to be paid in compensation to the owners was stipulated. This clause, unique in international legislation, signified concretely that from the sum to be paid according to the December 1970 book value of Anaconda, Kennecott and Cerro Corporation deductions should be made corresponding to the sum total of all so-called 'excess profits' reaped by the companies during the last fifteen years, plus the value of all installations that the Chilean state (i.e. the *Contraloría General*) found poorly maintained or obsolete as a consequence of negligence on the part of the former owners. 'Excess profits' were calculated as net profits exceeding a norm of twelve per cent a year which was established as a 'reasonable' rate of return. The Chilean state assumed, however, the responsibility for the whole 774 million dollar debt that the mixed Chilean–American companies had contracted in connection with 'expansion programs' in the late sixties.[25] The results of the compensatory calculations are given in table 6.9.

Thus, while the Allende government's complete nationalization of the

Table 6.9 *Net compensation to be paid for the Gran Minería companies:*
book values minus deductions (millions of dollars, rounded figures)

	Chuquicamata	El Salvador	El Teniente	Exótica	Andina
Book value	242.0	68.4	318.8	14.8	20.1
less excess profits	300.0	64.0	410.0	—	—
less other deductions	18.5	5.9	219.2	4.8	1.9
Subtotal deductions	318.5	69.9	629.2	4.8	1.9
Compensation, net[a]	−76.5	−1.6	−310.4	10.0	18.3

[a] Minus sign signifies debt to the Chilean state.

SOURCE: ODEPLAN, *Nueva Economía* no. 1, September–December 1971, p. 18.

127

Gran Minería of copper came as the logical culmination of Frei's 'Chileanization', the procedures applied in the two cases were totally different. While the Christian Democrats 'Chileanized' with the express consent of the American companies – in the case of Kennecott even in accordance with the company's own proposals – and paid a price for the Chilean holdings which by far exceeded the sum total of the mine's book values, the UP's nationalizations clashed directly with the interests of the foreign owners, who not only lost all their assets in Chile but who even found themselves owing the Chilean state several hundred million dollars.

The Kennecott, Anaconda and Cerro Corporation quite naturally protested against the calculations made by the Contraloría General. Though the American companies could do little about the constitutional amendment, they did have the right to appeal to a 'copper tribunal' set up in order to settle the very likely conflict over the amount of compensation to be paid for the companies' assets. In August 1972 this copper tibunal – whose decisions were final and whose verdict both sides beforehand had promised to respect – confirmed both the legality of the Chilean state's measures and, with only a few minor modifications, the calculations made by the *Contraloría General*. The legal road was thus effectively blocked for the US companies.

The nationalization of copper was bound to have repercussions upon Chile's international relations, and the compensation issue was soon converted into an open dispute between the governments of the United States and Chile. A vital part of American foreign policy – manifested in, for example, the so-called 'Hickenlooper amendment' and in a host of official statements of various kinds as well as in innumerable concrete cases of diplomatic, economic and military pressure on countries expropriating US property without paying 'prompt and adequate compensation' – is to protect American business. In the case of the Gran Minería of copper the US government also became directly involved at once since the US companies' assets in Chile were insured against expropriations through the public agency OPIC (Overseas Private Investment Corporation). The US government responded to the Chilean proceedings with considerable concern; not so much because of the amount of money involved, perhaps, but rather out of fear that the Chilean example would initiate a chain reaction among Third World countries which could be tempted to start deducting 'excess profits' when nationalizing foreign property.[26]

The attitude towards Chile thus turned cool, if not outright hostile, although reprisals were kept on a far more discrete level than, say, was and is the case with Fidel Castro's Cuba, which has had to endure an almost total US economic blockade. Against Chile the American government preferred to act with more caution, the principal form of retaliation being the curtailment of Chilean access to credit from US banks and credit institutions and from various international organizations under US control.

Exactly how much the copper conflict contributed to making the United States suspend new lending to Chile is difficult to tell, of course. The US-UP relations were strained long before the Gran Minería was nationalized in July 1971, and American economic and political pressure against Allende had, as we recall, been initiated even before Allende took office. And because of the economic policies pursued by the UP Chile's creditworthiness rapidly declined. There were good commercial reasons for being careful in granting Chile new loans. Among international credit agencies the Allende government's capacity to handle development projects was seriously questioned.[27]

The 'invisible blockade' undoubtedly contributed to aggravating the overall economic situation in Chile in 1972 and 1973. The Chilean position over foreign trade was less vulnerable, since Chile had the great advantage of not being too dependent on the United States as a trade partner. Less than 10 per cent of exports went to the US in 1970, and most of the import trade could be redirected, albeit not without certain difficulties, towards other suppliers.

There was, however, an informal 'trade blockade' against Chile as well. There were many instances when Chilean companies were frequently denied spare parts, machinery, etc. from former US suppliers (and from many a company in Western Europe as well). In part as a result of this discreet, unofficial blockade, the US share of total Chilean imports fell from 37.2 per cent in 1970 to about 10 per cent in 1972.[28] The effects of the problems thus created were felt mainly in mining, and especially in copper mining to which sales of American capital goods were drastically curtailed and for which certain specialized machinery and equipment could not so easily be obtained from other suppliers. Before November 1970 over 95 per cent of all capital goods to the Gran Minería of copper came from the United States; two years later this had virtually been reduced to nothing.[29] But in addition, in the case of Chile's import problems purely commercial reasons were often important. With her foreign reserves approaching zero Chile found it increasingly difficult to get even current commercial credit and was more and more forced to pay in cash to American suppliers.

In addition to the problems encountered in obtaining goods and loans from the United States the Allende government soon became involved in a struggle to protect Chilean interests abroad from various forms of attack by the expropriated copper companies. Both Kennecott and Anaconda tried – successfully – to get a court in New York to block several assets belonging to Chilean state agencies operating in the state of New York. The battleground was extended to other countries as well. Claiming that all copper coming from El Teniente was 'stolen property' Kennecott repeatedly tried to seize Chilean export earnings by urging the purchasers of copper to pay not to Chile but to Kennecott.[30] These and similar legal actions directed against Chilean copper sales created uncertainty among buyers and were ever-present sources of apprehension in Chile, and in three test cases (France, Holland and Sweden) Kennecott got consumers of El Teniente copper to block payments to Chile. The quantities affected were small, but as a result of Kennecott's actions Chilean sales of El Teniente copper to France, Holland and Sweden had to be suspended, and Chile temporarily ran into problems when trying to sign new contracts with other purchasers (up to March–April 1973 the world market for copper was depressed; after that date, it became a seller's market).

Evaluation

It is of course impossible to quantify the damage done to Chile through the United States' and Kennecott's and Anaconda's retaliation. The income side of the UP's nationalization without compensation of the Gran Minería is perhaps easier to assess, at least in terms of foreign exchange. When the American companies were the owners of the mines annual profit remittances would amount to some 50 to 100 million dollars, depending on the level of copper prices. The nationalization of Kennecott and Anaconda was, in this respect, a good illustration of the argument advanced twenty years ago by Martin Bronfenbrenner, who maintained that the appeal of confiscation should in no way be discarded as '"pure propaganda" in the sense of economic fallacy'; confiscation was, quite the contrary, often likely to bring 'the pragmatic results desired' by 'shifting income to developmental investment from capitalists' consumption, from transfer abroad, and from unproductive "investment"'.[31]

But to evaluate the 'pragmatic results' of the Gran Minería takeover we also need to take into account what happened *within* the mines. As well as international repercussions and foreign economic aggression, should the 'costs of nationalization' include any direct costs associated with problems for the new owners in running the mine? To try to estimate such costs would be difficult indeed, but a few words must finally be said about the performance of the Gran Minería under the new Chilean administration.

The UP had many difficulties with its copper mines. First, there was the problem of the flight of technicians. In Chuquicamata, for example, all the 54 American managers and technicians who had held important posts in the company left Chile after the nationalization. Ninety-seven Chilean professionals, offered jobs elsewhere by Anaconda, also left in 1971.[32] Repercussions were similar in all the mines, and not only top management positions had to be refilled but a large number of both American and Chilean technical and administrative staff had to be replaced. Transition problems necessarily arose, although technical difficulties caused by the lack of trained personnel appear to have been far less serious than many people, including high CODELCO officials, had initially feared, and also less serious than problems caused by the lack of spare parts and equipment.

Still more troublesome were the attitudes of the mine workers and the conflicts that arose with the Chilean technical staff. The rigid capitalist discipline that ruled under American administration was in no way replaced by socialist discipline; absenteeism increased markedly on all levels, and the comparatively privileged miners of the Gran Minería – politically much to the right of the great majority of Chilean workers – had endless disputes over wages with the UP government. In Chuquicamata, where these problems were most pronounced, 67 partial work stoppages are said to have taken place in 1972 alone[33], and in El Teniente, for a long time renowned for its good working conditions and for the responsible and conscientious spirit of its workers, a large group of miners went on strike for two months in April–June 1973.[34] From mid-1972 the technical and office staff openly began to show hostility towards the new administration, and minor strikes were very common.

What role the possible incapacity of the new management played in these conflicts is impossible to assess, however. The trade unions for supervisors, technicians and office personnel were traditionally controlled by Christian Democrats, and the strikes were basically directed against the UP government in general.

But despite these and similar problems output was maintained and, thanks to the good performance of the El Teniente workers, even slightly increased in 1972.

Table 6.10   *Gran Minería of copper, production levels 1970–72*
(thousands of metric tons)

	1970		1971		1972	
Chuquicamata	263		250		235	
El Teniente	177		147		191	
El Salvador	93		85		83	
Sub-total old mines		533		482		509
Exótica	2		35		31	
Andina	6		54		54	
Total	541		571		594	

SOURCE: CODELCO. The junta's provisional figures for 1973 (*El Mercurio*, International Edition, January 20–27, 1974) show a 2.1 per cent decline of output during the first nine months of the year.

Mining other than copper

Chile's gaining of control of her iron, nitrate and coal mines was carried through after direct negotiations with the foreign interests involved and was thus much less dramatic than was the case with copper.

The UP decided to act at once. In 1971, when almost all the above negotiations were concluded, the Allende government's political power reached a peak, a circumstance which was bound to affect Chile's bargaining position positively. Since the foreign companies' desire to remain in Chile under the new regime was usually limited, it was not difficult to convince them to sell out, and a common opinion in Chile was that the agreements that the UP reached were highly advantageous to Chile.

Most of the nitrate industry, formerly very prosperous but during recent decades rather stagnant, was nationalized early in 1971 as a result of the Chilean state's purchase of the American majority holder's 61 per cent controlling interest in Anglo Lautaro Co., the most important nitrate company in Chile. The second largest nitrate establishment, Salitrera Victoria, was already owned by the Chilean state which, through the incorporation of Anglo Lautaro, acquired control of over 95 per cent of the total production of nitrates and nitrate products. The price paid for the Anglo Lautaro shares amounted to eight million dollars, to be paid over a period of two years – a sum which could be compared with the cost of the Frei administration's 'Chileanization' of the same company: 24.6 million dollars for little more than one-third of the share capital and with no direct control over the administration of the company.[35]

A similar deal was reached with the main foreign investor in the field of iron, Bethlehem Iron Mines Co. (a subsidiary of Bethlehem Steel). For twenty million dollars the Chilean state bought the totality of Bethlehem's mining interests, and after the acquisition of the huge steel and metallurgical complex, Pacific Steel Company (CAP), a mixed company with CORFO and a couple of American mining enterprises as major shareholders, and of most of the remaining metallurgical industries, the Chilean state became the owner of almost the whole iron and steel sector.

The UP government also purchased the large Chilean-owned coal mine Lota-Schwager, accounting for more than 95 per cent of Chile's total output of coal (most of the remainder was produced by an already nationalized mine, Arauco). Like many other Chilean mining companies Lota-Schwager had, during the last few decades, entered a period of decline and the 14,000 workers – living in perhaps the most miserable of all Chile's urban agglomerations – had for long struggled to get the state to take over the mine. The owners offered little resistance when the poorly managed and loss-making company was sold to the state at a very low price only a few months after Allende took office.

Numerous similar deals were negotiated. By early 1972 the mines exclusively owned by the state had increased to 34, as against only one in December 1970. Four more had passed to the area of mixed state–private ownership.[36] One of the prime objectives of the UP for its first year was thus virtually reached. Allende had promised to nationalize all basic mineral resources before the end of year one, and in fact no private mining interest of importance had survived any longer. The small-scale mining (mainly of copper) which remained in private hands accounted for less than ten per cent of the value of Chile's mineral production. The projected increase in the integration of the mining sector with the rest of the economy was also initiated. No more 'enclaves' were to be permitted, and the Allende government transferred almost all major mineral-processing industries to the area of social ownership and began to launch ambitious investment plans for their future development.

This 'constructive' phase of the UP's mineral strategy did not have time to advance very far, however, and our only safe conclusion with respect to the government's policy towards the mineral sector is that it did achieve all its major nationalization objectives within a short period of time.

The formation of the social area of the economy

A final word should be said about the development of output in mining other than copper. My data are provisional, especially for 1973, and they do not distinguish between private and state-owned companies, but even if they are only approximately correct they reveal a general pattern. The good or acceptable performances in 1971 were followed by great difficulties in 1972 and 1973. The problems that arose were usually attributed to the lack of spare parts and machinery, particularly of foreign origin, but other factors, the relative importance of which I have no way of assessing, certainly contributed. But what is clear is that political problems of the kind that affected the Gran Minería of copper were totally absent in the iron, coal and nitrate mines. Here the Chilean Left had a solid and fervent core of adherents, and no strikes or major labor conflicts broke out.

Table 6.11   *Percentage variations of production (volume) in iron, coal and nitrate mining 1971–3*

	1971	1972	1973[a]
Iron	−0.4	−20.0	+7.2
Nitrate	+18.9	−13.0	−7.0
Coal	+6.9	−9.0	−3.9

[a] January–September compared with the same period in 1972.

SOURCES: 1971: Banco Central, *Boletín Mensual* no. 540, February 1973, p. 223. 1972: *Panorama Económico* no. 276, April 1973, p. 11. 1973: *El Mercurio*, International Edition, January 20–27, 1974. No primary source indicated.

INDUSTRY

It was in manufacturing industry that the most bitter fights between the Left and the rightist opposition took place after December 1970. The struggle for and against the incorporation into the 'social area' of those 'strategic monopolies' that the UP had undertaken to expropriate was conducted on all fronts with an intensity that perhaps no other political issue could arouse. The Congress, the mass media, the courts of justice, the streets, and the factories themselves were convereted into battlefields over the question of the state area of the economy.

It is quite understandable that the UP met with such determined resistance here. The strategic importance in the national economy of the manufacturing sector was recognized by government and opposition alike, and no other point in the UP program so directly affected and clashed with the Chilean bourgeoisie's immediate economic interests as did the one promising the rapid elimination of private ownership of all industrial 'monopolies'.

A few other circumstance contributed to make the Allende government's policy towards private manufacturing likely to produce contradictions and confrontations. First, there was the lack of clear-cut criteria within the UP itself with respect to the dimensions of the nationalization program. What should be understood by 'strategic industries', 'monopolies', etc.? And should the UP program be interpreted as merely anti-monopolistic or should the outright socialist connotations be stressed as well? The legal and institutional situation was, furthermore, considerably less favorable to the government in manufacturing than in, say, mining and agriculture, where the opposition's chances of blocking the realization of the program were smaller. In mining mainly foreign interests which were either anxious to sell out or so discredited that no leading Chilean politician could oppose their nationalization were involved, and in the agrarian sector there already existed legislation which permitted the complete abolition of all large *fundos*. In manufacturing, however, the situation was far more complicated.

Legal and political aspects

'The limits of the private, mixed and social sectors of the economy will be established with precision', Allende declared in his first state-of-the-nation address to Congress.[37] In order to try to avoid what the UP regarded as unjustified insecurity among small and medium-scale entrepreneurs, the government, at least in the beginning, repeatedly announced its willingness to give companies not included in the category of 'strategic monopolies' absolute guarantees against expropriations if the opposition, in turn, would allow new legislation regulating the legal rules of the game for the three-sector economy to be passed in Congress. But the congressional deadlock was complete. By the time the government presented its first expropriation bill it was already too late to reach an agreement with the congressional opposition (if this possibility every existed, and I believe it never did).

In October 1971 a detailed legislative project was presented in

Congress by the UP. The bill proposed that a number of important activities – large-scale mining, air and road transporation, banking, postal and telegraphic services, electricity, and a few others – should be exclusively reserved for the public sector. Private stock companies, in manufacturing and elsewhere, with a capital exceeding 14 million escudos by December 1969[38] were to be wholly or partially expropriated – i.e. would be transferred to either the social or the mixed area of the economy. Smaller companies were, according to the proposed legislation, to be given absolute guarantees against expropriation.

The bill suggested that the amounts of compensation to be paid to the owners should be equivalent to each company's book value at the end of the year preceding its nationalization. As a rule indemnification was not to be paid in cash but in so-called social area bonds to be amortized over a longer period of time, but which could, under certain circumstances, be exchanged for ordinary shares in companies within the private or mixed area.

Small shareholders were favored, while the larger ones were offered disadvantageous terms. For holdings up to 20 *sueldos vitales* a full compensation for inflation would be added each year to the value of the bonds, while the bonds exchanged for larger stockholdings were to get only a 70 per cent adjustment for inflation.[39] All 'social area bonds' were to carry an interest of three per cent per annum.

With the bill briefly described above the UP wanted to fulfil two of its old electoral promises: first, to nationalize the 'strategic' industries while giving guarantees to small and medium-scale business and, second, to safeguard the interests of all small shareholders.

Although not explicitly stated, it was taken for granted that all or almost all enterprises whose share capital exceeded 14 million escudos were to be transferred to the social area, and it is thus of interest to see what the UP bill would have signified in figures. Altogether the number of companies satisfying the size criterion of 14 million escudos comprised 253 individual enterprises (some of which had already been nationalized by October 1971, for instance the large-scale mining companies), which accounted for approximately 90 per cent of the whole share capital of all the 1,978 joint-stock companies in Chile.[40] Of these 253 slightly more than 150 were manufacturing industries; a tiny minority of the 35,000 industrial establishments that existed, of course, but a very powerful minority in terms of shares of employment and, particularly, of output. According to the conservative daily *El Mercurio*, this time anxious to exaggerate the Chilean economy's degree of monopolization, the UP's nationalization bill would, if accepted, signify the 'virtual suppression of the whole private sector by means of a law'.[41] It would also, according to the same source, transfer to the public sector over 95 per cent of all commercial advertising in television, radio, and other mass media.[42]

The latter point is not without importance for an understanding of the unified political opposition's fierce resistance to the social area of manufacturing. Although the *El Mercurio* figure of 95 per cent appears far too high there can be little doubt that the expropriation of the 150 largest industrial enterprises would threaten to wipe out most of the commercial advertising supporting the rightist mass media. This was, no doubt, one of the reasons why the opposition always attacked the industrial expropriations much more violently than it attacked the UP's virtual elimination of privately-owned mining companies and *latifundios*.

Let us return to the stalemate in Congress. In view of the vital interests that were involved for the Chilean non-socialist opposition, it is hardly surprising that the government's legislative project was rejected by the congressional majority. And in spite of the fact that the number of companies to be expropriated was being reduced by the government all new proposals continued to be rejected. In January 1972 a list of only ninety enterprises to be transferred to the social and mixed areas was released by the UP.[43] A number of firms had already come under public control, but many strategic companies with share capital exceeding 14 million escudos which remained in private hands had now been excluded from the government's expropriation plans.

The UP's clear retreat from earlier positions was heavily criticized by the UP Left, but was imposed on the group and defended by Radicals and Communists who wanted to give an unmistakable demonstration of the government's good will with respect to adherence to a strictly anti-monopolistic strategy. The new legislative project was officially backed by the National Association of Small Manufacturers (whose members had nothing to fear from Allende's bill – the seventy-four manufacturing establishments that were on the list of the ninety employed an average of 755 workers each), a circumstance which was heavily utilized by the PR and PC in their propaganda against the UP Left. It proved, they argued, the viability of the alliance between the working class and the petty-bourgeoisie.

However the government's conciliatory gesture, which was accompanied by a cautious policy in other fields as well, in no way appeased the rightist opposition, whose response was prompt and negative. A 'constitutional reform' which would impede the government from expropriating or taking control of private companies through other means without congressional approval in each individual case was presented by two Christian Democrats[44] and accepted by the congressional majority. The 'reform' was clearly unacceptable to the UP (not only did it block the further formation of the social area, it also contained a retroactive clause calling for the return to their owners of all companies which had come under state control since 14 October 1971) but the government, in an effort to reach an agreement with the 'progressive sectors of the DC', took up conversations with a number of Christian Democratic senators.

No compromise was ever made, however. After several months of negotiations the talks were unilaterally interrupted by the DC and Allende, in turn, later vetoed all important points in the opposition's constitutional amendment. These vetoes were never accepted by the rightist parties or the Constitutional Court (*Tribunal Constitucional*) to which the dispute was finally submitted,[45] but Allende insisted on the government's (in this author's judgement quite correct) interpretation of the Chilean Constitution and acted as if the opposition's 'reform' had never existed. The legal situation thus remained unchanged. It continued to be what it had been before the UP's assumption of power and the government had to continue to make use of the old legislation. Legislation which, as both sides were well aware, was flexible enough to permit a substantial expansion of the social area of the economy.

Most important among the legal prerequisites at the government's disposal were two 40-year-old laws which Marmaduke Grove's Socialist Republic of 1932 had passed. The legislation that came into existence during this short-lived (thirteen day) experience had not been repealed by subsequent governments, and a completely forgotten and never used law, the so-called DFL No. 520, was found to be useful to a socialist administration.[46]

According to DFL 520 any private enterprise producing or dealing with 'goods of prime necessity' could be expropriated as a result of non-compliance with the law. And the laws were plentiful: both 'price speculation' and 'stockpiling' could, for example, attract the sanction of expropriating. In cases of interruption of production or refusal to use installed capacity in times of 'shortages' of the commodity in question the DFL 520 also permitted expropriation to take place. Through simple decrees from DIRINCO (Dirección Nacional de Industria y Comercio), a public agency supervising the price control system among other things, the government could also oblige firms producing goods of prime necessity, under the threat of expropriation, to raise the level of output by a certain percentage (the so-called production contingents).

In short, DFL 520 was flexible enough to allow the expropriation of virtually all existing industrial and commercial establishments. The only problem was that full compensation had to be paid to the owners, and it had to be paid in cash and in quantities determined by a civil court (which was almost always firmly controlled by conservatives).

The first expropriation by the Allende government took place in December 1970 and affected the large textile company Paños Bellavista Tomé, whose activities had been paralyzed. The political effects of the government's resolute action were considerable – the opposition's legal experts were all taken by surprise – but the inconveniences in having to pay in cash, and pay well, made the UP reluctant to use this legal tool very often. During the first two years only seven companies, of which five had a share capital over 14 million escudos, were expropriated this way.

DFL 520 stipulated another possibility, however: for the same offences that could result in expropriation a company could be 'requisitioned'. According to later and little known legislation from the 'Popular Front's' administration in the 1940s another mechanism, 'intervention', with the same legal consequences as requisition, could be applied in cases of serious labor conflicts such as prolonged strikes. Both requisitions and interventions were conceived as temporary solutions only. Via an interim manager, the state took control of the administration of the plant in question but could not become the owner of the company through this procedure.

At first the Allende government regarded interventions and requisitions mainly as expedient means by which industrialists could be forced to obedience. One of the crucial preconditions for the success of the short-term reactivation program was that private business should refrain from economic resistance, and the drastic sanctions that DFL 520 made possible were initially used as threats (blackmail, the Right said) in order to safeguard output and employment against obstruction. These measures soon lost their emergency character, however. No legislation facilitating nationalization was passed, and since both the government and the workers were anxious to attack private business and implement the UP program, more and more companies were subjected to intervention and requisition. In practice the interventions and requisitions either tended to be indefinite or resulted in the old owner selling out to the state. They became, in fact, the UP's prime instruments for increasing the number of companies under public control.

Although always accounted for separately the enterprises that had thus been put under 'temporary' state management were referred to by most people as belonging to the 'social area'. The owners of the factories, mobilizing the oppositional parties, 'public opinion' (i.e. the rightist mass media), the courts and the *Contraloría General*,[47] naturally launched violent campaigns against the use of DFL 520 and the other 'legal roads to socialism' that the UP legal experts had unearthed, but interventions and requisitions continued to take place in spite of all the inconveniences that were connected with the use of these means.[48]

In many cases, however, and especially when foreign interests were involved, the government tried to avoid the more brutal methods described above. An arrangement often suggested by the UP to foreign investors was the creation of mixed companies, or joint ventures, with the Chilean state holding a 51 per cent controlling interest in the company in question.

Against North American property the attitude was tougher. From the very beginning the Allende government calculated on strained relations with the United States, and sanctions against US companies were common. The very first interventions that the UP undertook, in fact, affected two predominantly US-owned industries – the foundry NIBSA and the food-processing industry Purina. In both cases the motivation claimed by the UP for the intervention was cessation of production. Other interventions in American interests which attracted much attention involved Ford Motor Co. in May 1971 (the plant had been closed down by the owners) and the International Telephone and Telegraph Co. (ITT), where intervention occurred in September 1971.

In the cases where ownership and not only control was transferred to the state the most commonly used means was to buy the whole company in question after having reached an agreement with the owners. For the Treasury this procedure generally turned out to be much cheaper than expropriation, since in the latter case the civil courts were absolute rulers while in direct negotiations the government often had a very good bargaining position *vis-à-vis* the capitalists. With the state controlling import licences and, from 1971, also bank credits and with access to legal threats and penalties ranging from the establishment of 'production contingents' to intervention or requisition the government was in a favorable position, especially when, as was usually the case, full support could be counted on from the workers involved.

The bargaining strength of the owners, on the other hand, depended to a large extent on their own ability to take to economic retaliation against the government. Companies which relied heavily on foreign licences, royalties, spare parts, etc. or which were wholly or partially owned by foreign interests from countries with which the UP wanted to maintain friendly relations were in the best position to be well compensated. As indicated earlier, the industrialists could also count on an increasingly efficient support from the legislative and judiciary powers and, of course, from the rightist opposition and its mass media. The talks between the government and the industrialists often took place in a heated atmosphere, with various forms of pressure brought to bear by both sides. The workers themselves often went on strike or even occupied the plant during negotiations, for example, while the bourgeois press would openly accuse of treason those capitalists who agreed to sell out to the state.

Public acquisition of shares without previous negotiations with any of the owners was another method through which the state area of the economy was enlarged, and practically the whole commercial banking system was in fact purchased this way. Resistance to selling was quite stubborn when it came to industries, however. Early in 1972 when the government, through the state development organization CORFO, decided to start buying shares in a number of companies that were on the 'list of ninety', it was politically too late. The overwhelming majority of shareholders refused to sell, and not one industry was bought this way. Even the smallest shareholders, to whom very favorable prices were paid, were reluctant to accept the generous offer – in part, no doubt, as a consequence of the massive propaganda campaign launched by the rightist newspapers, a campaign which among other things consisted of letting the conservative daily *La Segunda*, part of the *El Mercurio* empire, publish lists of 'traitors' who had sold shares to CORFO.

The Allende government's purchases of companies through negotiations or acquisitions of shares were criticized from the revolutionary Left as well. 'Are they trying to *buy* capitalism?' was a typical remark,[49] and in many factories the workers grew impatient and seized the plants against the will of the Ministry of Economy. The government often found itself obliged to try to dissuade the workers from occupying an industry that it did not want to nationalize. For instance loss-making companies, foreign-owned industries, and small and medium-sized firms whose take-over would destroy the hoped-for alliance with the petty-bourgeoisie were placed in this category. But as worker militancy increased the government often gave way to the workers' demands and named a state *interventor*. It also happened that the workers presented two separate wage readjustment demands depending on whether the industry remained in private hands or not. This was the case in the copper-processing industry MADECO, where early in 1971 the workers put forward two alternatives: either a general 35 per cent wage increase or only 25 per cent plus state intervention.

Let us now summarize the legal and institutional aspects of the formation of the state area of the economy. There were five different alternatives for taking over private business: three (expropriation, direct agreements with the owners, and public acquisition of shares) which signified a real change in ownership, and two (intervention and requisition) through which control but not ownership was transferred to the state. Which method was used was a matter of circumstance and depended on such different factors as the size of the establishment in question, the attitude of the owners and the political position of the workers, the existence or non-existence of technological dependency and foreign ownership, etc. Every company that the government wanted to take over was subject to detailed analysis by the Ministry of Economy in the above respects, and often a combination of, say, intervention and negotiations with the owners was used. In the final analysis it was the political strength of the opponents, the correlation of forces – and here the militancy of the workers themselves was extremely important – that determined the outcome.

To illustrate the flexible strategy sometimes employed by the government an internal document elaborated by a group of officials (all members of MAPU) at the Ministry of Economy deserves to be quoted. The document, published in *El Mercurio*[50] (which had agents everywhere), discussed the situation of the companies on the 'list of the ninety' in March 1972 (that is, after it had become clear that the UP's nationalization bill would never pass Congress and before Pedro Vuskovic was suspended) and it also, albeit very briefly, recommended possible lines of action in the following way:

CCU. Requisitioned. Acquisition of shares initiated.
Cía Industrial. Acquisition of shares initiated. Agitation followed by requisition recommended.
Grace y Cía. Wait and see.
Mademsa. Acquisition of shares should be initiated.
Acero Andes. Requisition should be prepared.
Cía Chilena de Fòsforos. Conversations with the Swedes should be taken up.
Interoceánica. Negotiations finished. Agreement to be signed on 21 March.

Industry

Nieto Hermanos. Agitation among workers, to be followed by requisition.
Caupolicán. Requisitioned. Acquisition of shares initiated.
Induro. Negotiations with the SIRCO group should continue.
CIMAT. Wait and see.

. . .

The few examples given above illustrate the opinion of the government, or at least of part of the government, with respect to how one should proceed with these companies – 'the ninety', which all the UP parties had agreed to nationalize in one way or another. But most divisions of the UP were by no means content with taking over such a reduced number of industries only, and within the UP and the whole Chilean Left there were sharp differences over the question of the size of the social area and the forms of struggle for it. The divergencies that thus arose were only natural expressions of the strategic differences that have been presented several times above. We recall that the PC and PR defined the UP program as democratic and anti-monopolistic rather than anti-capitalistic, while the majority faction of the PS, MAPU and the whole revolutionary Left outside the UP (the MIR, above all) stressed the revolutionary and socialist aspects of the struggle.

This debate turned especially heated when medium- and small-scale industry was affected by strikes or occupations. In line with their general strategic outlook the 'consolidationist' sectors of the UP feared that such actions would render impossible the hoped-for anti-monopolistic alliance between the working class and the petty-bourgeoisie, while the UP Left discarded this way of reasoning as reformist while often supporting both state interventions of non-monopolistic firms and the workers' own actions directed against medium- and small-scale business as well.[51]

In practice the industrial working class sided with the revolutionary line. Strikes and occupations continued, and most workers in small and medium-sized establishments could see no reason why they should not be allowed to participate directly in the struggle against capitalism. Objectively this latter sector of the working class had – and herein lies an important aspect of the failure of the UP's strategy – much more to win from a radical change of the economic system than had the large-scale industrial workers who enjoyed much better economic and social conditions.

An exclusively anti-monopolistic struggle would, then, affect but a small part of the industrial population, leaving the majority of workers – and the poorest ones, too – without any immediate prospects for a different future. (Similar phenomena, producing similar political contradictions, were very well reflected in the problems that confronted the UP in the agrarian sector.) An outright anti-capitalist strategy would, on the other hand, clash at once with the interests of the whole bourgeoisie and would thus leave the working class without vital support 'from above', from those petty-bourgeois sectors which the PC and PR especially considered as both indispensable and possible allies.

We thus see that one of the basic structural characteristics of the Chilean economy – the existence of a relatively modern and high-productive manufacturing sector employing only a small minority of the labor force – gave rise to contradictions which the UP program had not taken into account. And this will become even more clear when we look at the size of the state area of industry in terms of relative shares of output and employment.

The social area in figures

Available statistics on the rate at which industries were integrated into the social area of the economy are incomplete, at least for the last year of the Allende government. But despite certain shortcomings they are sufficiently clear for our purposes, and in what follows aggregate data on the pace of the UP's implementation of its nationalization program will be presented.

In table 6.12 we can see how the number of industries brought under state control through either transfer of ownership or permanent intervention or requisition grew between November 1970 and May 1973. Table 6.13, which is mainly of political interest, illustrates the distribution in time of the government's use of the methods of intervention and requisition. Here not only manufacturing establishments but also companies in other sectors have been included, and another difference from table 6.12 is that temporary interventions and requisitions have not been omitted.

During most of 1973 – and especially during periods of military presence in the cabinet – the rate of intervention and requisition declined appreciably. Shortly after the aborted military coup on 29 June the government made a final decision to take over a large number – about fifty – of mostly small and medium-sized companies which had been occupied by their workers in response to the attempted coup and which the workers refused to give up.[52]

The UP's own official figures on the total number of companies

Industry

Table 6.12 *Number of industrial establishments controlled by the Chilean state*

Form of control	Nov. 1970	Dec. 1971	Dec. 1972	May 1973
State ownership[a]	31	62	103	165
Under intervention or requisition	—	39	99	120
Total	31	101	202	285

[a] Both social and mixed areas and including six new industries that were created by the Chilean state after November 1970.

SOURCES: November 1970 and December 1971: Instituto de Economía, *La Economía Chilena en 1971*, pp. 455ff.
December 1972: Instituto de Economía *La Economía Chilena en 1972*, p. 135.
May 1973: Article by Pedro Vuskovic in *Ultima Hora*, 7 June, 1973.

It should be observed that the sources are of different quality. The data from the Instituto de Economía are based on detailed specifications of all individual companies, while Vuskovic in his June 1973 article gives only aggregate figures on the number of industries taken over by May 1973.

brought under state control during the whole Allende period will probably never be known, but a little more than three hundred would be a fairly good estimate. According to the Pinochet junta the sum total of expropriations, purchases and permanent interventions and requisitions had reached 323[53] by 11 September 1973. Compared with the 35,000 odd industrial establishments then existing in Chile, this was less than one per cent. But in terms of capital, output and employment the social area of the economy naturally became much more important than this statistic indicates. 'Strategic monopolies' were the most sought-after objects for nationalization, and although quite a few of those defined as monopolies escaped,[54] while several small establishments were taken over, the average size of companies under state control was far above the average for the economy as a whole.

Exactly how much above average is not known. No reliable and up-to-date quantitative analysis of this aspect of the situation was ever presented. According to estimates by the Institute of Economics at the University of Chile the state-owned sector's share of all industrial production in December 1972 was about 22 per cent, and a common hypothesis in mid-1973 was 'some thirty per cent', but nobody really knew. In some branches state industries undoubtedly reached a 'dominant' position, to use a phrase often used by the UP when defining its objectives, but in others the private sector's supremacy continued.

Table 6.13 *Number of requisitions and interventions by time periods, November 1970 – November 1972*

Period	Interventions	Requisitions	Total
November–December 1970	37	1	38
January–February 1971	23	—	23
March–April 1971	1	5	6
May–June 1971	12	12	24
July–August 1971	9	6	15
September–October 1971	24	7	31
November–December 1971	21	9	30
January–February 1972	13	6	19
March–April 1972	14	7	21
May–June 1972	16	3	19
July–August 1972	7	18	25
September–October[a] 1972	23	48	71
November 1972	2	4	6
Total	202	126	328

[a] During the 'October events' a large number of enterprises were subjected to intervention or requisition for participation in the general lockout. Most of these companies were later returned to their owners.
SOURCE: Based on Instituto de Economía, *La Economía Chilena en 1972*, pp. 116ff.

146

In order to get a notion of the impact of the UP's nationalization program we can, however, draw upon calculations made in a study[55] of the relative importance of the public sector in the manufacturing industry 'in the future', i.e. *if* the plans of the government had really been implemented. The companies that were considered when defining the 'UP's plans' were those which were either already owned by the state in 1970 *or* had been purchased by the Allende government by the time the study was made (early in 1973) *or* were on the 'list of the ninety' *or* had been explicitly mentioned in a bill that Allende (vainly) presented to Congress in January 1973. All subsidiaries to companies satisfying one of the above criteria were also included.

Two tables from the above study will be presented below. Table 6.14 shows the relative importance of state-owned companies (including mixed companies) in different subsectors of manufacturing in 1970 and after a complete carrying through of the UP's nationalization plans as defined above. The material thus indicates which branches the UP considered 'strategic', and indirectly it also tells us something about which branches were most monopolistic.

Table 6.15 provides aggregate information about the ('future') role of the social and mixed areas in terms of their shares of the whole manufacturing sector's output, capital, exports, imports and employment. This table gives yet another illustration of the high degree of concentration in Chilean industry (we recall that the state controlled sector would comprise at the most one per cent of all industrial establishments) as well as of the great differences in productivity between large- and small-scale industry.

Let us finally turn to some important socio-economic and political implications of the figures presented in tables 6.14 and 6.15. We see that the state-owned sector's very low 'planned' share of the whole industrial work force – 22.2 per cent of the total – adds further evidence to our previous remarks on the limitations of the Allende government's nationalization program in terms of number of workers directly affected. The amount of industry included in table 6.15 goes considerably beyond the Communist Party's strictly anti-monopolistic strategy, but nevertheless almost four-fifths of all industrial workers would, after the full implementation of these far-reaching plans, continue to be employed by private enterprise.

The essence of the UP strategy thus amounted to trying to nationalize some two-thirds of the whole industrial capital with the active help of only about 20 per cent of all industrial workers. The remaining 80 per

Table 6.14   *Relative importance of the state-owned sector of manufacturing in 1970 and according to UP plans (percentages of gross value of production)*[a]

Industry	1970	Planned
Food	13.8	30.4
Beverages	1.5	33.6
Tobacco	—	100.0
Textiles	—	38.5
Clothing	—	18.0
Footwear	—	18.8
Leather and leather products	—	8.0
Wood and wood products	5.3	18.5
Paper and paper products	10.7	85.0
Printing and publishing	2.3	14.3
Industrial chemical products	23.2	64.8
Other chemical products	3.1	35.7
Refined petroleum	79.7	100.0
Petroleum and coal derivates	83.3	89.2
Rubber products	—	75.3
Glass and glass products	—	55.2
Other non-metallic mineral products	0.4	72.0
Iron and steel	49.5	76.2
Non-ferrous metals	—	93.0
Non-electrical machinery	14.4	44.8
Electrical machinery	0.4	46.5
Other metal products	1.9	33.0
Transport equipment	21.4	97.2
Miscellaneous	10.9	10.9
Total, weighted average	11.8	43.9

[a] Percentage estimates based on production values in 1967. The choice of 1967 as base year thus signifies that the estimates given above correspond to the 'true' percentages only if all industries developed in a parallel way from 1967 and onwards. The procedure used for companies created after 1967 is not indicated in the source, *Panorama Económico*.

cent, the vast majority of the Chilean workers, should vote for socialism, and defend the government in confrontations with the Right, and support the 'struggle of production', but they should not undertake any militant actions against their own employers who were, in theory, their own allies, allies of the working class.

But it did not, and could not, work this way. The Chilean working

Table 6.15 *Estimates of the social and mixed areas' relative shares of fixed assets, gross value of production, employment, and foreign trade (percentages of manufacturing total) 1970 and according to UP plans*

Share of	Social area[a]		Mixed area[b]		Social and mixed areas	
	1970	Planned	1970	Planned	1970	Planned
Value of fixed assets[c]	16.9	53.3	11.5	16.1	28.4	69.4
Gross value of production[c]	7.6	27.7	4.2	15.2	11.8	43.9
Industrial employment[c]	4.6	15.4	1.9	6.8	6.5	22.2
Industrial exports[d]	3.2	34.7	17.9	33.6	21.1	68.3
Industrial imports[d]	14.3	41.4	2.3	25.9	16.6	67.3

[a] Public ownership exceeding 80 percent.
[b] Public ownership falling between 51 and 80 per cent.
[c] Base year 1967 (cf. Table 6.14 above).
[d] Base year 1969.

149

class, and wide sectors within the UP leadership as well, did not accept the above philosophy, and for this reason – and for several others – the contradictions inherent in the UP's political and economic strategy became more and more manifest as the overall polarization in society proceeded.

Without denying the importance of purely ideological factors we can thus conclude that the failure of the UP's strategy was in part only the political expression of the underlying economic conditions in Chilean society which gave rise to contradictions which the UP could not solve and which could never have been solved within the narrow confines of the 'Chilean road to socialism'. For either this road was to be solely 'Chilean' – strictly anti-monopolistic, parliamentary and with much use of state repression against the great majority of the working class not content with the PC's anti-monopolistic strategy – or it had to be social-ist, but in the latter case the 'Chilean' road would have to be replaced by something quite different from what was envisaged in the UP program, namely socialist revolution.

So far our discussion has dealt with the *formation* of the public sector's share of manufacturing: its legal, political and socio-economic pre-requisites and the quantitative growth of state controlled industries. But how did the companies actually work after they had been taken over? What criteria did the UP apply in price and investment decisions? What were the effects of the 'social area' on the overall economic situation in Chile?

It is not easy to give accurate answers to these questions. Only very vague guidelines were given to the state-appointed managers, and conditions varied appreciably from plant to plant. Statistics from the state-controlled sector – growing in size and always changing in com-position – are incomplete or non-existent, particularly for 1973. We will, then, have to confine ourselves to general observations on problems connected with the economic performance of the social area of manu-facturing. But first a few remarks on the formal organization of manage-ment in the typical state enterprise and on the achievements made in the field of industrial democracy.[56]

Worker participation

As we have seen, in the struggle for the creation of the social area the workers themselves often took the initiative while the government lagged behind, and once the battle of a particular factory was won the workers demanded not a mere change of masters but a genuine transformation of the social relations and power structure within the plant. The government's official policy, as reflected in the UP program and in statements and documents of various kinds, was to support these aspirations, to avoid bureaucracy and paternalism and to provide scope for democratic forms of management. Industrial democracy was an ever-present issue in Salvador Allende's Chile, and in spite of constant and well-founded complaints about bureaucracy and inefficiency in the forms of participation that were tried, a great deal was in fact accomplished in the state-controlled industries.[57] It should be emphasized, however, that the issue was *participation* and little more; the role of the state as an institution and final decision maker was questioned only by the most leftist contingents within and outside the Unidad Popular.

In December 1970 the Allende government and the CUT (Central Union of Workers) had already signed a general agreement regulating, among other things, norms for economic democracy. Representatives of the CUT were granted participation and influence in the overall planning of the economy (a planning which by and large failed to materialize), and within the individual industries power and responsibility were to be shared between the workers themselves and the state managers. According to the formal organization model agreed upon, factories should be run by 'administrative councils' made up of one government-appointed president and five representatives of the workers[58] and five of the state. This system thus gave the government more votes than the workers in the top decision-making body of the enterprise but the workers could, on the other hand, force the government to recall any one of its representatives at any time subsequent to a censure vote in the general 'workers' assembly'. (Many politically unfit or otherwise incompetent state-appointed managers were in fact ousted by the workers in this way.)

In addition to this formal worker representation in the administrative council, there was also a host of other committees, councils and more informal channels for worker participation in plants. The role of the trade unions also changed in the state-controlled companies. Their traditional 'economistic' tasks declined somewhat in importance, but now the unions began to take a very active part in matters concerning production targets, cultural and educational activities, etc. They also did conciliation work when, as often happened, conflicts between management and workers arose.

In practice the general CUT–government blueprint was seldom

copied in detail, and concrete forms of participation varied enormously from plant to plant. The system of formal representation in the administrative council often remained a scrap of paper, while other, more informal expressions of industrial democracy flourished. As from 1972, and particularly after October 1972 when the danger of a rightist military coup was first felt to be imminent, the organs of worker control that gained importance were to an increasing extent those which were directed towards broader and more explicitly political objectives than the economics of the individual plants. 'Defense committees', 'distribution brigades', 'coordination committees', etc. mushroomed, while interest in administrative matters stagnated. Whole areas were becoming integrated into so-called industrial belts (*cordones industriales*) comprising all industry within a particular region. The *comandos comunales* were in charge of such different matters as distribution of foodstuffs, health services, defense against rightist sabotage or military attacks, and united both workers, students, housewives, unemployed and others within a whole community. 'People's power' (*poder popular*) became the battle cry of Chile's revolutionary Left, but, despite their having gained much importance during the last few months of the Allende regime, the industrial belts, *comandos comunales*, etc. were never really accepted by the most reformist groups within the UP, which argued that the authority of the government was jeopardized by the embryonic organs of 'dual power' that proliferated.

But this is another story, and let us return to the situation within state-controlled enterprises. We have seen that the social area of manufacturing was at least a partial success in terms of worker participation and mass mobilization. The picture becomes less favorable when we turn to economic performance. This was certainly not the fault of industrial democracy. In factories where this worked well production and cost control also tended to be better handled than in plants where the system of participation was poorly developed. It was rather due to the vacillating and contradictory industrial policy followed by the government and to circumstances connected with the overall economic and political situation that prevailed which were far beyond the control of each individual industry.

Neither plan nor market

'Planning will be our principal instrument for the allocation of our productive resources' – this and similar phrases frequently recurred in the speeches and writings of the UP leaders.[59] Through planning the 'anarchy of the market' was to be at least partially overcome, and by means of planning the UP's medium- and long-term development objectives, such as downgrading the external sector as the engine of growth and restructuring production so as to correspond to a new, more egalitarian pattern of demand, were to be achieved. Within the social area imperative planning was to rule, and well defined investment criteria were to be established. The investable surplus generated within the state enterprises would constitute the pillar of the capital accumulation process in the future. This was, in very few words, the Allende government's blueprint. But things did not work this way. The anarchy of the market was replaced by the anarchy of neither plan nor market.

Guidance to the socially owned companies was exceedingly vague. The social area should be oriented towards 'raising the standards of living of the poor majority of the people', in the words of Amérigo Zorrilla (Minister of Finance, November 1970 – June 1972), who by adding 'while keeping the requirements of accumulation in mind' admitted the existence of a trade-off between these objectives.[60] The expression used by Zorrilla clearly indicates where emphasis was put, and to increase output while keeping costs and prices low became the prime criterion of success in the running of a state-controlled enterprise. The output goal dominated; to 'produce as much as possible' was a rule of thumb oft repeated by managers and workers alike.

And production did rise, particularly during 1971 when output in the state-controlled industries increased by 14.9 per cent over 1970.[61] The policy of massive mobilization of idle industrial capacity and manpower gave very good results initially, but it was not followed by a more sophisticated development policy when the easy period of 'extensive' growth came to an end and bottlenecks began to increase.

With the new situation disguised unemployment appeared and work discipline – already weakened as a result of easily understandable political circumstances – was further relaxed. Total employment in the social area of manufacturing increased about ten per cent in 1972 over 1971, or considerably above the rise of output.[62] Part of this decline in labor productivity could perhaps be explained by various bottlenecks and particularly by the greater needs of manpower caused by difficulties in getting spare parts and machinery from abroad. A highly labor-intensive important substitution was forced upon many industries. But in part it was also the result of scarcity of experienced administrative personnel. It was, of course, necessary to fill almost all high managerial posts in the state enterprises with people of confidence, but political dedication and responsibility did not always compensate for lack of economic and technical training among the new industrial leaders. Adaptation problems necessarily arose.

It is, however, very difficult to apply ordinary efficiency criteria to the UP's social area of manufacturing, and this not only for political reasons. The violent inflation beginning in 1972 and concomitant distortions in relative prices made planning and accounting in monetary terms both difficult and almost meaningless. Rightly or wrongly, both workers and managers soon got used to thinking in physical units rather than in escudos when assessing whether a particular industry was doing well or not, and in many companies even elementary economic controls such as book-keeping and cost calculation became deficient or almost absent. Neither was easy access to cheap state credit conducive to economic discipline, though this built-in distortion should be blamed on the UP's general economic policy. Another built-in waste mechanism was the fact that enterprises kept under intervention or requisition continued to be the property of their private owners. In part it was the owners' money that was being spent, and who cared about the capitalists' capital?

Many formerly highly profitable companies began to incur heavy losses after having been taken over by the state. According to informed guesses[63] seven out of the ten major industrial sectors in the social area ran cash deficits in 1972, deficits which altogether amounted to some 20,000 million escudos.[64] Instead of being able to 'generate its own surplus', as the UP had conceived, the social area became a leaking bucket, adding fuel to the money supply and the galloping rate of inflation.

Some of the reasons behind the substantial financial deterioration of most state-controlled enterprises have been indicated above: shortages of managers, impaired work discipline, production bottlenecks, and difficulties caused by inflation and by the undefined legal status of companies run under intervention and requisition. To assess the relative importance of these more or less interdependent factors would be hard and to give figures impossible, but nevertheless I believe that two other causes deserve to be singled out as even more important when explaning the losses made in the social area: the good but expensive improvements in material benefits to the workers and, last but not least, the price policy pursued by the government. As illustrations of some crucial weaknesses in the UP's industrial policy these two aspects deserve explanation.

The bargaining position of the workers in state enterprises can be described as excellent. The government, happy to be able to improve miserable working conditions and anxious to avoid conflicts, offered little resistance to many of the workers' demands, especially since the entire rightist opposition willingly sided with the working class by fomenting, through its mass media and organizations, virtually all wage claims presented in the social area.[65] Wage-drift above the periodic general readjustments was common.

It was not primarily higher wages that characterized the state-owned companies, but rather a wide range of fringe benefits that did not exist in private business. Child care centers were created, and women workers were given time off during their shifts to visit their children. Good, nutritious and cheap meals were served at the work-place. Medical and dental services were introduced in all factories employing more than a minimum number of workers. In-plant libraries were installed, and space and money for various other educational and cultural activities were put at the workers' disposal, etc.

All these facilities did not exist everywhere in the social area, of course, but a truly admirable – and for the individual companies, which were charged all the costs, expensive – effort was made to ameliorate work conditions. Apart from providing striking benefits for the workers, many of these improvements should also be regarded as badly needed investments in human capital.

These were the positive aspects, but again we must consider some of the deeper implications of the UP's anti-monopolistic strategy. The policy of 'nationalizing' no more than some twenty per cent of the industrial labor force, giving these twenty per cent vast material and non-tangible privileges (influence, prestige, etc.) while leaving the situation for the great majority – and, let me repeat, the poorest section – of the workers more or less unchanged was bound to give rise to new inequalities and to generate (or, perhaps, accentuate) splits within the working class. The UP was certainly not totally unaware of what its industrial strategy was leading to in this respect, but as in the case of the agrarian reform – where the above tendencies were even more pronounced and inequality greater – it lacked the political strength to carry through more egalitarian policies. The workers remaining outside the social area were promised wage increases, social reforms and new legislation regulating their working conditions, but most reform projects were either not passed in Congress or insufficiently implemented. Profits arising in state enterprises were intended to be used to build new factories and to improve living standards for all workers and unemployed. The problem was, however, that profits disappeared and were converted into losses. As inflation and shortages grew worse it was the real wages of privately employed workers, who received poor fringe benefits or none and whose bargaining positions remained poor, which first began to deteriorate.

The masses grasped these contradictions much better than the UP leadership, and it was only natural that a large number of small-scale workers, unemployed and *pobladores* abandoned the anti-monopolistic strategy and called for a socialist revolution, thus further undermining the official strategy of class alliances upon which the UP program rested.

Before leaving the social area of manufacturing a final word should be said about how the government's price policy contributed to turning profits into losses. The cornerstone of the price policy was simple, and aimed at favoring consumers rather than producers. To keep the prices of products from 'its own' industries low was a matter of special honor for the UP, and since companies belonging to the social area also stuck to official price guidelines to a far greater extent than did private businesses, losses were bound to arise as official prices became increasingly unrealistic. Instead of being granted decent price rises the state-owned companies were given bank credits to cover their losses.

The effects of the government's price policy were quite arbitrary and often unwarranted. The concentration of public ownership in sectors like energy, transportation, intermediate industrial goods and heavy industry rather than in the consumer goods industry, for example, meant that large subsidies were being given to private companies using cheap inputs from the state sector. In addition, within the private sector thus favored it was large-scale, modern industry using little labor (which was relatively expensive) that was inadvertently most privileged.[66] And with respect to the general aim of subsidizing consumers it must be said that a clearly undesirable side-effect of the artificially low prices of consumer goods was the enrichment of a large but unknown number of speculators.

The list of explanations of the cash deficits that arose in the state controlled industries has now been exhausted. We have seen that the 'socialist embryo' which the UP tried to create in the midst of a hostile political and economic environment was an expensive undertaking, but in no way should we pretend to evaluate its significance with reference only to profit-and-loss accounts in escudos. If a Chilean industrial worker were to read the above picture and argue that it was very biased and 'economistic', that the innumerable unquantifiable advances that the Chilean working class made precisely in the socially owned factories have been neglected, I would whole-heartedly agree. But to analyze these questions would require another study.

The critical appraisal of the social area's economic performance should not be interpreted as an attempt to put the blame on the individuals running the plants. The situation within state-controlled industries was difficult: the 'rules of the game' were thoroughly changed, and workers and managers could not – and were, despite recurrent government calls for financial discipline, not expected to – act in accordance with capitalistic, profit-maximizing criteria. It was rather the political struggle and the confrontation between planning and market forces – or, we could say, between administrative improvisations and black markets – which gave the economics of the social area such a chaotic character. The capitalist rationality was not replaced by a socialist rationality, whatever is to be understood by the latter. What ruled was neither plan nor market, but a combination of the two whose results could be described by means of an expression often used by Allende when explaning the difficulties that confronted the economy: 'We suffer from all the disadvantages of capitalism without enjoying any of the benefits of socialism.'

On the political level the half-way implementation of the nationalization program expressed itself as a strategic failure: the bourgeoisie was neither defeated nor appeased. Or in Pedro Vuskovic's Chilean version of the old Oskar Lange dilemma:[67] 'During this period', Vuskovic wrote at the end of 1972, 'the advances in the implementation of the [UP] program have been great enough to provoke furious reactions on the part of imperialism and the bourgeoisie, but quite insufficient to deprive the domestic bourgeoisie of its ability to use the economic power that it still retains for all kinds of obstruction and economic sabotage.'[68]

OTHER SECTORS

Mining and large-scale manufacturing were not the only activities that the UP had planned to nationalize in order to take control of the 'commanding heights' of the Chilean economy. Banking and 'monopolies' in the fields of distribution, communications and foreign trade were also regarded as being of vital importance for the creation of a dominant state-owned sector capable of directing the economy along planned lines. We should therefore complete this overview of the formation of the social area of the economy with a brief account of the UP's achievements in these sectors.

The Banking system was an obvious target, and already in December 1970 President Allende made public the government's plans to take over all domestic and foreign banks operating in Chile.[69] The method suggested was simple: public acquisition of shares.

This initiative shocked the opposition, which despite a violent campaign against the UP's unexpected offer was unable to prevent the shareholders from selling out. The prices paid for the shares were high[70] and the government had a powerful arsenal of reprisals to resort to against banks whose owners were unwilling to sell. It was made clear that the government could easily force any bank offering resistance into liquidation, and that it was prepared to do so. Concerns about employment, production and know-how were less present in banking than in the directly productive sectors, and the number of individual banks that were to remain did not matter very much since it was part of the UP's intentions to merge all commercial banks into one single state-owned bank. The shareholders were in effect offered a choice between selling voluntarily or being left with worthless stock in bankrupt banks.

Subsidiaries to foreign banks operating in Chile – Bank of America, First National City Bank, Bank of London and a mixed French-Italian bank – found themselves in equally awkward bargaining positions and decided to sell out rapidly following direct negotiations with the Chilean government.

With the exception of the Bank of Edwards – which immediately after Allende's taking office went into bankruptcy, reporting a loss of seven million dollars, while its principal owner, Augustín Edwards, left for the United States to become Vice-President of the Pepsi-Cola company – all major banks were gradually bought by the state.[71] In November 1971 the Minister of Finance, Amérigo Zorrilla, could announce that 'the nationalization of the banking system is practically completed. The state now controls sixteen banks which together provide over ninety per cent of all credit ... This process of nationalization ... means that the links between financial and industrial monopoly capital have been broken'.[72] A little later no commercial bank of importance remained in predominantly private hands.

To break the links uniting the dominant sectors of the Chilean bourgeoisie was one important objective of the government, but not the only one. Credit policies were to be changed in accordance with the UP's development priorities, and a redistribution of bank credit favoring mainly state controlled enterprises, agriculture, export industries and small-scale business was initiated. Real – in 1971 even nominal – interest rates were drastically lowered, and the overall volume of bank loans expanded.

The government's plans to merge all banks into one in order to centralize the provision of credit and provide scope for strict control of investment decisions were never realized. In part as a result of opposition from the bank employees the original project gradually became modified. In 1973 the UP agreed on the amalgamation of the individual banks that existed into three large state banks: the Banco Central was to be in charge of monetary policies and external transactions, the Banco del Estado would specialize in agricultural credits, and the Banco Nacional would finance investments in other sectors, mainly industry and commerce. But the application of this three-bank formula was also delayed, and the banking system continued to operate in the same, relatively decentralized way as before.

The following frank answer given early in 1973 by Fernando Flores, then Minister of Finance, indicates why advances were so slow in the above respect (and in some others as well, perhaps):

Interviewer: Why haven't you made any progress in centralizing the banking system?

Flores: One and a half years ago nothing could be done because of PIR [i.e. because of staunch opposition from the *Partido de Izquierda Radical*, at that time participating in the cabinet]. And after that, well there were other reasons. As you know we are often very good at talking but when it comes to achieving concrete results we are not quite as good.[73]

Transport and communications were sectors where public ownership was substantial even before 1970, and where private interests dominated the UP failed to increase the relative scope of the social area. For example, railroads and airlines had been run by the state since their very start, but in the highly strategic field of road transportation nothing was done to break the almost complete control that private companies held in both freight and passenger traffic.

Although the UP eventually became perfectly aware of the political dangers connected with letting such a vital activity as road transportation remain in private hands, there was little that the government wanted to do against a sector which was not classified as controlled by 'monopolies'.[74] After October 1972 it became increasingly urgent but also politically more difficult to intervene. The agreement which put an end to the 'October crisis' and which was supervised by three high military officials who entered the cabinet contained guarantees against expropriations of anything that had to do with road transportation. And without support from the mass of small proprietors – who decidedly sided with the large companies in the struggle against Allende's government – the UP was effectively trapped, and the self-assured *transportistas* of truck and bus owners knew how to make use of the situation. The entire last year of UP rule was characterized by escalating confrontations following a very simple scheme: lockouts and blackmail, concessions from the government, new lockouts and new concessions. The military take-over in September 1973 was preceded by a seven-week paralysis of road transportation. After the coup the head of the Chilean Association of Truck Owners was immediately appointed a travelling ambassador by the Junta.

The main telecommunications networks had long been controlled by private foreign investors, headed by the US giant ITT, which monopolized the telephone network in most of Chile.[75] For political and nationalistic reasons this company with its many subsidiaries was an obvious target for take-over by the UP. In September 1971 ITT was intervened, and later it appeared at the top of the UP's list of the ninety companies to be nationalized.

After the publication of the ITT Documents revealing the role played by ITT in the late 1970 plots against Allende, the government decided to expropriate the company with all its subsidiaries. According to the bill presented to Congress – where it was passed as a gesture by the rightist majority just a few weeks before the military take-over – no compensation was to be paid as a penalty for the anti-Chilean activities that company had indulged in.

All other private firms engaged in the field of telecommunications – that is, Transradio Chilena, Cables West Coast and All American – were also to be nationalized, and negotiations with the foreign owners were almost completed by September 1973.

The crucial importance of distribution escaped the attention of neither the government nor the Right, and the UP's advances in reducing the private sector's supremacy in this field were erratic and met with fierce opposition. A firm alliance between the *gremios* of truck owners, wholesale traders and small merchants was soon created to defend their members against real or imagined threats. With help from the rightist political organizations – which found a fertile ground for extreme right-wing propaganda among frustrated self-employed workers – this coalition became strong enough not only to protect private business but to play a very active role in precipitating the overthrow of Allende. To these conflicts, and to some of their causes, we will have occasion to return.

In wholesale trade the government undertook to compete with the private sector. A new state company DINAC was founded through the merger of four private distributing enterprises (Duncan Fox, Agencias Graham, Gibbs and Williamson Balfour) which were gradually being purchased after direct negotiations with their British owners. DINAC's field was groceries, where its market share early in 1973 reached about 29 per cent; the remainder was wholly handled by private firms.[76] In some lines of distribution, particularly in perishable foodstuffs, the UP established completely new state-controlled enterprises – SOCOAGRO for the distribution of meat, ENAVI for the distribution (and production) of poultry, SACOOP for the buying and selling of vegetables, etc. But most of these new companies experienced substantial setbacks and managed to take over only a very small share of the trade. With black markets for all kinds of food flourishing, the state distributors had great difficulties in competing with private intermediaries offering the producers much higher prices than the official ones.[77] Political factors were also involved, and market shares remained generally very low for the public sector, which rose to importance only in imported commodities.

Retail trade was dominated by small-scale merchants who constituted the Chilean petty-bourgeoisie *par excellence*, and in addition to the 125,000 odd retail establishments, there was a huge army of ambulant traders of all kinds. Large supermarkets or chain stores were essentially non-existent.[78]

An aggressive policy for retailing would have signified the death-blow to the UP's strategy of class alliances. The small merchants were supposed to be closely allied with the working class in the struggle against monopolistic interests. But here, too, contradictions emerged. The JAPs (Price and Supply Committees) were actively fostered by the government, and in relations between organized consumers and traders frictions inevitably arose.

Behind the growth of the JAPs stood the UP government's price decrees. In order to enforce official prices speculation and hoarding were attacked both from below (the JAPs) and from above (DIRINCO's price inspectors). And although most tradesmen – and of course particularly the unscrupulous ones – were far better off under Allende than ever before, tensions were becoming aggravated, and as in so many other cases in history the petty-bourgeoisie tended to side with the extreme Right as polarization in society as a whole intensified. From mid-1972 onwards the powerful National Association of Merchants, headed by Rafael Cumsille, initiated and intensified strikes and boycotts directed against the government. In October 1972 most shopkeepers in Chile went on strike, together with the *gremios* of truck owners, wholesalers, professional trade unions, etc.[79]

The government did not quite know what to do. One innovation which first arose spontaneously during the 'October events' and which later developed in a more organized form was a system for the direct distribution of goods of prime necessity (above all groceries). This elimination of intermediaries was originally envisaged as nothing more than an emergency solution to problems caused by the shopkeepers' closing down, but the consumers, the obvious beneficiaries, were quick to realize the great advantages in getting their food without the mediation of retailers.[80] In some *poblaciones* the consumers, organized in JAPs, managed to force the government to continue to deliver goods in the same way as when the shops were kept closed, and many a tradesman who re-opened his shop after the 'October crisis' had been solved had to face the fact that trucks from DINAC now provided his old customers with groceries far more cheaply than he himself had ever been able to do.

DINAC's low priced 'popular baskets' (*canastas populares*) were naturally looked upon with great concern by established commercial interests, but DINAC's capacity was limited and it could only cater to a small part of the population's needs. In 1973 the number of families in Greater Santiago (in the *poblaciones* where the system was most developed) receiving commodity baskets from DINAC once a week or once every two weeks never exceeded 100,000 to 130,000, and the baskets received were relatively small, containing only a limited selection of groceries. The importance of this form of direct distribution was above all political. The *pobladores* themselves mobilized to raise demands and to take care of the concrete on-the-spot delivery of the commodities, and the JAPs thus vested with new functions often turned into nuclei around which other, more far-reaching embryos of 'popular power' were created. Within the government the attitudes towards the *canastas populares* ranged from enthusiastic support to hostility, and the directors of DINAC were incessantly fired – now for having 'done too little', now for having 'gone too far'.

After October 1972, when the dangers of being overly dependent on the unreliable private sector in such a vital field as distribution of foodstuffs had become evident, the UP gradually began to establish state-owned supermarkets. Early in 1973 a chain of slightly over one hundred 'popular supermarkets' had been created throughout the country[81] – considering the number of retail establishments that existed in Chile this was only a drop in the ocean, but it was quite enough to cause a further deterioration in the Allende government's relations with private tradesmen and their powerful *gremio*.

In retail trade, as in so many other fields, the UP's strategy thus turned out to be politically very dangerous. The general economic policy was, to begin with, bound to create apprehension among merchants, despite the fact that commerce as a whole benefited – at least initially – thanks to the sellers' market that emerged. The combination of inflationary pressures, price controls, and supervision by government officials and by JAPs was pregnant with tensions of all kinds. Producers, consumers, merchants and government all had some reason to complain, and they often blamed one another for the spectacular growth of black markets and the ensuing disruptions of established distribution channels that took place. Stockpiling, infrastructural bottlenecks (above all lack of storage and transportation facilities) and recurrent strikes and lockouts among merchants and truck owners contributed to making the delivery of goods erratic, and the political costs of the government's failure to cope with distribution problems were high. A surprising number of people thought, for example, that the easily visible shortages of several products 'proved' that the total supply of commodities, and especially of foodstuffs, actually declined dramatically during the Allende government. Scarcities and queues were time-wasting and provoked widespread irritation, and since no serviceable system of rationing was ever developed (an undertaking which would have met with huge political and administrative obstacles) arbitrary injustices frequently occurred.

With the above general background in mind it is easy to understand that relations between the Allende government and the merchants became strained, and the measures undertaken by both sides only served to aggravate the situation. Although no part of the UP had initially intended to let the public sector compete with private retailers, the latter's fears – nurtured by the Chilean Right – eventually turned into self-fulfilling prophecies. The merchants' protests and strikes 'forced' the government to intervene more directly than was ever envisaged at first, and the rightists' propaganda thus 'proved' to have been true. The UP's encroachment upon the private sector's control of retail trade was thus quite sufficient to cause alarm within the petty-bourgeoisie, whose reactions occasioned further public interference, but the methods used by the UP (DINAC and *canastas populares*, 'people's supermarkets', JAPs, etc.) further increased antagonisms without being drastic enough to permit any rational solution along socialist lines.

Similar failures were, as we have seen, characteristic of the whole UP strategy towards the private sector. Wanting to attack 'monopolies' only, while maintaining good relations with the small and medium-sized entrepreneurs, the Allende government nevertheless found itself in open conflict with the most modest layers of the petty-bourgeoisie. The struggles had ideological aspects, of course, but they were also the result of contradictions inherent in the 'Chilean road to socialism', contradictions which made the middle-of-the-road solution sought by the dominant factions of the UP an illusion.

In the UP's agrarian policies, which will be studied in the following chapter, these contradictions were no less manifest than they were in the fields of industry and distribution.

CHAPTER 7

The agrarian sector

In the late 1960s agriculture accounted for only about eight per cent of GDP and employed less than one quarter of the whole work force. Its modest size in the Chilean economy makes Chile quite exceptional in the Third World. In this limited sense, Chile would also appear to be the country with the most 'modern' economic structure among those countries where a transition from capitalism to socialism has been attempted. But being the result of a long and deep stagnation, the low statistical weight of agriculture indicates the agrarian sector's decisive role in the future development of Chile rather than the economy's modern, industrialized character.

Ever since the 1930s Chilean agriculture has become less and less capable of satisfying the domestic demand for food. A high and rising share of total export earnings has, as will be shown below, been absorbed by agricultural imports. Once a large net exporter of agricultural products, Chile has gradually become heavily dependent upon imports. To make Chile self-sufficient in foodstuffs in ten years would require, if we look at the situation by 1970, a more than doubling of the historical rates of growth of domestic production, and if the Chilean people were to enjoy nutrition standards comparable to those in Western Europe even higher rates would be necessary.

This was the nature of the task confronting Chilean agriculture. The gap between deficiency and self-sufficiency had grown steadily for over four decades and had taken a heavy toll in both undernourishment and burdensome food imports. Clearly the most important long-range objective of agrarian policy in Chile must be to reduce this gap and bring production closer to the needs of the country.

An almost equally crucial, and interrelated, aim must be to achieve an expansion of the agrarian sector's manpower-absorbing capacity. Unemployment and underemployment have been an ever-present yoke in rural areas, and migrating job-seekers have greatly exceeded the number of urban occupational opportunities. Merely to provide employment for the mass of unemployed and marginally-employed people in the Chilean cities would entail huge efforts. Chile has long been hyper-urbanized, and infrastructural bottlenecks – particularly abundant in Greater Santiago – also make a geographically more evenly distributed population desirable. The availability of housing and sanitary facilities, means of communication, etc. is inadequate in all urban areas, and little progress can be made unless the sparsely inhabited countryside starts absorbing a larger share of Chile's population growth. For these reasons, too, better employment opportunities in agriculture and in rural-based activities are required.

An augmentation of output and employment in agriculture is, then, of utmost importance for Chile's overall economic development. One purpose of this chapter is to study whether, or to what extent, the Allende government's agrarian policies, and above all its land tenure reform, were likely to provide scope for such improvements.

Much of this discussion should be relevant for countries with agrarian structures similar to Chile's. However, most will be devoted to the specific conditions prevailing in Chile between 1970 and 1973. A detailed analysis of how the UP's agrarian reform was implemented will be presented, and we will also analyze some of the political restrictions which limited the Allende government's freedom of action, restrictions which helped to make the development of a consistent agrarian reform policy difficult, if not impossible. In view of the agrarian sector's importance from a political point of view and the UP's heavy stress on explicitly political objectives, we will also study some of the more important aspects of rural political development under the Unidad Popular.

THE SITUATION PRIOR TO 1964

Whether basing their arguments on social justice or on economic efficiency the advocates of agrarian reform had an easy case in the early 1960s. Inequality in land ownership was startling. Most of the agricultural population – comprising a work force of some 700,000–750,000 people – had no land at all, and, as seen in table 7.1 the 11,000 largest estates occupied about four-fifths of all land and covered an area over one hundred times larger than all *minifundios* together.

Since yield per hectare – but not per worker – was higher on the small farms than on the large estates (see tables 7.2 and 7.3), agricultural income was not quite as unevenly distributed. The 11,000 odd large landholders received an income substantially higher than all agricultural workers and *minifundistas* together.[1]

165

Table 7.1 *Distribution of agricultural land by farm size 1965*

Size	Number of units	%	Surface covered (thousands of hectares)	%	Average size (ha)
Sub-family	124,000	48.7	207	0.7	1.7
Family	97,000	38.4	3,000	9.9	30.0
Multi-family, medium	22,000	8.7	3,200	10.4	145.0
Multi-family, large	11,000	4.2	24,200	79.0	2,200.0
Total	254,000	100.0	30,600	100.0	120.5

SOURCE: Ministerio de ODEPA Agricultura, *Plan de Desarrollo Agropecuario 1965–80*, Vol. I, pp. 1–40.

Table 7.2 *Distribution of agricultural land, agricultural work force and value of agricultural production by farm size (percentages), 1955*

Size group	Agricultural land	Agricultural work force	Value of production
Sub-family	—	13	4
Family	8	28	16
Multi-family, medium	13	21	23
Multi-family, large	79	38	57

Table 7.3 *Relative value of production as percentage of that of sub-family farms*

Size group	Per hectare of agricultural land	Per hectare of cultivated land	Per agricultural worker
Sub-family	100	100	100
Family	14	47	165
Multi-family, medium	12	39	309
Multi-family, large	5	30	437
Total	7	35	292

SOURCE: Barraclough, 'Agricultural Policy and Land Reform,' p. 928; and CIDA, *Tenencia de la Tierra*, p. 327.

Conditions of life were miserable and deteriorating prior to the Christian Democrats' agrarian reform. Agricultural workers' real wages, which had already declined in the 1940s,[2] fell by 23 per cent between 1953 and 1964,[3] and what social and economic progress had been made in Chile was out of reach of the great majority of the agricultural population[4] – a fact for which the continual exodus from the countryside and the concomitant transfer of rural poverty into urban slums provided ample proof.[5]

The polarization in the countryside was reinforced rather than counteracted by the earlier administrations' agricultural policies. The voice of the poor *campesino* was weak and seldom heard. While the big landowners had a firm control of legislation and policy implementation at all levels the agricultural workers and smallholders remained poorly educated, badly organized[6] and without representation in decision-making institutions. Under these circumstances it is quite natural that the economic gulf separating the two poles existing in rural Chile continued to widen. Agricultural policies consistently tended to serve large landowners and urban pressure groups, not agricultural workers and *minifundistas*.[7]

Credit policy can serve as an example. Although the agricultural sector as a whole received benevolent treatment when it came to access to capital – in 1964 agricultural loans made up 35 per cent of all public and private institutional credit – small producers had little or no contact with the organized credit market. The bulk (93 per cent) of all credit went to the *latifundistas*, not to the family-sized or minor producers who instead of benefiting from the negative real rate of interest the former enjoyed through institutional loans, were forced to the black market run by storekeepers and other local moneylenders where the nominal rate of interest generally exceeded 50 per cent.[8]

Tax policies also served the interests of the wealthy. Virtually all taxes were indirect, and the extremely light taxation on land, capital, income, and inheritance enabled the large estates – and especially the idle ones – to get off almost scot-free.[9] A study made in 1961 of tax-paying and consumption habits of twenty large landowners (each with tax assessments exceeding the equivalent of 150,000 dollars) revealed that of an average income of 45,865 dollars a year 42,600 remained as disposable income after taxes. Of this, some 84 per cent was spent on personal consumption.[10]

Smallholders and agricultural workers, on the other hand, suffered badly from heavy use of sales and turnover taxes. With average *per capita* incomes of less than 100 dollars a year almost all of these groups' commercial transactions were in foodstuffs, and since the tax system changed the terms of trade between consumption and production to their disadvantage they were penalized both as producers and consumers.

The growing realization of the necessity for agrarian reform and of a revision of agrarian policies was however not only the result of compassion for the pauperized *campesinos*. The small and shrinking agricultural sector – accounting for some 10 per cent of GDP and occupying slightly above 25 per cent of the economically active population – had for long been unable to satisfy the people's demand for foodstuffs – let alone their needs – and poor agricultural performance came to an increasing extent to be held responsible for the stagnation of the economy as a whole. Agricultural production *per capita* declined at an annual accumulative rate of 0.4 per cent between 1936–8 and 1963–5,[11] and the deficit in Chile's foreign trade balance in agricultural products spiraled up-wards.[12] While idle land and manpower were abundant, foodstuffs produced in Chile were not. Production of livestock products had become especially critical. While the population practically doubled between the mid-thirties and the mid-sixties, the stock of animals remained about the same: 2.6 and 2.9 million cattle, respectively.[13] Despite heavy imports, consumption of meat *per capita* fell considerably during the whole post-war period,[14] thus causing the agricultural crisis to be felt not only by the poor, who had always suffered from malnutrition, but also by wide sectors of the middle classes who found it increasingly difficult to maintain their traditional food standards.

A few facts will illustrate the extent of under-utilization of the Chilean soil. According to René Dumont only some 1.8 per cent of the land area was ploughed in the early 1960s 'although it could reach at least 7 per cent'.[15] Other studies[16] confirm that only about one-quarter of the arable land was actually being cultivated intensively. Even in the irrigated parts of the extremely fertile Central Valley one-third of the land was not ploughed but kept as unimproved pasture.

Along with the prevalence of poorly utilized *latifundios* there was a superexploitation of the land in the hands of smallholders, whose parcels – covering less than one per cent of Chile's arable land – produced four per cent of total output and employed thirteen per cent of the agricultural work force. With a labor productivity far below the sectoral average – which, in turn, amounted to no more than some 30 per cent of the national average – these *minifundistas* can hardly be said to have been rationally occupied. As indicated by tables 7.2 and 7.3, the potential gains from a reallocation of manpower within the various divisions of the agricultural sector were considerable.

In their ambitions to reform the Chilean agrarian structure president Frei and the Christian Democrats could, as we have seen, count on support from wide but utterly heterogeneous interest groups. Urban industrial workers, as well as their employers, wanted agricultural efficiency so as to reduce the inflationary pressures originating from an insufficient supply of foodstuffs; the *campesinos*, when asked, and the radicals urged for justice and decent living conditions for the rural poor; liberals in Chile and abroad advocated reform in order to contain peasant radicalism and forestall revolutionary upsurges, etc. Among the political parties, only the *latifundista*-dominated conservative parties[17] showed their opposition to agrarian reform – first by refusing to make use of their own laws from 1962, later by trying to impede any revision of the old legislation.

The agrarian sector

THE CHRISTIAN DEMOCRATS' LAND REFORM

Legal aspects

The legislation from 1962 – which the Frei government had to work with until 1967 when, after almost three years of debates, compromises and bureaucratic transactions, the Congress finally accepted the Christian Democrats' reform proposals – only permitted the expropriation of estates which were 'badly run' by the owner or 'abandoned'. The number or estates subject to these conditions was considerable, however, which made it possible to initiate expropriations without having to wait for the new laws to come into force. During the first three years of Christian Democratic rule 562 *fundos*,[18] covering about 1.2 million hectares, were taken over by CORA, the land reform agency.

The legislation of 1967 made expropriations easier mainly for two reasons:

1. It was no longer necessary to prove that a *fundo* was badly run or abandoned. Excessive size was added as a legal ground for expropriation. The upper limit was set at 80 'basic hectares' (b. ha) – that is, the equivalent of 80 hectares of good, irrigated land in the Central Valley, which in less fertile, non-irrigated districts could amount to several hundred hectares. Every *fundo* larger than this was a potential object for expropriation, but the owner was, if he wished, free to keep 80 'basic hectares' for himself (the so-called *reserva*).

This important modification of the old law also meant that the beneficiaries could take possession of the land and begin to cultivate it much earlier than before, since the landowners' ability to delay the handing over of the estates through various legal procedures was now curtailed.

2. The 1967 legislation also made it possible to compensate the owners with long-term bonds, running up to thirty years, while that of 1962 stipulated full compensation in cash. This released an important financial constraint. Now only between one and ten per cent, depending on the cause of expropriation, had to be paid in cash.

Implementation

Despite the new legislation, the execution of the land reform was slow and partial. About the same land area was affected between 1968 and 1970 as during the first three years. The initial political target of creating 100,000 new peasant proprietors in six years remained what it had perhaps always been: an electoral promise and nothing more. By the end of 1970 1,408 expropriations had been carried out, some 18 per cent of the arable land had been reformed, and the number of beneficiaries amounted to no more than 20,970 families.

Relatively little use was made of the new opportunities of expropriating land because of excessive size. Of all the estates taken over during the first five years about three-quarters were either expropriated because they were badly run or abandoned or were offered voluntarily to CORA by the owners.[19]

Public expenditures for the reform were high. Cash outlay amounted to between six and ten thousand dollars per *campesino* family. Of this, more than half constituted credits to the beneficiaries (credits which very often had the character of gifts, since repayment rates were low). Administration costs were also high: almost twenty per cent of total cash outlay, approximately equivalent to indemnity payments to the owners of the expropriated property.[20]

A partial reason for both the high costs and the low number of expropriations can be found in the extraordinary institutional mess found within the administration. Even if the Christian Democrats had had a clear reform strategy – which they, always compromising with someone as they were, did not – their chances of implementing it were reduced due to the complexity of the decision-making apparatus within the agricultural bureaucracy which the Christian Democrats lacked the political power and/or will to destroy. As pointed out by Jacques Chonchol (Minister of Agriculture, 1964–8 and 1970–72), in 1964 when the new government took over agricultural policy was decided by twenty-one different public institutions dependent upon five different ministries. In several important areas – for example the granting of credit to the agricultural sector – the influence the Ministry of Agriculture could exercise was almost nil.[21]

However, the shortcomings of the Christian Democrats' agrarian reform were not limited to the fact that it was slow, bureaucratic and expensive. The way of selecting the beneficiaries and of organizing the reformed areas had such serious defects that it can be doubted whether the cautious steps that were taken to 'revolutionize' the land tenure system were even steps in the right direction.

The asentamiento system

The cornerstone of the reform was the transformation of each expropriated estate into a so-called *asentamiento*,[22] which was a transitional system of managing the estate until the land, after a lapse of three to five years, was to be put at the disposition of the beneficiaries who were then to decide whether to run the farm collectively or to split it up into individual holdings. CORA and other public institutions were officially neutral with respect to the *campesinos'* decision on how to organize the estate after the *asentamiento* period, but in practice they often tended to favor some kind of cooperative solution.[23]

The *asentamiento* system was very favourable to the beneficiaries. The *asentados* who were to become individual or collective owners of the land consisted almost exclusively of tenant farmers and sharecroppers (*inquilinos*[24]) who 'belonged' to the expropriated estate by virtue of their living on the *fundo* in question, and the *fundos* were, as we have seen, in general both very large and underutilized. The average land area per *asentamiento* family amounted to 14 hectares of irrigated land plus 155 hectares of non-irrigated land. A new rural elite thus arose, a class of comparatively well-to-do *asentados* who enjoyed both a large holding of land and benevolent treatment from the government, which poured money and technical assistance into the reformed areas. At the same time very little was done to improve the situation for the poor majority of *campesinos* whose status disqualified them from becoming *asentados*. As described by Solon Barraclough: 'The permanent laborers on expropriated estates, and a few others who received land, obtained welfare, employment, and income. But the more than two-thirds of the *campesinos* who are *minifundistas* or unattached landless laborers had no prospects of benefiting from the reform, and many became even worse off as a result.'[25]

Performance

Historically, experience with agrarian reform in different countries and under different circumstances indicates that our expectations of the short-term effects on production should not be high. The reasons why production can be expected to fall immediately after the initiation of the reform are many and compelling (uncertainty, organizational and distributional disruptions, etc.). This did not happen in Frei's Chile, where production increased,[26] presumably because of the fact that in Chile, in contrast to most other countries where agrarian reforms have been carried through, no institutional break in the form of a social revolution preceded the reform. The uncertainty that undoubtedly existed among many landholders seems instead to have been beneficial for production, since the legal arrangements put some pressure on the *latifundistas* to work their estates better. (Compensation was given at considerably less favourable terms when estates that were 'badly run' were expropriated.) Indeed, the most positive short-term effects of the reform were attributed to the *fundos* which were *not* taken over. The threat of expropriation was said to have produced a substantially better performance among those who were threatened, especially with regard to land utilization.

Evaluations[27] made of reformed areas reveal that progress was fairly small on the expropriated estates, however, in part due to the substantial de-capitalization that had taken place. Since only the land was taken over, the *latifundistas* were quick to sell all existing capital, including the stock of animals, on the future *asentamientos*, or to transfer it to their own *reservas*. Production rose slowly, if at all, and the marketable surplus from the *asentamientos* actually declined. The beneficiaries tended to take out much of their economic gains in large increases in their own consumption of foodstuffs, thus accentuating the country's dependence upon food imports.

This is, of course, a problem which every change in agricultural policies that improves living standards of poor and underfed peasants must confront, but in Chile it was aggravated by the fact that the *asentados*' heavy indebtedness constituted a strong incentive against marketing the output. All cash incomes had to be shared with the creditors.

A more serious problem involving the way the reform was conducted was that it promised no solution for the eternal Chilean problem of poor land utilization. The total area under cultivation was not raised through the 1965–70 land reform; in 1969–70 it was, in fact, slightly lower than in 1964–5.[28] The limitation of beneficiaries to tenant farmers and permanent workers on the large estates meant that the man–land ratio remained practically unaltered. The extremely irrational allocation of manpower was thus perpetuated through the *asentamiento* system, the ideological foundation of which was the traditional populist slogan: 'The land to those who work it!' (which, we note, can never be the motto of a viable land reform in countries with the Chilean type of land tenure structure). Fearing that their holdings would have to be split up among more individuals, the *asentados* were in many cases even more reluctant to accept new permanent settlers on their land than the old owner had been, and the workers employed by the *asentados* were mainly temporary day-laborers lacking both land and job security.

Work incentives on the *asentamientos* were also unsatisfactory. Each member received a state-guaranteed minimum wage, quite high and independent of his own work efforts – a renumeration principle which resulted in high leisure preferences. On many *asentamientos* work performed by hired labor exceeded that of the *asentados*, who often came to constitute an inflated group of collective employers and supervisors. Thus, in many cases an important consequence of the agrarian reform was the replacement of one idle person with several who did little – a good example of the old *cliché* 'one step forward and two steps back'.

It is, however, no longer possible to make an evaluation of the long-term effects of the Christian Democrats' agrarian reform. We know that the government failed to come even close to its own quantitative goals – which, in turn, promised a solution for only a small minority of the rural population – and we also know that their method of organizing the reformed areas contained several doubtful aspects which, if unchanged, would have guaranteed the persistence of a considerable amount of both inequality and inefficiency in the Chilean countryside. But we will never know whether the Christian Democrats, if re-elected, would have been able to elaborate and implement a new agrarian strategy. 1964–70 was, as Eduardo Frei liked to put it, only to be the beginning of a long era of Christian Democratic rule in Chile, and although towards the end of the sixties the PDC had to recognize that the agrarian 'revolution' had been delayed, they did promise to correct some of the mistakes made and to accelerate the agricultural transformation.

But the acceleration of the process became the responsibility of the government of Salvador Allende which, as will be seen below, had to work with exactly the same legal tools as its predecessor but under different circumstances and inspired by different intentions.

Before leaving the 1964–70 agrarian reform we must, however, give credit to the Christian Democrats in one important respect: they did succeed in stimulating the active participation of the *campesinos*.

Campesino mobilization

The rapid abolition of all remaining legal bans on agricultural trade unions was one of the first steps taken by the new government in order to permit the *campesinos* to express their opinions and fight for their interests collectively. Encouraged by active support from CORA and other public institutions, as well as by a virtual invasion of the Chilean countryside by cadres from different political parties anxious to gain influence in the awakening *campesino* movement, the rural poor did not fail to grasp the opportunity.

Not only trade unions underwent a spectacular growth. *Campesino* cooperatives and similar organizations, non-existent before 1964,

The Christian Democrats' land reform

Table 7.4 *Agricultural trade unions 1964–70*

Year	Number of unions	Number of members
1964	24	1,658
1965	32	2,118
1966	201	10,647
1967	211	47,473
1968	325	71,721
1969	385	101,232
1970[a]	488	127,680

[a] June 1970.

SOURCE: Alaluf *et al.*, 'El sector agrario en el gobierno de la Unidad Popular' in Instituto de Economía, *La Economía Chilena en 1971*, p. 493.

absorbed another 100,000 members, mainly *minifundistas* and small tenant farmers. The cooperatives' concrete economic achievements were insignificant but they did serve as educational centers for large groups of peasants who had earlier been almost deprived of both elementary education and regular contact with other *campesinos*.

During the first few years the Christian Democrats monopolized almost all organizational activity in the countryside, and as late as 1970 about two-thirds of all agricultural trade union members belonged to unions led by the governing party. A shift was under way, however. *Campesino* disappointment increased as promises were betrayed, and with the emergence of militant, revolutionary movements even the traditional Left had to face the fact that it was unable to control wide sectors of the rural proletariat. The situation became more and more explosive, and the last two years of the Frei regime witnessed confrontations, sometimes violent, of an intensity which few political leaders had foreseen when they had supported the organization of the *campesinos*. The latters' interpretation of the Christian Democrats' slogan 'participation' diverged more and more from that of the government, which often responded with severe repression against illegal strikes, land seizures, etc.

This is not to say that the process of radicalization had reached all rural areas and sectors. The *campesino* movement was badly split into rival organizations, and fear of or respect for *el patrón* still prevented many from engaging in activities directed against the still powerful landowners.

The agrarian sector

One of the results of the discriminatory selection of beneficiaries was, furthermore, that the conflict of interests between diverse *campesino* groups tended to grow. The creation of 'collective *latifundistas*' through the *asentamientos* tended to divert many *campesinos*' attention away from the remaining individual ones, and in many cases the large landowners and the rightist political parties managed to create alliances with the *asentados* against the groups whose interests lay in a radicalization of the agrarian reform.

But despite the political and organizational weaknesses of the *campesino* movement, the incorporation of hundreds of thousands of people into trade unions and cooperatives must be considered a very important achievement. This is the main reason why the years 1964 to 1970 will be remembered as an extraordinarily dynamic period in the Chilean countryside. For subsequent events in rural Chile the existence of an organized mass of *campesinos*, increasingly aware of their new possibilities, was of far greater importance than the Christian Democrats' 1,400 expropriations and creation of 20,970 petty *kulak* families.

THE AGRARIAN REFORM 1970–73

'Agrarian reform', Salvador Allende argued, 'is, in itself and seen in isolation, recognized as one of the so-called bourgeois-democratic transformations ... In our case, however, the agrarian reform is not carried through within the context of preserving capitalism, but within that of destroying its basic nucleus: domestic and foreign monopolistic capital. For it is not a question of developing capitalism in the countryside, but of making agrarian relations march towards socialism.'[29]

We thus see that – and this was heavily emphasized in the UP's 1970 program as well – the agrarian reform was to be implemented as but one part of a general strategy aimed at transforming the whole of society along socialist lines. From the point of view of political power this was often put forward in a crude, slightly mechanical way. The destructive phase of the land reform, the expropriation of all large land holdings, would, it was said, eradicate the material base of rural conservatism. Deprived of their economic base the *latifundistas* would be forced to give up their strongholds in the countryside. The positive side was, of course, to provide opportunities for the poor *campesinos* to take their place in economic and political matters and for the political parties of the UP to gain influence as well as votes in future elections at the expense of the PN and PDC. The general democratic aspects of the agrarian reform played a very important role in the UP's program, and to give power to the *campesinos* ranked as high as the other objectives, i.e. above all to increase production and employment and improve the living standards of the rural poor.

Besides the expropriation of all *latifundios* the program of the UP also called for the transfer of all agricultural supply, marketing and processing 'monopolies' to public or cooperative ownership. Together with the nationalization of all commercial banks and private credit institutions, this would guarantee a more or less direct state control of all major financial and commercial transactions connected with the agrarian sector. Agriculture was to be integrated with the overall planning of the economy, although state farms would be of only marginal importance. Expropriated land would preferably be organized on a cooperative basis, and with the exception of those small garden plots to which all *campesinos* in the cooperatives would be entitled, individual ownership of land was to be permitted only in 'special cases'.

As regards overall agrarian policies the UP program was very vague. All peasants and agricultural workers (i.e. not only those who benefited directly from the land reform) were to be favored, and rural incomes were to be raised to levels equal to those of urban industrial workers. Credit on advantageous terms and in large quantities was to be provided to agriculture, and the producers would be guaranteed high and stable prices, known to them in advance, for all crops produced in accordance with the plans made up jointly by the government and representatives of democratically elected 'Peasant Councils'. The relative position of agriculture *vis-à-vis* the other sectors of the national economy was to be improved considerably, and this could, according to Jacques Chonchol (Minister of Agriculture 1970–72), take place only if agriculture received subsidies from the remainder of the economy. Whereas other socialist countries had to a certain extent financed their development in industry and other sectors with surpluses extracted from agriculture, Chonchol argued, the outstanding characteristic of the Chilean socialist model lay in the circumstance that for a long period of time Chilean agriculture would be unable to finance even its own development, and that capital for agricultural investment thus would have to be drawn from elsewhere.[30]

Not so in the future, however. The constant underexploitation of Chile's rich agricultural natural endowment was emphasized in the UP program as well as in most of Chonchol's interventions, and rather than acting as a brake on the overall economic development agriculture ought to be able to play the role of one of its driving forces. Exploitation of idle land, intensive cultivation, crop specialization and a close integration with domestic industry was Chonchol's formula, a formula which would help to solve both production and employment problems and would provide scope for a better utilization in domestic and foreign trade of certain regions' natural advantages.[31]

Little was accomplished in terms of Chonchol's formula, however. Despite the many great achievements that were no doubt made during Allende's three years, the UP's land reform promised no solution to Chile's agrarian problems even if the reform had been allowed to be completed along the 1970–73 lines. A different strategy – and a different political environment – would have been required, and the reasons for the Unidad Popular's relative failure will be the focus of the analysis presented below.

The legal heritage

The UP's 1970 agrarian program was constructed on the assumption that the existing agrarian reform legislation of 1967 would be revised, since a large number of the program's vital points were clearly impracticable in terms of the existing legal framework. But having failed to take over parliament shortly after having assumed office – the UP did not, as we know, even make an attempt – the government was obliged to accept the old legal provisions and try to make the best possible use of them. To delay the initiation of the reform and expect the parliamentary opposition to carry through a new and better proposal was for many reasons out of the question.[32]

The government's intentions were thus at odds with the legal framework. With the exception of 'badly run or abandoned' estates only those huge *fundos* covering more than 80 'basic hectares' (b. ha) could be expropriated, and a sizable and well-to-do class of farmers was thus left out of reach.[33] In the eyes of most of the UP leaders this was politically dangerous, and it clearly reduced the scope for 'socialist' relations of production, although nobody denied that a large number of those medium-sized farms were quite efficiently run and accounted for a disproportionately large share of the marketable surplus of foodstuffs.

The obligation to grant the expropriated landowner a *reserva* of 80 b. ha was an even greater hindrance to the realization of the UP's agrarian objectives. The UP had argued that the future planning of the reformed part of the agrarian sector was to be conducted not on an artificial estate-to-estate basis but by whole areas. This was rendered impossible by the right of the former owner to retain his *reserva* and by the fact that the agrarian reform law stipulated that every expropriated *fundo* was to form a unity of its own and that only permanent workers and sharecroppers could become members of the cooperatives that were to be established, save in cases when the affected *campesinos* themselves agreed to take in others. If CORA and the beneficiaries were in agreement, they could organize the expropriated areas as they liked. Furthermore, the law allowed the expropriation of land only. Buildings, machinery, equipment, inventories, cattle, etc. were not included. Neither was the control of irrigation works. By choosing his *reserva* suitably the landowner could, and in many cases did, direct and re-direct the supply of water.

The legal restraints on a more radical agrarian reform were thus numerous, and since the correlation of forces in the countryside and in Chilean society as a whole did not develop favorably enough for the Left, the UP's ambitions had to be reduced. What could, at best, be achieved was a successful bourgeois-democratic agrarian reform, not a socialist one, and in most vital aspects the reform of the UP was only an extension and acceleration of the work initiated by the Christian Democrats.

IMPLEMENTATION

The destructive phase: the death of the latifundio

In two years Chile will be liberated from all *latifundios*; this was the promise given by the new government when taking office. Both in order to respond to the strong pressure from the *campesinos* and to pre-empt the spread of uncertainty the UP decided to act immediately,[34] and more *fundos* were expropriated in the first fourteen months than during the whole Christian Democratic administration. By the end of 1972 virtually no estate liable to expropriation due to excessive size remained, although the actual taking possession of the land by CORA and the *campesinos* was very often delayed for six months, or even a year, while in the meantime a tremendous decapitalization occurred.

It was in a climate of social turmoil that this massive expropriation took place. The electoral victory of the UP had given the *campesino* movement a new impetus, and rural conflicts – now over wages and working conditions, now over the question of land – greatly increased.

The forms in which the peasants expressed their discontent also grew more militant as fear of violent repression faded away, and the number of land occupations (*tomas de fundos*) multiplied. In 1967 9 *tomas* took place; in 1969, 148, and in 1971, 1,278.[35] The immediate objective of these *tomas* was generally the expropriation of the estate in question, but a large number of *tomas de solidaridad* also occurred – a clear sign of the qualitative change in class consciousness and organization that the *campesino* movement was undergoing.

The time had thus come to eradicate the *latifundios* from Chile (temporarily, we could add today, with hindsight). Possessing the necessary legal tools, the executive power and support from below, from the mass of workers on the large *fundos*, the Unidad Popular had both the right and the power to set to work. The big landowners had to face the fact that their vast holdings were to be drastically reduced, and quite a few of them drew desperate conclusions. They slaughtered their cattle, sold their tractors and packed their bags. Others, who did not want to sell out so cheaply, engaged in a capital flight of a somewhat unusual kind. It is estimated that some 160,000 cows undertook a long march over the Andes and crossed the Argentine border during the months that followed the presidential election.[36]

But the majority of landowners stayed to protect their interests. They were, after all, guaranteed good-sized *reservas* (a right which was, however, frequently disputed by the militant *campesinos*) to which they were soon to withdraw most of their cattle and machinery, and compensation for the land was given on appreciably more favorable (less disadvantageous) terms if they stayed.[37]

No land tenure reform which really hurts the interests of powerful groups (and if it does not, it is hardly worth the name) can be an altogether peaceful process, and Chile 1970–73 was certainly no exception. But by and large the government complied scrupulously with all legal requisites of the Land Reform Law of 1967, and in view of the antagonism involved and the number of confrontations that did occur the immediate social cost of the elimination of Chile's *latifundios* must be said to have been relatively low. Despite the Right's efforts to create uncertainty and even panic among medium-scale producers, no serious disruptions in production took place, let alone massive material destruction. The violence, destruction and killing took place afterwards, when the *latifundistas* took revenge after 11 September 1973.

In March 1973, when the first phase of the land tenure reform can be said to have been completed, a sum total of 5,036 *fundos* had been

expropriated since 1965. Of these over 70 per cent were taken over
after November 1970, and in terms of surface area and number of beneficiaries the UP's share amounted to slightly over 60 per cent (table
7.5).

If converted into 'basic hectares' the total surface area that was
expropriated corresponded to slightly less than 800,000 b. ha; that is,
between eleven and twelve physical hectares were, on average, estimated
to be equivalent to one basic hectare. Since the size of the landowners'
reservas was based on those calculations (the lower the estimate of the
value of the land was in terms of b. ha, the larger would the *reserva* be),
these figures indicate that the landowners were quite successful in their
attempts to get favorable land evaluation coefficients, and their success
in this respect was a constant source of complaint from the UP and from
the *campesinos*.[38]

But even more important for the reduction of the land area liable to
expropriation was the process of subdivision of large estates that had
taken place after 1965. Rough estimates of the magnitude of these
efforts by the *latifundistas* to avoid becoming expropriated by splitting
up their *fundos* indicate that some 1,500 subdivisions were made after the
Christian Democrats' initiation of the land reform, and the area covered
by estates between 40 and 80 b. ha increased its share of total agricultural
land dramatically.[39] In 1965 it was estimated that some 55–60 per cent
of all Chile's agricultural land was subject to expropriation for excessive
size, and as late as in 1971 Chonchol asserted that by 1972 more than
half of all land would have become integrated into the reformed area.[40]
When, however, practically all *fundos* over 80 b. ha had been expropriated it turned out that almost two-thirds of all productive land still
remained in private hands (see table 7.6).

Subdivisions and generosity when calculating the size of the *reservas*
thus made the reformed sector's share of land fall appreciably short of
the UP's early expectations. By 1972, when the 'destructive phase' of the
land reform was virtually completed, the medium-sized multi-family
estates between 20 and 80 basic hectares large had a clear dominance
over the other two poles of land tenure in existence, *minifundios* and
reformed cooperatives.

And *campesino* pressure for land continued. The 34,000 families which
were the direct beneficiaries of the Allende government's rapid elimination of Chile's remaining *latifundios* constituted but a tiny minority of
the whole agrarian population. The strictly anti-*latifundista* strategy
advocated by the dominant sectors of the UP could not satisfy the

Table 7.5 Expropriations 1965 – March 1973

| Period | Area covered (hectares) | | | | Number of beneficiaries (families) |
	Number of estates	Irrigated land	Dry-farming[a] land	Total	
1965–November 1970	1,508	290,601	3,273,952	3,564,553	20,976
4 November 1970–22 March 1973	3,628	394,777	5,190,850	5,585,327	33,948
Total	5,136	685,378	8,464,802	9,149,880	54,924

[a] Including non-cultivable land.

SOURCE: Allende, *Third Message*, p. 272. An additional number of some 300–400 medium- and small-scale estates were 'intervened' as the result of prolonged labor conflicts or sabotage by the owners.

Table 7.6   *Estimate of land tenure structure in Chile[a] by size groups.*
July 1972

Size (b. ha)	Number of units	%	Total area covered (b. ha)	%
< 5	190,000	79.3	200,000	9.7
5–40	35,000	15.1	510,000	24.6
40–80	9,800	4.1	566,000	27.3
> 80	200	—	60,000	2.9
Subtotal	235,000	99.9	1,336,000	64.5
Reformed sector	4,564[b]	0.1	731,818	35.5
Total	239,564	100.0	2,067,818	100.0

[a] The data cover, to be exact, only the provinces from Coquimbo in the north to Llanquihue in the south, but outside this 'Greater Central Chile' very little agricultural production is carried on. The exclusion of the geographical extremes of Chile cannot affect the estimates materially.

[b] Does not correspond to the number of reformed units, since some estates were merged into larger holdings.

SOURCE: ICIRA, 'Diagnosis', p. iii–2.

aspirations of the mass of smallholders and landless day-laborers, and tens of thousands of poor *campesinos* mobilized to struggle for a radicalization of the reform. Dissatisfaction with the pattern of land ownership that had emerged was widespread within the government as well, although the PC and PR were reluctant to try to carry the land reform further to an attack against the medium-sized landowners. Such an attack would no doubt destroy the very foundation of the official UP strategy of rural class alliances. Late in 1972 a UP compromise was reached, however, and the government began to call for a lowering to 40 b. ha of the upper limit of private estates to be permitted. In this initiative the UP had the obvious support from the *campesino* organizations, which constantly demanded a more drastic expropriation policy, but not from what counted in legislative matters, namely the Congress.

Land tenure structure by 1972

No agricultural census which could have provided us with exact information about the relative importance of the various forms of land tenure that existed after the full implementation of the UP's land reform was ever undertaken. The best estimates available are those made by Barraclough and Affonse in ICIRA, 'Diagnosis', which are presented in table 7:6. Although their study refers to the situation by mid-1972 the fact that only about 200 fundos over 80 b. ha then remained to be expropriated means that the data are good enough to illustrate the possible impact of carrying through a land reform in the absence of new legislation.

If we divide agriculture into three types of exploitation – smallholders (*minifundios* and family farms up to 20 b. ha), medium and large farms (*medianos* between 20 and 80 b. ha), and the reformed sector – we get the picture shown in table 7.7 of the relative importance of each category in terms of land area, employment, output and marketable surplus.

The disproportions in the various sectors' shares of land, employment and output thus remained very large, with concomitant huge differences in productivity per agricultural worker and per hectare. If data on the distribution of capital were available these would undoubtedly also show great differences in this respect. The *medianos* – including all *reservas* – would rank by far the highest in capital intensity,[41] followed by the increasingly mechanized reformed sector.

Little was thus achieved in terms of a modification of the very uneven distribution of labor in relation to available land. Operating within basically the same legal structure as the Christian Democratic government, although more determinedly and with different aims, the UP failed to alter the man–land ratio significantly. To achieve such a change a

Table 7.7 *Hypothesis concerning the approximate distribution by sector of agricultural land, work force, agricultural production and marketed production in July 1972 (in percentage of total)*

Category	Land (b. ha)	Work force[a]	Gross value of production	Value of marketed production	Share of sector's production marketed
Smallholders	22	60	28	15	45
Medium and large farms	42	22	43	56	95
Reformed sector	36	18	29	29	80
Total	100	100	100	100	76

[a] Including temporary laborers and unemployed.
SOURCE: ICIRA, 'Diagnosis'

different kind of land reform would have been necessary, a reform which could have brought forth a real *re*distribution of land and labor and not merely a change in the titles of ownership of the large, sparsely populated *fundos* (however important the latter was for other reasons). Between 1965 and November 1970 the average amount of land per beneficiary family amounted to 169 physical hectares, of which 13.8 were irrigated. In the period November 1970 – March 1973 the corresponding figures dropped only insignificantly, to 165 and 11.6 hectares respectively.[42] The 100,000 smallest *minifundistas*, on the other hand, continued to have at their disposal less than two physical hectares of land per family, and they continued to overexploit their tiny holdings just as before, while vast amounts of land in other parts lay idle.

From table 7.7 we also note that the expropriation of all *medianos* in itself would have changed little in this respect. The abundance of land in relation to manpower was as pronounced on the estates between 20 and 80 b. ha as it was in the reformed area (the man–land ratios were, in fact, almost identical). Only the full integration of smallholders and unattached day-laborers as beneficiaries would have made possible a radical improvement in the poor and irrational utilization of rural Chile's land and manpower. Such an integration would also have been required to relieve the misery of the hard core of rural poor, who benefited little or not at all from the Unidad Popular's land tenure reform.

THE CONSTRUCTIVE PHASE OF THE AGRARIAN REFORM

Obstacles to a clear strategy

That mere expropriations were not enough was quite clear to the UP, and the separation of the powerful and not very productive *latifundistas* from their vast landholdings was seen as a necessary, though far from sufficient, condition for the future development of Chile's agriculture.

In this the whole Chilean Left agreed. But what next? Who were to replace the *latifundistas*, how was production to be organized, how could those who had been marginalized from the benefits of the expropriations be employed rationally and be given decent incomes, and how were future relations between agriculture and the rest of the economy to take shape? To these questions, and many others, the UP's 1970 program had only very vague answers or no answer at all, and it is hardly an exaggeration to say that in no other field of economic policy were inconsistency and internal disagreement so pronounced.

There were several reasons for this. 'The agricultural problem has never been thoroughly discussed within the UP,' complained Chonchol in April 1972,[43] manifestly disappointed at the lack of interest and/or knowledge of agrarian problems exhibited by the governing parties.[44] The urban industrial dominance in the UP's social base and the parties' close contacts with their cadres in the factories of Santiago and Concepción had molded the whole Chilean Left's way of thinking,[45] and instead of leading and directing the militant but ideologically quite heterogeneous *campesino* movement the UP usually found itself tailing behind. The UP was also unable to control the huge agrarian bureaucracy – in which the majority of officials were Christian Democrats but where anything from friends and relatives of *latifundistas* to revolutionaries could be found – in a coherent way, and the confusion as to what the government's agrarian policies really consisted of added to the always present party rivalry and sectarianism in the offices of CORA, INDAP, ODEPA, SAG, INIA, ICIRA, IDI, CORFO, etc.

There also existed profound ideological and strategic divergencies within the UP coalition. The 'right wing' – mainly Communists and Radicals – put their main emphasis on the 'battle of production', prescribed an alliance with the medium-sized landowners and maintained a very negative attitude towards land occupation and other 'excesses'. They argued, moreover, that the majority of the *campesinos* were not ideologically ready for collective forms of ownership, and that private land-ownership therefore might be necessary during a transitional period. The Left, on the other hand, denied the possibility and even desirability of reaching political agreements with the *medianos*, emphasized the primacy of the class struggle over the 'battle of production', called for collective forms of working the land, for planning rather than relying on market forces, and worked for an integration of the rural 'subproletariat' into the struggle for land – and for socialism.

There was, in short, ample room for friction within the UP, whose freedom of action was also limited. Confronted with a strong political opposition and with serious and in part unforeseen economic problems *ad hoc* measures often had to replace conscious, strategic action. Let us now look at the result of all these wills and circumstances.

The reformed sector: forms of organization

The *asentamiento* system, the weaknesses of which were indicated above and which constituted the cornerstone of the Frei government's agrarian reform, remained in fact, though not always in name, the model used by the UP in organizing expropriated estates. Of the three other forms of organization that were introduced after 1970 one, the so-called *Comités Campesinos* or *Comités de la Reforma Agraria*, had a structure almost identical to that of the *asentamientos*, the only difference being some minor organizational innovations. The *comités* were also transformed into cooperatives with joint CORA-*campesino* management, and they shared the *asentamientos'* fundamental weakness of being organized on an estate-to-estate basis which impeded both zonal planning and specialization and the integration of landless laborers and *minifundistas* who lived in the area without being attached to the particular *fundo* in question. The system was, of course, very advantageous to those workers and former sharecroppers who became members and who, in general, were quite reluctant to let the other sectors of the rural proletariat enter the cooperatives and share all the benefits.

New privileges and large differences in economic status and security were thus inevitable consequences of this new social stratification introduced on all *asentamiento*-like settlements. To overcome these and other deficiencies the UP sought to replace the above system with 'Agrarian Reform Centers' (*Centros de la Reforma Agraria*, CERAs), which were also of an essentially cooperative character but which differed from *asentamientos* and *comités* is that they were formed through the merging of several neighboring farms into larger units. (There were several other differences as well, but these had mainly to do with questions concerning decision making. The CERAs were thus much more democratic than the *asentamientos*; women and men had equal rights, the *afuerinos* had a higher degree of participation, etc.) This was not always possible, however. The landowners' *reservas* hampered the full integration of whole areas, and the CERAs also met resistance from many of the *inquilinos* who were in a much better bargaining position than the mass of unattached day-laborers and smallholders. The violent campaigns against the CERAs from the political opposition frightened many *campesinos*. The story was told that the CERAs were to be converted into state farms with not even private garden plots permitted. Even within the Unidad Popular knowledge of the CERAs (which also were provisional forms of organization only and which could not be transformed to state farms unless the *campesinos* working there so accepted when the transitional period of three to five years had come to an end) was lacking and scepticism widespread, and the Communists especially were afraid that the CERAs would constitute a too advanced form of collective farming.[46]

The fourth form of settlement that arose, the 'Production Centers'

(*Centros de Producción*, CEPROs), was radically different from the others, however, in that the state was made definite owner of the land. Defined by the UP as an 'exceptional' form of operation, the number of CEPROs established was very limited (54 up to March 1973), but they were large and covered an area representing some 14 per cent of the whole reformed sector.[47] The CEPRO was the only kind of production unit which made no distinction whatsoever between 'members' and 'non-members' and where all workers were guaranteed steady employment and social security. The distribution of units between the different forms of organization is shown in table 7.8.

With regard to working conditions and wage principles the systems introduced on the cooperative settlements were rather similar to each other, although the CERAs tended to develop the most radical forms of collective farming. In general, however, local political and economic circumstances rather than official designation of a particular form of organization determined the differences that existed. They all shared the basic defect of having a renumeration system providing very poor work incentives.

All *socios*, full members of the cooperatives, were guaranteed a minimum basic income for their participation in collective work, and in addition to this they were to receive a share in the profits made by their cooperative.[48] Although the beneficiaries were often very proud of this egalitarian character of the cooperatives – a typical remark was: 'We are all equals here!' – it is quite clear that the majority of them were not prepared for such advanced distribution principles, and neither was Chilean society as a whole, with all its flagrant inequality.

There also existed a third source of revenue, a source which was of far greater importance than the share in common profits (which were usually non-existent), namely the sales from the *socios*' individually owned garden plots. These 'plots' were quite large – in 1972 they

Table 7.8 *Organization of the reformed area in 1971 and 1972.*
Number of units

Year	Asentamientos	Comités	CERAs	CEPROs
1971	246	628	25	18
1972	752	779	238	36
Total	998	1,407	263	54

SOURCE: *Allende, Third Message*, pp. 272ff.

occupied 13 per cent of the whole surface area of the reformed sector[49] – and with the high prices prevailing on the parallel, black markets for foodstuffs the fortunate members of the cooperatives were able to increase their cash incomes appreciably. Many peasants gave priority to working these private plots: *afuerinos*[50] as well as tractors provided by CORA often did the collective work while the members dedicated themselves to individual farming. This practice also reinforced the tendency to use the collectively owned land area mainly for extensive cultivation, with a resultant loss in employment opportunities.[51] These private parcels were thus essentially competitive *vis-à-vis* collective farming rather than complementary to it,[52] with negative consequences both for agricultural planning and for the promotion of socialist consciousness in the countryside.

Campesino resistance to the introduction of accounting systems on the cooperatives was another problem. In part due to lack of knowledge – many of the adult members, until very recently working under the semi-feudal system of *inquilinaje* , were illiterates – and in part out of fear that CORA would use the results against them in their negotiations, the peasants were reluctant to accept cost calculations and profit-and-loss accounts, and little concern was generated for profitability and productivity in collective work. The distorted price structure – including the cost of credit, which fell sharply in real terms as prices sky-rocketed – also hampered the making up of cost calculations worth the name, of course, and the arbitrary character of almost all estimates based on current prices increased the *campesinos'* scepticism towards bookkeeping in general.

Although the UP became more and more aware of these and other shortcomings of the *asentamiento*-like cooperatives they could nevertheless do little to transform the reformed estates into both ideologically and economically more suitable forms of organization. The Unidad Popular was too weak politically to be able to resist the 'spontaneous' drift towards the old type of settlements, which had the support both from the rightist political opposition and from most of the beneficiaries themselves. The verdict that Rolando Calderón (socialist, Minister of Agriculture November 1972–March 1973) gave upon the *asentamientos* in an interview would perhaps not have been shared by the whole UP, but the magnitude of the discontent that existed is indicated by Calderón's harsh words:

Question: Which forms of organization in the so-called reformed sector do you think ought to be promoted?

Answer: There is, to begin with, one form of organization which ought *not* to be promoted: the *asentamiento*. All the peasant organizations agree in that on the *asentamientos* there are no incentives for the worker; that irresponsibility, alcoholism and absenteeism develop there: that they are a failure from the point of view of production, that the *asentados* start exploiting their own class brothers, etc. ... There are exceptions, but in general it works that way ... I would like to make clear that I am not criticizing the individual *campesinos* who are members, many of whom have made great efforts to raise production, but I am criticizing the *very system of asentamientos* ... Secondly, frankly speaking, I believe that the *Comités Campesinos*, CERAs, etc. are to a large extent mere armchair products. In practice, you go to a CERA and you notice that it works in much the same way as an *asentamiento*.[53]

Credit policies and mechanization

The members of the reformed cooperatives were in no position to finance necessary purchases of machinery and equipment, seeds, fertilizers, etc. They also lacked the means to renew the stock of cattle, which had been either brought to the former owner's *reserva* or else stayed at the *fundo* but had to be paid for in cash. The UP was thus obliged to provide the reformed sector with financial and technical assistance so as to satisfy the needs for working capital and funds for reinvestment. The normal working of the land alone called for vast public support.

But the actual assistance to the cooperatives very soon greatly exceeded the requirements dictated by these circumstances. The UP, in fact, decided upon a policy aimed at promoting rapid mechanization and allocating financial support through huge subsidies to the whole reformed sector. The total amount of credits granted to the agrarian sector is estimated to have increased by 56.9 per cent in 1971 over 1970 in real terms and by another 19.2 per cent in 1972; of these, over three-quarters went to the reformed areas.[54] The members of the cooperatives received in 1971 an average of almost 32,000 escudos per family;[55] that is, a sum equivalent to the wages of one man working for over 1,000 days at the legal minimum wage rate.[56] Interests on the loans were kept down (see table 7.9), and so were prices on agricultural inputs of all kinds.

Nevertheless, the cooperatives had great difficulties in repaying the credits. The entire reformed sector was like a leaky bucket, and the 'rate of recovery' of interest and amortization payments on the credits granted by CORA fell from 25.1 per cent in 1970 to 15.6 per cent in

The constructive phase of the agrarian reform

Table 7.9 *Nominal interest rates on credits to the reformed sector and increases in the consumer price index in 1971–2 (percentages)*

Period	Rate of interest	Rate of inflation
1971	12	22.1
January–September 1972	12	163.4
September–December 1972	75	

SOURCE: Banco Central, *Boletín Mensual*, various issues.

1971.[57] The *campesinos* came to regard the funds as handed over to them almost gratuitously, like the land had been;[58] a circumstance which impeded the development of an awareness of real costs and which reinforced the *campesinos'* preference for asking for new credits in order to finance labor-saving investments.

To assess the exact value of all the different forms of subsidies involved in the UP's assistance to agriculture is a difficult task indeed, but in order to get an idea of the magnitudes we could compare the total amount of credit granted the agrarian sector in 1971 with the gross value of total agricultural output the same year: 5,200[59] and 8,500[60] million escudos, respectively. For the reformed sector, which received the bulk of public support, credits considerably exceeded the value of production, and the gift element in these credits must have been greater by at least 30 per cent of the value of total production on the co-operatives.

That agricultural development was to be in part financed with surplus from other sectors in the economy was, as we recall, emphatically pointed out by Jacques Chonchol. But certainly nobody in the UP had expected the subsidies to take such gigantic forms. The production response from agriculture, and above all from the reformed cooperatives, was a clear disappointment to the government; capital productivity fell noticeably.

The destination of the credits granted differed greatly. Large infrastructural investments were made, housing and sanitary facilities on the cooperatives were improved, and seeds, cattle, pesticides and fertilizers were purchased. Many *campesinos* grasped the opportunity to equip themselves with clothing and other badly needed consumer goods. Much of the short-term credit was nothing more than a (quite irrational) form of consumption subsidy. The larger part of the credits was used to mechanize the reformed areas, however, a process symbolized by the mounting importance of the tractor.[61]

In 1970 some 10,000 tractors were in use in all Chile, or about one for every 75 people working in agriculture. In 1971 the number of tractors reached 14,500, in 1972 over 20,000. Of those that were put into use during 1971/2 the majority (some 70 per cent) went to the reformed sector, and the rest to private *medianos* and to public tractor-stations put at the disposal of smallholders.[62] According to President Allende,[63] one objective of the UP's mechanization program was to increase the number of tractors in the reformed sector to 50,000 units over a period of five years. The realization of this goal would thus have resulted in the cooperatives and CEPROs, controlling some 36 per cent of Chile's agricultural land and 18 per cent of the agrarian work force, gaining possession of five times as many tractors as existed in the whole of Chile in 1970. This in turn would have meant that the members of the reformed settlements would then dispose of an average of almost one tractor per family.

How should this veritable technological revolution be evaluated? To begin with it should be pointed out that the initial direct costs of mechanization, even on this massive scale, were not insurmountably high. A good tractor could be bought for 4,000 dollars, and even the full implementation of Allende's 'tractorization' program would have cost no more than some additional 160 million dollars, or considerably less than 50 per cent of Chile's annual food imports.

But to these direct costs of mechanization we should add several others: the training of tractor drivers and mechanics, infrastructural investments and, last but not least, maintenance costs such as spare parts, oil, etc. The import-intensity of agricultural production rises rapidly as mechanization proceeds, and the dependence on the external sector increases. Agricultural workers have to – or, at least, ought to – be maintained whether they work or not, while the use of machinery requires extra imports.[64]

Finally, a few words should as well be said about the likely effects on employment. Apparently, the UP did not see a conflict between the goals of increasing production through mechanization and raising employment, although a conflict undoubtedly existed. There was a trade-off, and if the UP did recognize this trade-off they gave priority to the production objective. This is clear from most public statements as well as from the policies actually followed. It is very likely that the gradual deterioration in the overall economic and political situation and the acute shortage of foodstuffs pushed the UP further and further in this direction. A serious drop in production would have been felt almost immediately in the large cities while a decrease in agricultural employment would not, and the cynical propaganda[65] from the opposition made it difficult to turn the attention from the housewives lining up outside Santiago's grocery stores to unemployed *afuerinos*.

The UP felt it to be an economic and political necessity to increase agricultural output rapidly and to gain (or avoid losing) political support from the *campesinos* in the reformed sector; hence the heavy reliance on mechanization policies. An alternative, more 'Chinese' model with massive undertakings of collective works in land improvement, reforestation, soil-erosion combatting, irrigation, draining, residential construction, etc. would no doubt have given much better results in terms of employment creation and, in a few years, also in terms of production. But too many institutional and political obstacles stood in the way of more systematic efforts to implement agrarian policies along these lines.

Price policies and marketing

In theory, price policy played an important role in the UP's agrarian project. Prices were to meet three fundamental requirements: they should serve as instruments in the struggle for a change in the income distribution, they should stimulate agricultural producers to raise production and, last but not least, they should guide the producers in their choice of crops, preferably towards exportable and high manpower-absorbing products.

Producers and consumers should both benefit in the distribution of incomes. Public subsidies should, and did in many cases, help to achieve these apparently contradictory objectives, but it was also thought that they could be achieved simultaneously at the expense of intermediary profits.

Prices on agricultural inputs were to be kept down; which was intended to act as an additional means of stimulating production.

The abnormal monetary situation that arose soon made the application of more sophisticated price policies impossible. Official prices to producers were raised more and more often and more and more drastically, but they almost always tended to lag behind those prevailing on the parallel, black market. To take one example: between January 1972 and January 1973 official potato prices were raised several hundred per cent, from 80 to 420 escudos per 100 kilo, but even so they remained much below the prices paid by private purchasers on the parallel market.

Official prices to consumers were raised from 2.5 to 10 escudos per kilo in the same period, but it would have been difficult to find someone who bought potatoes for less than 15 or, towards the end of the year, 25–35 escudos per kilo on the streets of Santiago. This is an extreme example – the potato shortage was notorious – but it does indicate the magnitude of the figures that were sometimes involved, the violent inflation, the large differences between official and unofficial prices both for producers and consumers, and the large profit margins obtained by intermediaries. The middlemen who were most fortunate – those who managed to buy at official and sell at unofficial prices – could indeed make handsome profits.

Under these circumstances speculation and stockpiling became the order of the day, and very little could be done by the government to cope with the situation. Price decrees and other administrative measures could attack the symptoms only. They were arbitrary and quite inefficient and the share of transactions closed in official prices declined steadily. Governmental efforts to force the *campesinos* to sell directly to state agencies at fixed and regulated prices were largely inoperative.[66]

The public sector's share of the distribution of agricultural products was small (except for imported foodstuffs, in which the wholesale trade was mainly handled by a state company); far too small to permit a stricter implementation of the official price policy. Extensive state influence over distribution channels would not have prevented prices from rising rapidly, and neither would it have prevented the distortion of relative prices that took place (quite the opposite, perhaps), but it would have permitted the Treasury and/or the consumers to absorb part of the profits that now arose from trade in agricultural products. But the government failed to come to grips with the private sector's dominance in distribution. The gaining of control of the 'monopolies' engaged in the processing and distribution of agricultural products was an integral part of the UP's agrarian strategy, but despite pressure from the government the owners of the firms that were to be taken over refused to sell out, and state companies were of only marginal importance.

The marketing of foodstuffs was, then, handled by pretty much the same companies and individuals as before, although the chaotic price situation caused a disruption of many old distribution channels, and the products often had to find their way to the consumers in new and illicit ways.[67] Exactly what prices were paid and how the gains were shared between producers and intermediaries is, of course, impossible to tell, but the latter, with their superior knowledge of market conditions and means of transportation, were in a very good position. The hypothesis that it was they who grasped the lion's share of the profits made is supported by the huge differences in producers' and consumers' prices on the parallel markets. Even the reformed sector traded primarily with private interests, as is evident from the figures in table 7.10.

Table 7.10   *Estimated distribution of the reformed sector's sales of agricultural products by category of buyer, May 1971– April 1972 (percentages)*

Category	Share
Private firms and middlemen	55.3
Mills and industries	16.1
State organizations	14.1
Agrarian cooperatives	7.3
Campesino organizations	4.5
Traditional forms of distribution[a]	2.7

[a] Fairs, markets, etc.

SOURCE: ICIRA, 'Diagnosis', anexo 12.

Policies towards the rural poor outside the reformed sector

While some 50,000 families were integrated into the reformed sector as members of cooperatives and about 5,000 as wage earners on CEPROs, the problems of land, employment and social security for the vast majority of the agricultural population were in no way solved by the land reform. The over 100,000 *minifundistas* continued to work their sub-family holdings and continued to try to get some incidental earnings through odd-jobs on neighboring estates, and some 350,000 landless workers continued to sell their labor-power, when jobs were available, to private landowners and now also to reformed cooperatives. For the miserably poor, indigenous Mapuche Indians, a people bearing the additional burden of constant discrimination,[68] the direct benefits of the land reform also remained out of reach. Of a rural Mapuche population of some 450,000 the great majority lived in 'indigenous reservations' (*communidades* or *reducciones indígenas*) outside the expro-priated estates, the rest being mainly day-laborers unable to enter the *asentamientos* as members.

We already know the reasons why the land reform failed to benefit these groups. They were, nevertheless, affected in many ways by the government's overall agrarian policies, and at least the smallholders were, in comparison with the situation in the past, paid considerable attention.

Smallholders

The most important ingredient of the UP's policy towards smallholders was actively to support the formation of cooperatives, and both economic and ideological persuasion was applied to make the *minifundistas* merge the plots and work the land collectively. The response from the small-holders was positive, often enthusiastic, and over two thousand co-operatives or 'Committees of Small Producers' were established during an apparently very successful campaign.[69]

The mere formation of cooperatives does not increase land area *per capita* by one single acre, however, and the main problem on those mini-ature cooperatives was hardly lack of work incentives, as on the larger ones, but of work opportunities. Underemployment remained high, despite considerable efforts to create new jobs through the undertaking of various infrastructural projects: drainage, irrigation, land improve-ment, etc. The formation of cooperatives widened the scope for these types of undertakings, which were badly needed from the point of view of raising productivity, but even with the very intensive cultivation and vast improvements in soil and production techniques the majority of these cooperatives were too small to be able to provide decent incomes and employment opportunities for their members.

A sizeable increase in financial and technical assistance, including education, was also part of the UP's program for smallholders. The amount of credits granted to this sector more than doubled in two years (see table 7.11), though it still received but a fraction of what went to the reformed sector, and tractor stations whose services the *minifundistas* cooperatives could buy inexpensively were established in some areas.

Literacy campaigns, courses in farming techniques, in tractor driving, in bookkeeping, etc. were initiated. Much attention was paid to the indigenous population. Schools were constructed on the reservations and the number of scholarships to Mapuches was raised drastically.[70] The people were stimulated to organize themselves to fight for their interests.

Table 7.11   *Credits to smallholders 1970–72*

Year	Number of beneficiaries	Total amount (escudos of 1971)	Average per beneficiary
1970	38,841	78,544,277	2,022
1971	74,124	177,660,100	2,396
1972	90,048	n.a.	n.a.

SOURCE: 1970–71: ICIRA, 'Diagnosis', Anexo I, table 15-A, 1972: Allende, *Third Message*, p. 299.

In short, a lot of good work was done, and compared with the achievements of earlier administrations the UP's deeds and, above all, intentions, undoubtedly constituted one step forward – but only one, perhaps.

The rural proletariat

As regards the landless farm workers, it is very difficult to assess the effects that the agrarian reform and the UP's policies in general might have had on their working situation. They neither received nor could lose any land; they formed no cooperative and were given no credits; they were affected only indirectly, through their situation as sellers of labor-power and buyers of commodities. In contrast with the small-holders, they were affected mainly by changes in the market. However the violent inflation beginning in 1972 and the lack of statistics even in nominal terms make estimates of the movement of real wages for the rural proletariat almost impossible.

But a few points should be mentioned. The first one relates to the institutional change that took place on the labor market, especially as manifested in the workers' activity in the trade unions, which continued at an increased rate. By 1972, 277,000 agricultural workers, or more than twice as many as in 1970, were organized. Supervision of minimum wage and social security legislation was improved both from above and from below, and implementation was, at least in the reformed sector, comparatively strict.[71] The political situation that prevailed in 1970–73 was also likely to improve the bargaining power of the rural proletariat, since the landowners were anxious to avoid labor disputes with many unpredictable consequences. Neglecting to pay the legal mini-mum wage, which was raised drastically by the UP in 1971, could also occasion either state intervention or, when the *fundo* was to be expropriated, more unfavorable terms when compensation was paid.

As for the employment situation, the higher wages that private landowners were forced to pay should have stimulated a substitution of capital for labor. The political climate reinforced this tendency. The rural bourgeoisie feared the workers, fired 'agitators' and were reluctant to contract unknown workers they could not 'trust'. For both economic and political reasons private landowners tended to prefer tractors to manpower.

The preference for labor-saving technologies was, as we have seen earlier, very pronounced in the reformed sector as well. The first phase of the agrarian reform, the expropriation of the *latifundios*, witnessed a rapid decapitalization of the expropriated areas and a subsequent mechanization of the *reservas*. In the next stage, the first tendency was more than amply compensated, however, since assistance from CORA soon exceeded the initial losses. Both the private multi-family estates and the reformed cooperatives (i.e. the agricultural workers' only possible employers) were thus becoming more and more capital-intensive, and Allende's promise of 50,000 tractors to the reformed sector pointed to further development in this direction.

Labor productivity in Chilean agriculture was indeed very low, only about one-third of the national average, and needed to be increased. Mechanization is a blessing for those who benefit from it. It lightens the burden of labor; it raises labor productivity; it is the necessary condition for all long-range economic progress. But were the unemployed and underemployed mass of landless day-laborers in rural Chile able to share these benefits, or was the surplus of men over jobs to be perpetuated or even increased by the developments that took place? This we will never know with certainty, but it is quite conceivable that the Allende government's way of promoting technological progress in the long run could have served to accentuate unemployment and poverty among large peasant groups.

AVAILABILITY OF FOODSTUFFS 1970–72

Domestic production

We have seen earlier that agricultural production went up markedly in 1970/71, and that a modest increase followed in 1971/72. But in 1972/3 there was a very poor harvest. As table 7.12 shows, the total area under cultivation fell by almost 20 per cent, with consequent drops in the production of most major crops.

It is difficult to assess the relative importance of the various reasons behind the relatively good harvests of 1971 and 1972 and the serious crop failure in 1973. Weather conditions affected output, of course. These were very favorable in the agricultural years 1970/71 and 1971/2, but adverse in 1972/3. But several other factors interacted.

It might have been expected that the most serious production problems would arise during the initial phase of the land reform, when uncertainty was widespread and ownership of more than one-quarter of Chile's agricultural land changed hands, and that the situation would stabilize when all *latifundios* had been expropriated. But the pattern was,

Table 7.12   Area under cultivation (thousands of hectares) and harvests (thousands of metric tons) of major crops 1969/70 to 1972/3

Crop	1969/70		1970/71		1971/2		1972/3[a]		Index 72/3 (69/70 = 100)	
	Cultivated area	Production	Cultivated area	Production	Cultivated area	Production	Cultivated area	Production	Area	Production
Wheat	740.3	1,306.9	727.4	1,368.0	711.8	1,195.0	470.0	827.2	66.4	63.3
Barley	47.4	97.4	52.5	113.6	67.1	139.0	67.0	147.4	141.5	151.4
Rye	8.3	10.7	8.9	12.3	9.2	12.4	9.0	12.5	108.4	116.8
Oats	72.6	110.5	75.3	112.0	83.8	111.3	70.4	97.5	96.1	88.1
Rice	25.2	76.2	27.3	67.1	25.7	86.3	18.0	61.2	71.4	80.3
Maize	73.9	239.1	77.0	258.3	84.5	283.0	108.0	388.8	148.8	162.6
Pulses	96.5	89.6	114.2	99.8	131.1	113.6	112.2	105.3	116.3	117.5
Potato	71.7	683.8	80.0	835.8	79.2	733.0	70.4	605.4	98.1	87.1
Sunflower	20.2	28.2	15.3	20.3	14.8	19.9	13.4	16.0	66.3	58.2
Rape	53.7	69.9	49.4	82.1	56.1	78.0	40.0	52.0	74.5	74.4
Sugar-beet	41.7	1,655.1	35.1	1,390.7	31.4	1,201.6	26.0	936.0	62.3	56.5
Total	1,251.5	—	1,262.4	—	1,294.7	—	1,004.4	—	—	80.3

[a] Preliminary data.

SOURCE: 1969/70–1971/72: INE, Encuesta Nacional Agropecuaria de Mayo de 1972, pp. 3ff. 1972/3: Allende, Third Message p. 278.

as seen, quite the opposite, the main reason probably being that outside the agrarian sector the former half of the Allende period was characterized by relative tranquility, while from mid-1972 galloping inflation, infrastructural bottlenecks, political turbulence and rightist sabotage occasioned much more disruption and disorganization than the social struggles in the countryside over the land question had caused earlier.

We can distinguish three main factors which in particular affected the 1972/3 harvest adversely:

1. *Bad weather conditions.* Huge rainfalls in the south during the Chilean spring (September–November) delayed or even impeded completely the sowing of several major crops (wheat, rape and sugar-beet, above all). This was the prime reason for the decline in the area under cultivation that took place in most of the southern provinces.

2. *The 'October events'.* The prolonged transportation strike (or 'lockout', as it ought to be called) occurred during the busiest agricultural season, or when spring sowing was in progress. The delivery of seeds, fertilizers, pesticides, etc. was cut off almost totally for more than three weeks, and the time that was lost could only partially be recovered. According to very rough and preliminary estimates by CORA, about three per cent of the whole year's crop was lost due to difficulties directly caused by the 'October events'.[72]

3. *Disorganization.* Here we must include a great many factors which influenced the normal farm work in a negative way: continuing strikes, land seizures and social struggles of various kinds, outright sabotage from former *latifundistas* and *medianos* linked to the political opposition, the disruption of traditional marketing channels, transportation difficulties, the poor organization and lack of work incentives in the reformed sector, etc. Naturally, the effects of these different but in part interrelated circumstances cannot be isolated, let alone estimated in quantitative terms.

The comparatively good performance of the livestock sector in 1972/3 may indicate a fourth reason for the substantial drop in production of foodgrains. The UP's agrarian policies and the changes in relative prices that took place might have turned many *campesinos*' attention to high-priced animal products (on which price controls were less effective and competition from imports not so pronounced) at the expense of cereals and industrial crops. But without a better knowledge of how the government's policies and the black market prices affected the relative profitability of different agrarian activities (and how this, in turn, affected the *campesinos*' production decisions) this can be no more than an untestable hypothesis. What is certain, however, as is shown in table

7.13, is that production of several livestock products was sustained or even increased in 1973.

Table 7.13 *Livestock production 1969/70 to 1972/3*

	1969/70	1970/71	1971/2	1972/3[a]	Index 1972/3 (1969/70 = 100)
Beef and veal[b]	127	125	111	119	94
Lamb and mutton[b]	34	30	27	26	76
Pork[b]	48	43	50	53	110
Poultry[b]	62	67	81	92	148
Milk[c]	1,071	1,169	1,242	1,329	124
Eggs (millions)	903	1,104	1,300	1,391	154

[a] Preliminary figures
[b] Thousands of tons
[c] Millions of litres
SOURCE: 1969/70−1970/71: Allende, *Second Message*, p. 244. 1971/2−1972/3: Allende, *Third Message*, p. 279.

Foreign trade

We could illustrate the mounting importance of agricultural imports for Chile after 1970 in two ways. First, imports as a share of total consumption of domestic agricultural products rose. Chile's degree of self-sufficiency in agricultural products dropped from about 80 per cent in 1965−70 to 74 per cent in 1971 and 67 per cent in 1972.[73] This took place despite a significant rise in Chile's own production and was, then, a mere reflection of the virtual explosion of demand for foodstuffs[74] (stimulated not only by wage increases and income redistribution but also by the UP's exchange rate policy which made imported foodstuffs very cheap). In 1973, when domestic production did fall off, the dependence on imports rose further.

To get an impression of the agrarian sector's increasingly crucial role in Chile's balance of payments situation we should also relate agricultural imports to total export earnings. While the former rose fast, the latter dropped. On average 1965−70 agricultural imports[75] absorbed 13.3 per cent of all goods export earnings; in 1972, this figure had risen to 56.0 per cent (table 7.14).

The dramatic rise in the above indicator was, however, to a very large extent a mere reflection of the changes in relative prices that took place

Table 7.14   *Exports of goods and agricultural imports 1965–70 (yearly average), 1971 and 1972 (millions of dollars)*

	1965–70	1971	1972
Exports of goods	939	964	836
(of which agricultural products)	(24)	(29)	(19)
Imports of agricultural products	184	311	468
Agricultural imports as percentage of total export earnings	19.6	32.2	56.0

between the late 1960s and the early 1970s, which were very disadvantageous for Chile. Thus, while copper prices in 1971 decreased by about 25 per cent below their 1970 level, which, in turn, was lower than in 1968–9, and remained equally low in 1972, foodstuffs rose sharply. Prices of a weighted average of Chile's agricultural imports increased by 8 per cent in 1971 and by another 41 per cent in 1972. 1972 was, then, an extreme year for Chile, with the terms of trade between copper exports and food imports falling to nearly 50, if 1970 is set at 100.

Early in 1973 copper prices started to recover spectacularly; in July, copper sold at twice the price (in current dollars) for the previous year. But wheat and other heavy items in Chile's import trade did not lag far behind.

Total supply of foodstuffs

That the serious food shortage that began to develop as of early 1972 was conditioned by a massive increase in demand and not by a reduction in supply is obvious from the data on production and imports presented above. The overall availability of foodstuffs in Chile is estimated to have been some 27 per cent higher in 1972 than in 1970.[76] Some smuggling to neighboring countries took place[77] and stockpiling of non-perishable goods such as sugar, rice, edible oil, coffee and tea, etc. was notorious. Actual consumption may thus have increased somewhat less rapidly, but there can be little doubt that the Chilean people had both more and better food at their disposal in 1971 and 1972 than before. This is also confirmed by the data on *per capita* supply of foodstuffs given in table 7.15.

POLITICAL DEVELOPMENTS

The main political tendencies from the preceding period were all confirmed after 1970. *Campesino* mobilization accelerated, and more

Political developments

Table 7.15 *Apparent consumption – domestic production plus imports, smuggling and hoarding disregarded – of major crops and livestock products 1970 and 1972 (kilos per capita)*

	1970	1972	% change
Wheat	152.7	178.1	16.6
Maize	54.1	64.0	18.3
Rice	9.7	11.8	21.6
Potato	51.6	55.8	8.1
Sugar	32.0	39.6	23.8
Edible oil	7.0	7.6	8.6
Wine[a]	47.0	52.6	11.9
Beef and Veal	17.4	15.4	−11.5
Lamb and Mutton	3.5	2.8	−20.0
Pork	4.9	6.1	24.5
Poultry	6.4	7.6	18.7
Milk[a]	123.9	171.8	38.7
Eggs[b]	93.0	117.3	26.1

[a] Litres
[b] Units
SOURCE: Allende, *Third Message*, p. 282.

and more militant forms of struggle were practised.[78] The reinforcement of the trend towards a strengthening and radicalization of the farm workers' organizations is evident from the rapid growth of strikes and land seizures and from the great headway made by the pro-UP trade unions (tables 7.16 and 7.17). Voting patterns in general elections confirm that the Left made substantial progress in widening its popular support in rural Chile, although they also reveal that the point of departure was disadvantageous and that the conservative forces continued to dominate. In the parliamentary election in March 1973 the UP's share of the votes was 37 per cent in the predominantly agrarian provinces, as against the 29 per cent reached by Allende in the same provinces in 1970.[79]

Together with the above trade unions, mainly pursuing 'traditional' objectives (aiming to protect the economic interests of the workers against their employers), there also developed a new form of *campesino* organization, the 'Peasants' Councils', with more extensive tasks. These provincial and country-wide Councils, whose membership was not confined to farm workers but also included *minifundistas* and members of the reformed cooperatives, should in theory have had a large influence in the actual carrying out of the agrarian reform. They were intended to develop into democratic organs of *campesino* decision-making rather

Table 7.16 *Number of rural conflicts resulting in strikes or*
land seizures ('tomas') 1967–1

	1967	1968	1969	1970	1971
Strikes	693	648	1,127	1,580	1,758
Tomas	9	26	148	456	1,278
Total	702	674	1,275	2,036	3,036

SOURCE: ICIRA, Diagnosis, pp. v–18ff, and Juan Carlos Marín,
'Las Tomas', *Marxismo y Revolución*, no. 1, July–September
1973, p. 59.

than to play a purely advisory role. Their implementation was delayed,
however, by opposition from the rightist forces within the UP which
long regarded the Peasants' Councils as a threat to the legal authority
of the government. Only late in 1972 did the formation of the Councils,
which were supported by parts of the UP, by the MIR and by the *campesinos* themselves, who began to regard the Councils as alternatives to
the hopelessly bureaucratic state apparatus, gain speed. A kind of 'dual
power' thus emerged in the countryside.

But not all *campesinos* took part in the general mobilization and radicalization. As to the direct beneficiaries of the land reform, the privileged
members of the reformed cooperatives, it must be said that this group
removed itself more and more from the rest of the *campesino* movement.
The *inquilinos*, formerly so militant, formed organizations of their own
once they had become integrated into the reformed sector. They reduced
their political activity appreciably and often came into conflict with
the landless laborers and with the smallholders. In general they tended
to side with the political Center, the Christian Democrats[80] (i.e. the
political force which best represented their objective interests against
possible attacks from the Right, vengeful *latifundistas* and their hangers-
on, and from the Left, all groups calling for a radicalization of the land
reform). The UP government's rapid expropriation of remaining *latifundios* and its policy of granting the reformed sector generous subsidies
made many members of the cooperatives very sympathetic towards the
UP, of course, but they could hardly be expected to work for a development along socialist lines. And since future interests count more than
actually received benefits in political matters the members of the cooperatives were, as a group, inclined to abandon the Left and pin their
faith upon the Center–Right. For the Christian Democratic/Unidad

Table 7.17 *Membership of farm workers' trade unions 1969 and 1972*

Organization	Political tendency	Number of members			
		1969	%	1972	%
Ranquil	PC–PS	30,912	29.8	132,294	47.6
Unidad Obrero-campesino[a]	MAPU	—	—	40,561	14.6
Sub-total	pro–UP	30,912	29.8	172,855	62.2
Libertad	'non-political'[b]	23,024	22.2	39,421	14.2
Triunfo Compesino	PDC	47,610	46.0	61,187	22.0
Miscellaneous	Anti-UP	2,098	2.0	4,432	1.6
Sub-total	Center–Right	72,732	70.2	105,040	37.8
Total		103,644	100.0	277,895	100.0

[a] Formed in 1971 as a consequence of a split within Libertad (and in the whole Christian Democratic Party).

[b] Formally 'non-political' but tended to support the PDC.

SOURCE: Based on Allende, *Third Message*, pp. 310ff.

Popular agrarian reform worked, as we have seen, to weaken the solidarity between different groups of *campesinos*. The obejcetive conditions for a split between the minority of beneficiaries and the great majority of 'outsiders' receiving no land or security at all were inevitably being created by the attempts to apply an anti-*latifundista* strategy on the socio-economic structure of Chile. And the ex-*latifundistas* and the rightist political parties, anxious to form an alliance between old and new privileges, understood perfectly well how to take advantage of the situation.

CONCLUDING REMARKS

The Chilean land reform of 1970–73 differed greatly from experiences in other Latin American countries (despite certain similarities in scope and extent with the ongoing land tenure reform in Peru). To begin with it differed from those projects (the majority) which remained reforms essentially in name only, those which were carried out reluctantly by bourgeois governments in order to forestall peasant radicalism and/or to qualify for US aid according to Alliance for Progress requisites. Today, more than ten years after the North and South American discussion of these types of reforms reached its peak, land reforms have been buried, even officially, in most countries on the continent.

The Chilean reforms also took place under completely different circumstances from those which did bring forth profound changes in existing land tenure structures (i.e. the Mexican, Bolivian and Cuban agrarian transformations). In these countries new land-holding relations were the result of social upheavals and ensuing changes in the overall power structure in society. In Mexico and Bolivia uprisings from below rather than legislation from above accomplished the bulk of expropriations, and in Cuba a social revolution preceded the land reform legislation. In Chile, however, it was neither armed masses nor post-revolutionary legislation but the combination of *campesino* pressure and bourgeois legislation which achieved the, temporary, extinction of all *latifundios* in Chile and the, also temporary, creation of semi-collective forms of ownership on more than one-third of the productive land.

As regards the kind of land-tenure structure that emerged, Chile also differed from other Latin American countries where, except in Cuba, land reforms have typically been characterized by an initial phase of expropriations of large estates and subsequent subdivisions of the land for further distribution among smallholders and landless laborers.

Concluding remarks

In Chile no such redistribution took place, the reformed sector being formed by production units whose boundaries almost always coincided with those of the expropriated *fundos* and whose workforce remained essentially the same as before.

But international comparisons are full of pitfalls. What can we, concretely, learn from Chilean agrarian experiences 1970–73?

It is easy, but also somewhat unfair, to point out all the shortcomings of the UP's agrarian reform. One can find faults almost anywhere: in the government's lack of clear strategy, in the system of selecting the beneficiaries of the land reform with its negative impact upon equality and land utilization, in the organization of the reformed sector with its lack of work incentives, in the bolstering up of the cooperatives with tractors and large consumption subsidies, in the price and import policy with all its arbitrary effects on relative prices, in the inability to cope with the serious distribution problems that arose, etc. The analysis of all those difficulties and inconsistencies has occupied most of the space in this overview of the Unidad Popular's agrarian reform, while the great achievements made have perhaps not been emphasized enough.

But what I wanted to illustrate above all was the huge obstacles confronting a left-wing government working with inadequate legal tools in a hostile political and chaotic overall economic environment. The UP's freedom of action was from the beginning very limited, later to become further and further reduced, and consistency in agrarian policies could not easily be achieved. What Dr Allende's government had to do was constantly to decide where to move on a specific trade-off between conflicting economic and/or political objectives, and the choices tended more and more to have the character of choices between the lesser of two evils.

The Unidad Popular, or at least part of it, was quite aware of the tremendous problems affecting the agrarian reform and Chilean agriculture in general, but few good solutions could be thought of or, when thought of, implemented. And, given the legal and political framework and the socio-economic heritage, did there ever exist any really good solutions?

Final reflections

The dramatic and, as it turned out, tragic development in Chile between 1970 and 1973 cannot easily be condensed into a few final pages. It remains however to summarize the political economy of Salvador Allende's aborted attempt to find a 'Chilean road to socialism', and some of the issues raised in the preceding chapters deserve to be brought together and emphasized once again.

We will begin by describing the general state of the Chilean economy after almost three years of UP rule, providing a sort of photograph of the economic panorama at the time Allende was ousted. An interpretation of the salient features of this situation will then be made in the light of Chile's earlier economic history, and we will thereby indicate the continuity with respect to earlier developments that the UP's economic policies, despite their many special characteristics, represented in the final analysis.

This aspect of continuity will also be used to illustrate the implications of the Unidad Popular's economic program in a more long-range perspective. Did the UP's 'structural transformations' really signify a difference in kind? What economic structure would have emerged if the Allende government had not been overthrown but allowed to continue to realize its program?

The question of the lessons to be drawn from the UP's ultimate defeat must finally be touched upon. Was the UP's failure the result of ordinary mistakes in the economic field, as some economists assert, or was it, as many socialists argue, the inevitable consequence of a reformist political strategy? Or was the whole project doomed from the very beginning, more or less irrespective of the policies that the UP leadership actually chose to pursue? Of course, these questions cannot be answered by a simple 'yes' or 'no'; nevertheless I will conclude by drawing attention to a number of substantive points of an essentially political character.

But first the economic situation during the last months of Allende rule.

Final reflections

The economic panorama in 1973 and its roots in Chile's past

Recapitulating the descriptive analysis of the previous chapters we know that the Chilean economy by mid-1973 found itself in the midst of a serious crisis. The symptoms were obvious: a pace of price increases exceeding one per cent a day, a pronounced tendency to stagnation in all major sectors of activity, mounting queues and shortages and a distribution system increasingly based on speculation and black marketing.

Beneath these easily visible indicators we encounter a series of other crisis symptoms. We could, initially, characterize the situation as one of widespread bottlenecks. The margins of idle capacity that existed earlier had been exhausted in enough sectors to render future growth of output difficult in the absence of large net investment in crucial activities. We could also point to all the deficits characterizing the economy: current imports exceeded exports by some 30 to 50 per cent, the fiscal deficit was immense and most of the state-controlled enterprises as well as the re-formed part of the agricultural sector were running at huge losses.

Disequilibria of all kinds flourished, and the distortions in relative prices were great enough to make meaningful economic calculations with the help of prevailing price relations almost impossible. As for the cost of capital, for example, the annual rate of interest on ordinary bank loans was in 1973 equivalent to the rate of inflation in only a few months. The price for foreign exchange could, by August 1973, range from 20 escudos to the dollar for food imports to 2,000 escudos for each dollar on the black market.

Most of the above features characterizing the economic situation in 1973 were not introduced by the Allende government but had existed for a long time, but they were accentuated dramatically under the UP regime. Inflation, shortages, balance of payments problems and fiscal deficits had for decades harassed the Chilean economy, and the policy measures – price controls, multiple exchange rates, cheap credit, massive foreign lending, etc. – applied to cope with these and other problems were simply taken over by the UP. The complex arsenal of administrative controls which the UP inherited had become part of 'common sense' in Chile ever since the great depression of the 1930s, but it was not primarily the result of a particular economic doctrine surviving administration after administration but rather it was rooted in the political rules of the game that prevailed and in the correlation of forces struggling for influence in the state apparatus. In the final analysis it was based upon a clientele system of attempts to satisfy different pressure groups and electoral coalitions without jeopardizing the process of capital accumulation as a whole. The Allende government took over the existing body of beliefs and policies, but made an effort to integrate the poor majority of the Chilean people into the traditional range of benefits granted by the state, without hurting the interests of the middle and upper-middle classes. But this could not be done without provoking a virtual collapse of the system, which had been created to provide *selective* favors but which could in no way be used to raise the living standards of the Chilean population as a whole.

When from early 1972 onwards it became increasingly difficult to satisfy everybody (i.e. all but the oligarchs) the UP responded by making even more drastic use of the old mechanisms that were most easily within reach. Wages, salaries and public expenditures were thus further increased, price controls were implemented in a stricter (but less realistic) way, imports were made even cheaper and the escudo correspondingly more overvalued, and real interest rates were lowered further so as to safeguard a continued capital accumulation, etc. But as the symptoms of the crisis were being attacked, their causes were strengthened.

Chile's productive capacity was, as we know, unable to meet all the demands that economic policies required it to meet. It could not provide all the favors that the UP tried to distribute – or, given the political circumstances, was 'forced' to distribute. Sooner or later someone would have to pay the price for the restoration of a more equilibriated economy. And such a restoration could not possibly take place without force, without a rupture of the impasse that characterized the Chilean political scene. In short: it could not take place without a drastic break with the gradualistic 'Chilean road'.

This truth was clear to both the bourgeoisie and the working class, but the dominant sectors of the UP leadership, to the very last hoping that some miraculous turn of events would palliate the crisis, refused to recognize it – at least in terms of action.

The significance of the UP program

For a different type of picture of the Chilean economy from the one presented above we could try to leave all the immediate crisis symptoms out of account in order to concentrate on more structural characteristics. What kind of economy was being created as a result of the Allende government's program of structural reforms?

Final reflections

The first outstanding feature to emphasize is related to the increased role played by the state. In this sense the UP program signified no break with past trends but an accentuation of old ones. Already before Allende's assumption of the presidency the public sector directly or indirectly controlled over two-thirds of all investments made, and state interference in the economic life of the country was significant enough to make some Chilean marxists maintain that the prevailing mode of production deserved to be classified as 'state monopoly capitalism'. The UP's 'structural transformations' were fundamentally based on a further promotion of the state as engine and director of growth, and the main difference with respect to previous administrations was that public ownership and centralized compulsory planning was to substitute – or, should we say, complement – many of the old mechanisms for indirect control.

Did this signify a difference in kind? We recall Dr Allende stating that the UP intended to make the public sector 'quantitatively even more important than it has been up to now, but also qualitatively different'.[1] By making it 'qualitatively different' Allende referred to, firstly, the system of centralized planning that was to dominate within the social area and, secondly, to the changes that were to be made in the managing of the firms: industrial democracy was to take the place of authoritarian capitalist rule.

Very little progress was made in the first of these two objectives, and only moderate progress in the second. What would have happened if the actual trend under Allende had been allowed to continue – a hypothetical question, since political developments ruled out such an alternative – is difficult to surmise, but probably few socialists would argue that the society that would have been created after the full implementation of the UP's program would have merited the designation 'socialist'.[2]

From the point of view of power the UP's program was, however, very far-reaching. Its realization would have deprived all the dominant sectors of the Chilean bourgeoisie of most of their economic base and power. The Unidad Popular's economic and political program was no doubt drastic enough to be totally unacceptable to the Chilean financial, industrial and agrarian oligarchy which for very good reasons felt seriously threatened.

Who were the main beneficiaries of the program? This is, I believe, one of the most important questions of all when evaluating the general significance of the UP's structural reforms. And here, too, serious doubts as to the viability of the UP's 'Chilean road' to development must arise.

For if we look at the likely socio-economic consequences of a complete carrying out of the UP's plans we cannot avoid drawing the conclusion that, even if the political circumstances had been such as to permit the Allende government to continue its reform program and even if the general economic situation had been under control, the UP's economic strategy as such promised no solution to Chile's basic development problems.

Obviously, we cannot make meaningful extrapolations from the experiences between 1970 and 1973. Neither is this the place to diagnose Chile's underdevelopment. But one crucial aspect dealt with on several occasions earlier deserves to be emphasized again: the number of direct beneficiaries of the 'structural transformations' undertaken by the UP was very small as a proportion of Chile's economically active population. This was particularly clear within the agrarian sector, where those who received land – either individually or, as was usually the case, as full members of reformed cooperatives – constituted less than 10 per cent of the whole agrarian work-force, and this after the process of elimination of all large *fundos* had virtually been concluded. In manufacturing perhaps 15 per cent of the workers had been incorporated into the social area by mid-1973, and if the UP had realized its whole expropriation program only some 20 per cent of the industrial work-force would have been integrated. As for mining, the nationalization of all large-scale mining companies had already been accomplished before 1972. But the miners were small in number: all Chile's copper, iron, nitrate and coal miners, producing over four-fifths of total export earnings, were easily outnumbered by, say, the number of domestic servants alone.

The sum total of workers (including clerical and technical personnel) directly affected by the UP's nationalization and agrarian reform programs – if these had been carried through as envisaged – can be estimated to have been somewhere between 230,000 and 260,000,[3] some eight per cent of Chile's labor force or approximately equivalent to the rate of open unemployment in 1970; or, to make another comparison, less than one-fifth of total employment in non-basic services.

This limited number of workers thus integrated into the social area of the economy and the reformed sector of agriculture received, for reasons we already know, a wide range of material and non-tangible privileges during the UP years. Their political influence was great, their economic role strategic. It must not be forgotten that they constituted the economic 'base' of the old American interests operating in

Chile and of the dominant, monopolistic sector of the Chilean bour-geoisie. Their bargaining power was therefore very strong. They already knew, or learned rapidly, how to fight for their interests. They would, had the UP's project been fully implemented, never have become wealthy, but they would undoubtedly have accentuated their general position of constituting a kind of labor aristocracy in Chile (with some noticeable exceptions such as the coal and nitrate miners).

This is not to say that almost all Chileans not directly affected by the UP's program of structural reforms were economically poor. Although Chile's 'very rich' were few indeed, the layer of professionals, medium-sized industrialists, landowners and merchants and relatively well-to-do public officials and private employees comprised perhaps one-fifth of the economically active population. But the point is that the vast majority of the Chilean people could receive no direct benefits from this part of the UP program, and this majority included the hard core of really poor: *minifundistas* and unattached *afuerinos* in the country-side, most of the indigenous population, workers in small-scale industry, *pobladores*, the mass of underemployed urban poor within the inflated services sector, etc. These large and underprivileged groups would continue to be dependent on market forces which would seldom favor them. They would continue to try to make a living as temporary day-laborers, small-scale workers, shoe cleaners, ambulant traders, domestic servants or, in quite a few cases, as petty criminals. It was not for these extremely under-privileged groups that the UP program was written, and it was not their voices that the government – and the traditional working-class parties – listened to. It was not they who could see a solu-tion to their problems in the UP's basically 'anti-monopolistic strategy'. Their political opinions varied between apathy, anarchy, revolutionary socialism and fascism.

It is true that the Allende government did far more for these groups than any previous administration. Almost all social services, which have been neglected in this study – like education, health, social security, free milk to children and cheap school breakfasts – were qualitatively improved and extended to cover a much larger share of the population than before. And, perhaps most important of all when judging the long-range effects of the political, social and economic processes during the Unidad Popular, expectations rose, and hitherto mostly passive masses mobilized to fight for a different and better future.

But our appraisal of the UP program must nevertheless be critical, even if mistakes made in its implementation and difficulties that arose as a result of the overall economic and political situation that prevailed in 1970–73 are disregarded. Not that it constituted a step back, of course, but to solve Chile's tremendous economic and social problems – the whole underdeveloped heritage – a qualitatively different strategy was needed.

The defeat: concluding remarks

Let me first stress one thing: the emphasis put in this study on economic matters should in no way be interpreted as if I wished to attribute the eventual military intervention to the economic crisis that developed under UP rule. I am perfectly convinced that although the economic crisis has often served as a rationalization for the *coup d'état* in the propaganda of the Right in Chile and abroad, the decision of the armed forces and *carabineros* to intervene was in no way *caused* by the economic problems that arose (although these economic problems in a variety of ways certainly contributed to prepare the ground for the victory of the Right). We know, for example, that this decision was taken long before the economic situation became critical. Plots were already being initiated toward the end of 1970, and, according to the junta's own statements, the key persons involved in the preparation of the coup reached preliminary agreement by mid-1972. We also know the Chile's military leaders, with a few exceptions who were gradually being ousted, did absolutely nothing to prevent the united rightist forces from sabotaging the economy and exacerbating the crisis. Particularly during the July–September 1973 waves of lockouts, sabotage, terrorist actions and massive material destruction, the military, first passively and later actively, supported the instigation of chaos, violence and economic dislocation. The revelation of the roles played by the CIA and Dr Kissinger add further evidence to our hypothesis that Salvador Allende's enemies hardly based their subversive activities on concerns for the Chilean economy.

However, the purpose of this study is to analyze the economic and, to some extent, the political aspects of the Chilean process from 1970 to September 1973, and our first conclusion from the whole preceding exposition must be that by the time the armed forces and *carabineros* won their easy military victory the UP had already been defeated on most other battlegrounds.

The most likely explanation of *why* the Unidad Popular was economically and politically defeated may be that the administration's economic policies simply did not work. This analysis is popular among liberal economists who put the emphasis now on devastating repercussions of the short-term program, now on mismanagement by the state administers in the social area or on distortive effects of the nationalization program and the agrarian reform.

All 'inflation-and-chaos' interpretations are full of pitfalls, however, and without a proper understanding of Chile's political reality and of the political reasons behind the economic crisis that developed they can lead to the ridiculous conclusion that the whole UP experiment failed for lack of good economists.

It is imperative to grasp the main political factors at work in order to understand all the limitations that existed in the Allende government's freedom of action. The analysis of these limitations constitutes one of the *leitmotifs* in this study of the UP's attempts towards a Chilean transition to socialism, and we know how the correlation of forces and the general political circumstances that prevailed after 1970 tied the hands of the UP government to an increasingly fatal extent. We also know that the program of the UP itself was pregnant with contradictions of all kinds which were reflected in increasing confrontations not only between the Right and the Left but between different factions of the Unidad Popular itself. And since the Allende government was a coalition of heterogeneous political forces representing different socio-economic strata, it was impossible to achieve a centralized, unified command of the process. Internal UP compromises often had to be made. It was not only the attacks from the opposition which made the government's margin of choice very narrow.

This is not to say, however, that the UP leadership was always 'forced' to act as it did, that all important decisions were predetermined. In both economic and political matters it is obvious that poor decisions were often made by the UP when a situation of choice existed.

The short-term program of 1971 is one example of a choice of policy which created more problems than it solved. This choice could in part be explained as a mere reflection of the UP's belief that it was possible to construct a new society without transitional material sacrifices, but whatever were the economic and political/tactical motives behind it, it turned out to have been a mistake, and the UP leadership gave proof of a serious lack of foresight in failing to assess correctly the medium-term consequences of the drastically expansionist policy with which it started. For what was visible to all by 1972, namely that a host of restrictions had arisen after the initial rapid recovery, should have been understood by the UP from the very beginning. The deep underdevelopment of Chile was known by the whole government, and in the Basic Program of the UP Chile's existing productive capacity and whole economic structure, which could not possibly be changed overnight, were repeatedly proclaimed as being incompatible with economic growth and responsible for the people's misery. But this truth was forgotten when the early advances made many a UP minister talk optimistically about continued expansion along the same lines. An important sector of the UP even believed that the deficient Chilean economic structure could serve to render possible a continued improvement in living standards not only of the low-income groups but also of the relatively well-to-do classes of professionals. This was the illusory corollary to the UP's fundamentally 'anti-monopolistic' strategy based on a hoped-for class alliance with all the 'middle strata' included in the list of enemies to the 'oligarchy'.

But while it is correct to say that the UP gave a huge overdose of traditional economic stimuli in its short-term policy, it is more difficult to agree with those who affirm that the government failed because it went too fast in its nationalization program. For in order to survive it should, I believe, either have given up altogether its expropriation project (except perhaps for the Gran Minería of copper and similar cases where a broad consensus could be reached) or it should have accelerated it further in a decisive attack against the most powerful interests of private business, including certain key sectors which traditionally had never been regarded as very powerful but whose strategic importance in sabotage actions was immense. (Road transportation is the most obvious example). Since the former option was out of the question – such a profound betrayal of the program never even occurred to any segment of the Left – the latter alternative might have been the least impossible one. Only a firm control rapidly gained over all crucial activities could have mitigated the effects of the rightist forces' economic obstruction and created the necessary, although not the sufficient, conditions for the UP to create a planned economy.

I need not repeat the detrimental effects on the economy which the UP's halfway nationalization program gave rise to. We know that both the agrarian reform and the industrial expropriations suffered badly from all the compromises that were made and the antagonisms that were accentuated. One conclusion must be that the Chilean experiences in 1970–73 illustrate very well the general dilemma that is likely to confront any left-oriented government taking over responsibility for an economy controlled by hostile economic interests. President Allende's position was necessarily precarious. He was elected on a program which was radical enough to provoke determined resistance from the domestic and foreign economic establishment, but his government was not strong enough to assume the direction of the economy and force the private sector to obey and neither were the different forms of 'popular power' created by the masses.

This dilemma was further accentuated by specific problems caused by Chile's socio-economic structure. We know that the few workers employed in industries classified as monopolies enjoyed comparatively acceptable living levels. A strict adherence to an 'anti-monopolistic' strategy would then have to clash with the aspirations of the great majority of Chilean workers, while such a limitation of the nationalization program could not possibly serve to placate the rightist opposition. Given the overall ideological and political atmosphere in Chile after 1970, the various contradictions that arose from the application of a basically 'anti-oligarchic' program to a socio-economic structure like Chile's were bound to intensify the political polarization. For the mass of workers had, let it be stressed once again, no objective interests in letting the government expropriate only a handful of companies while leaving all the rest in peace.

The government was challenged from both Left and Right, and it lost most of the control it had once had over the process. The class struggle was converted into a virtual class war, and no solution was possible within the old, constitutional framework. The question of power had to be settled. The gradualistic 'Chilean road' became blocked, and Chile was left with two quite distinct alternatives: revolution or counter-revolution, socialism or fascism. In the confrontation thus approaching, it was counter-revolution that held the winning cards. The overall combination of forces was unfavorable to the Left. It was utterly disadvantageous from an international point of view: under the patronage of the United States and Brazil a powerful rightist offensive swept over Latin America, and the installation of pro-Brazilian military dictatorships in Bolivia and Uruguay in 1971–3 no doubt had a profound impact on the Chilean political situation.

But even apart from the international development it was the bourgeoisie that was strongest. For it was not, as the UP had once hoped, the 'oligarchic' interests that became politically isolated as the struggle intensified; it was the industrial working class. The Left failed to neutralize, let alone win over, all those non-monopolistic and supposedly progressive sectors of private business which played such an important role in the UP's official strategy of class alliances. The alliances that took shape were of a different character; the political expression *par excellence* of medium and small business in Chile in 1972 and 1973 was the overtly pro-fascist *gremialismo* movement.

In this development strictly ideological factors played an important role. The rightist opposition maintained a firm control over the mass media industry, and its experienced anti-communist propaganda fell on fertile ground as the disintegration of the traditional society proceeded. But we also know that it was not without some very objective reasons that almost all small and medium-sized industrialists, landowners, merchants, truck-owners, etc. joined the extreme Right to precipitate the overthrow of Allende. They were quite right in seeing their, often very modest, positions as being threatened by the economic and political process that was taking place. (Although they did not realize that most of them would be far worse off under a semifascist military dictatorship representing the interests of the big bourgeoisie. But this is another story.)

When discussing the behavior of medium- and small-scale business it should also be emphasized that Chile's large industrial and financial groups had a power which went far beyond the control of their own 'monopolies'. Through a variety of economic and political means the few large corporations could exercise a dominant influence over a great number of non-monopolistic enterprises. Many UP leaders no doubt overestimated the latter's degree of independence, thereby underestimating the danger of a confrontation with the whole sector of private business when a 'handful of monopolies' were attacked.

It also appears that the distinction often made by the UP between 'imperialist interests' and the 'national bourgeoisie' was politically irrelevant. No segment of the bourgeoisie showed any inclination to unite with the 'popular forces' in their struggle against foreign dominance. No anti-US feelings were, for example, ever expressed by the organizations that represented medium- and small-scale business.

This should, on the other hand, hardly come as a surprise. From chapter 1, especially, we recall the heavy impact of foreign investment in strategic sectors of the economy by the time the UP took office, and subsequent economic and political events in Chile added proof to Salvador Allende's previously quoted diagnosis of the Chilean bourgeoisie: 'The penetration and domination of foreign capital has been so accentuated during the last few years [i.e. under Eduardo Frei] that it has made the so-called national bourgeoisie virtually invisible.'

To confine the influence of foreign capital only to direct foreign investment would indicate a kind of optical illusion. A far larger number of companies than those directly owned by foreign capital were thoroughly dependent on foreign patents and licensing arrangements and on imports of spare parts, machinery, fuels and equipment. The UP's denouncements of the United States for economic aggression against Chile – the ITT documents, the 'invisible blockade', etc. – only served to increase these groups' desire to improve Chile's relations with the United States by getting rid of Allende. Add to this the fears of the middle strata that the UP's policies were jeopardizing the availability of imported consumer goods, and we can more easily understand why the Chilean economy's foreign dependence made the number of allies in the anti-imperialist struggle fall appreciably short of many UP leaders' early expectations.

The Chilean Left had another handicap which was also in part only the political expression of economic factors inherited from the past. Chilean society's class structure did not facilitate the Allende government's task. In particular the low numerical weight of the industrial working class and the extreme heterogeneity with respect to socio-economic conditions and political consciousness among the 'popular forces' weakened the position of the UP tremendously, while the increasingly unified Right managed to mobilize large sectors of the petty-bourgeoisie and even of the urban subproletariat around a project which was so simple that internal contradictions could be temporarily buried. The solid core of UP supporters, the 'classical proletariat' of blue-collar workers in manufacturing, mining and construction, was both relatively small in number and insufficiently prepared to replace the bourgeoisie as the dominant class of the Chilean society. If we look for explanations of the UP's failure which go beyond 'erroneous strategic concepts', 'reformism' or simply 'mistakes' the following passage by Friedrich Engels indicates part of the answer: 'The worst thing that can befall a leader of an extreme party is to be compelled to take over a government at a time when society is not yet ripe for the domination of the class he represents and for the measures which that domination implies . . . He who is put in this awkward position is irrevocably lost.'[4]

The question of whether Allende was 'irrevocably lost' from the very beginning or whether he and what he represented *became* lost as a consequence of mistakes which could have been avoided can never be answered. What is, however, certain is that the Unidad Popular never came very close to reaching its overriding objective of gaining power in society as a whole. With the exception of the executive power, all vital branches of the state apparatus – the Congress, the judiciary, the armed forces, etc. – remained in the hands of adverseries, and this in a process of radical social change when all kinds of extra-parliamentary opposition and sabotage made control of the legislative and repressive organs of state power absolutely indispensable. But these opposition-controlled bastions were never conquered by the UP, whose leadership adopted a defensive, conciliatory line, thereby relinquishing all attempts to take state power. The offensive preceding and following upon the 1970 election continued on the *fundos*, in the factories and in the *poblaciones*, but on the governmental level it was gradually being replaced by a policy based on concessions. As the government was already on the defensive the UP's bargaining position became poorer and poorer. The concessions made did not serve to facilitate viable agreements with the opposition but to encourage the latter, making it more and more inclined to aggressive actions of resistance and sabotage.

The struggle for power was irrevocably lost. President Allende was in practice defeated long before 11 September 1973. Whether a different strategy by a different group of leaders would have succeeded in Chile in 1970–73 is impossible to tell; all we can say with certainty is that the policy actually pursued by the Unidad Popular was doomed to failure.

Notes

1. AN INTRODUCTION TO THE CHILEAN ECONOMY

1 For a more detailed account of Chilean economic history see S. de Vylder, *From Colonialism to Dependence: An Introduction to Chile's Economic History*, 1974.

2 Osvaldo Sunkel in Claudio Véliz (ed.), *Obstacles to Change in Latin America*, 1966, p. 119.

3 The following reflections from 1796 by Manuel De Salas, then Minister of Finance, show that this contradiction was clearly recognized almost two centuries ago:

'The Kingdom of Chile is, without comparison, the most fertile in all America; yet it is the most miserable of all Spanish Dominions. Possessing everything, it lacks the necessary...

The parks and streets are day after day full of robust workers who, underselling each other, offer their services in exchange for goods that are often useless and expensive ... Nobody can say that a work has been left unfinished because of lack of manpower. As soon as a job is offered, hundreds of people show up... In the mines, where work is hard, there are more people than work. It is not from indolence, but from lack of employment opportunities, that the people suffer... Instead of giving occupation to one-quarter of its inhabitants, this Kingdom should be able to employ at least seventeen times as many people as it already has...'

Freely translated from De Salas, *On the State of Agriculture, Industry and Commerce*, reprinted in Hernán Gódoy (ed.), *Estructura Social de Chile*, 1971, pp. 139ff.

4 Marto Ballesteros & Tom Davis, 'The growth of output and employment in basic sectors of the Chilean economy 1908–1957', *Economic Development and Cultural Change*, vol. XI, no. 2, 1962.

5 See Samir Amin, *L'Accumulation à l'Echelle Mondiale. Critique de la Théorie du Sous-developpement*, 1970.

Comparing today's underdeveloped countries with the old undeveloped, precolonial societies Amin notes that the latter, as well as modern developed countries, by the large were 'des societés cohérentes, caractérisées par un correspondance entre ses diverses secteurs'. An 'économie désarticulée', on the other hand, is characterized by an 'absence de communications entre des différentes secteurs' (pp. 25–6).

6 Cf. ch. 7.

7 In accordance with Anglo-Saxon convention the word 'American' will for simplicity

sometimes be used in this study when the Latin American expression would be *norteamericano*.

8 A. G. Frank, *Capitalism and Underdevelopment in Latin America*, 2nd edn., 1969, p. 102.
9 Next to the somewhat special case of Israel.
10 Frank, *Capitalism and Underdevelopment*, pp. 104–5.

2. THE UNIDAD POPULAR

1 See Patricio Manns, *Las Grandes Masacres de Chile*, 1972.
2 In Puerto Montt 9 March 1969. A squatters' camp erected after an illegal land occupation was attacked and burnt down by the riot police, and ten *pobladores*, including several children and pregnant women, were shot dead as they rose from sleep at 6.30 a.m.
3 The Radical Party supported and participated with ministers in every cabinet since 1938, with the exception of the Christian Democratic minority government, 1964–70.
4 For a discussion of the PC–PS divergencies, see pp. 38–40.
5 Cf. ch. 7.
6 Data from *El Primer Mensaje del Presidente Allende ante el Congreso Pleno*, 21 May 1971 (hereafter referred to as *First Message*), p. 603.
7 See Clotario Blest, 'Los trabajadores: su organización sindical', in *Punto Final* no. 108, July 1970.
8 Allende, *First Message*, p. 609.
9 Provoked by a rise in collective transportation fares – a not uncommon cause of riots in Latin America.
10 Naturally, Communists and Socialists had been working in the *poblaciones* for years, but without ever being able to organize much more than isolated land seizures by homeless families.

   The revolutionary potential of the *pobladores* was traditionally grossly underestimated by the Chilean Left, which often bunched them together under the disdainful – and erroneous – label *lumpenproletariat*. The extremely hostile attitude of Marx and Engels towards the so-called *lumpenproletariat* – 'this scum of depraved elements from all classes, with headquarters in the big cities, is the worst of all possible allies', etc. – probably exerted an influence, but the Chilean Left soon had to realize that Santiago's *pobladores* were quite different from the thieves and prostitutes of mid nineteenth-century Paris.
11 According to official data from the PDC's National Council of Popular Promotion, total membership in these organizations reached 2,467,000 in 1969, but these figures certainly include some double counting. C. Jorge Giusti, 'Political Participation in Chile. Three Types of 'Pobladores' Organization', 1971, p. 7.
12 To borrow Jorge Giusti's expression.
13 E. Labarca, *Chile al Rojo*, 1971, pp. 256–7.
14 The Senate, 50 seats, and the House of Deputies, 150 seats. At the time of the election the UP had 80, the PDC 75 and the Right 45 of the 200 senators and deputies.
15 The Chilean material on the events of September–October is abundant, and the

story was told over and over again in the Chilean press. Among the sources I have drawn most upon should be mentioned four, however: *Chile al Rojo* by Eduardo Labarca, *Chile: Una Economía de Transición?* by Sergio Ramos, articles in *Monthly Review*, vol. 22, no, 8, January 1971, and *Documentos Secretos de la ITT* (hereafter referred to as *ITT documents*). The latter, consisting of memos written by agents from the CIA temporarily employed at the International Telephone and Telegraph Company's branch office in Chile, are especially valuable. Their authenticity has been officially recognized, and they contain much, although perhaps not always accurate, information which is difficult to obtain from other sources.

16 For figures, see Amérigo Zorrilla, *Exposición sobre la Política Económica del Gobierno y del Estado de la Hacienda Pública 27.11.1970* (hereafter referred to as *First Exposition*), p. 78.

17 In September these sales reached 17.5 million dollars and in October 13.6 million, as compared with an average of 5.3 million during the first eight months of the year. Ramos, *Chile*, p. 139.

18 See *Monthly Review*, January 1971, p. 4. 'It is worth remembering,' the *MR* editorial points out, 'that the election of Labor Governments in Britain or Social Democratic governments in Scandinavia has never evoked a similar compliment from the local bourgeoisies.'

19 For a complete text of Zaldívar's report, known by the Left as the 'terror speech', see *El Mercurio*, 24 September 1970. Cf. also the *ITT documents* (especially p. 24) where the speech is referred to as if it were part of a general plan to provoke economic chaos, a plan which is said to be 'encouraged by some sectors in the business and political community and by President Frei himself'.

20 Supported by Washington, according to the *ITT documents* (p. 10): 'Last Tuesday night [15 September] Ambassador Korry finally received a message from the State Department giving him the green light to move in the name of President Nixon. The message gave him maximum authority to do all possible – short of a Dominican Republican action – to keep Allende from power.'

21 *Ibid.* p. 21.

22 Which is clearly recognized in the *ITT documents*.

23 See Banco Central, *Boletín Mensual* no. 515, January 1971, p. 23.

24 The *ITT documents*, p. 23.

25 *Ibid.* p. 14.

26 *Ibid.* p. 34.

27 *US News and World Report*, 30 November 1970, p. 39.

28 Naturally, we will often have to refer to other sources, such as authoritative statements by Allende and other leading UP politicians, when interpreting the program, and we will also see that although the whole UP always declared the execution of the program to be the government's prime objective, there was considerable divergence of opinion about how and at what pace this should be achieved.

29 Zorrilla, *First Exposition*, p. 9.

30 Speech made at an Alliance for Progress meeting in Washington on 22 February 1971. Reprinted in a Martner (ed.), *El Pensamiento Económico del Gobierno de Allende*, 1971, pp. 97–111.

31 See 'La experiencia Chilena. Problemas económicos', in CESO–CEREN, *Transición al Socialismo y Experiencia Chilena* (based on a symposium held in October 1971), p. 100.

32 *Ibid.*

33 *Ibid.* p. 101.

34 In Spanish *trabajadores*, which includes all working people: blue-collar workers, *campesinos*, etc. The Spanish word for (manual) worker is *obrero*.

35 Allende, *First Message*, p. vii.

36 *Ibid.* p. xii.

37 *Ibid.* p. vi. Naturally, the UP repeatedly emphasized that only through the realization of an anti-imperialist and anti-oligarchic transformation of society could the formal democracy guaranteed in the constitution be given a real and not merely formal content. An economic structure characterized by foreign control and monopolistic concentration was denounced by Allende as the 'very negation of democracy'. *El Segundo Mensaje del Presidente Allende ante el Congreso Pleno*, 21 May 1972 (hereafter referred to as *Second Message*), p. xi.

38 Allende, *First Message*, p. xi.

39 'Informe al Pleno del Comité Central del Partido Communista', November 1970, cited in Ramos, *Chile*, p. 30.

40 Hernán del Canto, leading Socialist and for some time Minister of the Interior. Speech given in November 1972, here taken from *Punto Final*, supplement to no. 172, 5 December 1972, p. 22.

41 'The realization of the social changes requires, above all, a mobilization of the masses' – a message repeated over and over again. This particular quotation is taken from a joint statement by the UP parties, published in *El Mercurio*, 2 February 1972.

42 See, for example, Allende's speech on 'Participation and Mobilization' in Juan Garcés (ed.), *Nuestro Camino al Socialismo – la Vía Chilena*, 1971, pp. 89–101.

43 With respect to small-scale business the UP program declared that the 'monopolistic firms' exploited the small ones through 'selling them their raw materials at high prices while buying cheaply', and that the state had so far served only the interests of the big monopolies. Under the UP government, small-scale enterprise would 'benefit from the overall planning of the economy'. The state should 'provide the necessary technical and financial assistance to the firms of this sector, enabling them to fulfill an important role in the national economy'.

44 As a very rough indication of the various political forces' strength we can look at the results of the municipal elections in April 1971, where the UP managed to get slightly over 50 per cent of the valid votes: PS, 22.9 per cent; PC, 17.4 per cent; PR, 8.2 per cent; other UP groups, 2.4 per cent. The opposition, 49.1 per cent.

It should be pointed out, however, that the PC's organizational solidity and discipline made the party far heavier politically than its electoral results would indicate. The PS, on the other hand, was comparatively poorly organized and consisted of a large number of different factions and tendencies. The fact that I often make use of the Socialists' documents and analyses when illustrating strategic differences within the Chilean Left should not be interpreted as if the PS pursued a consistent 'revolutionary' line against the Communists' 'reformism'. The policy of the PS was, in fact, very contradictory.

45 For a good overview of the positions of the PC and the PS during the 1960s see

James Petras, *Politics and Social Forces in Chilean Development*, 1969, pp. 182ff, or Carlos Cerda, *El Leninismo y la Victoria Popular*, 1971, pp. 107ff. A great many Socialist documents referring to the PS–PC controversies are found in Julio César Jobet & Alejandro Chelén (eds.), *Pensamiento Teórico y Político del Partido Socialista*, 1972.

46 It is significant that the PS, and even more the MIR, tended to emphasize the need of the industrial working class to get allies 'from below' – *campesinos*, unemployed, the laboring poor in the *poblaciones*, etc. – much more than the PC did. The Communists worked for alliances 'upwards', with the middle class of small businessmen and salary earners.

47 Cited in Cerda, *El Leninismo y la Victoria Popular*, p. 198.

48 The following remark by Allende, who should not be taken for a representative of the most radical wing of the PS, is quite typical: 'The penetration and domination of foreign capital has been so accentuated during the last few years that it has made the so-called national bourgeoisie virtually invisible.' In Regis Debray's interview with Allende in *Punto Final*, 16 March 1971, p. 31.

49 Which leaked out and was published in *El Mercurio*, 12 and 13 March 1972. Its authenticity was confirmed by the PS.

50 The party rivalry within the UP was in fact institutionalized through a rigid quota system for the distribution of posts, not only in the government but in the whole public administration. Every UP official far down in the hierarchy was appointed politically, and every one should have an immediate superior and an immediate subordinate from parties other than his own. While such a system might have created 'justice' within the governing coalition it was hardly conducive to efficiency, and the problems with the huge Chilean bureaucracy were further aggravated by the fact that almost all functionaries from preceding governments remained in their jobs, albeit deprived of much of their power.

3. THEORETICAL PROSPECTS OF THE 'CHILEAN ROAD'

1 There exists, on the other hand, an abundant Marxist literature dealing with the concept 'transition to socialism'. Since this discussion is of limited relevance for the present study I will not delve into this problematic area here. Suffice it to observe that there seems to prevail a general consensus in this 'transition debate' about at least one thing: in order to qualify for being in a stage of transition to socialism a society must meet two fundamental and necessary requirements: 1. The working class (in alliance with other non-bourgeois classes and sectors) must have taken power and have replaced the old state with a new, proletarian state. 2. The socialist mode of production must have become the dominant (albeit not the only) mode of production within the economy. These two criteria need further definition and clarification, of course – and here consensus tends to come to an end – but no Marxist arguing along the lines sketched above would maintain that Chile after a couple of years of Unidad Popular would deserve to be called a 'transitional economy'.

For recent contributions to this debate, see Charles Bettelheim, *La Transition vers l'Économie Socialiste*, 1968, and Luis Althusser and Etienne Balibar, *Lire le Capital*, 1968, and the Paul Sweezy–Charles Bettelheim discussion in successive issues of *Monthly Review* during 1968 to 1971. Special reference to the Chilean case is made in Ramos, *Chile*, and in CESO–CEREN *Transición al Socialismo y Experiencia Chilena.*

2 O. Lange, *On the Economic Theory of Socialism*, 1938, pp. 123–4.

3 *Ibid*. pp. 125–6.

4 *Ibid*. p. 126.

5 The one in force during the UP regime dated from 1925, when the constitution of 1833 was revised (but not fundamentally changed). The modifications made after 1925 were primarily designed to strengthen the position of the president *vis-à-vis* the parliament.

A revised text, up to date at August 1971, is found in Francisco Complida & Cecilia Medina, *Constitución Política de la República de Chile*, 1971.

6 The *Tribunal Constitucional* was established only in 1970, and nobody really knew its exact function. Between 1970 and 1973 it intervened on only a few occasions – always at the request of Allende, who wanted the *Tribunal* to support the executive's view (which it almost always did). Its political role was quite insignificant in comparison with the other state authorities mentioned in the constitution.

7 The Congress had, for example, no influence whatsoever upon the designation of ministers, and the members of the Supreme Court could only be nominated by the Supreme Court itself.

8 For military appointments the approval by the Senate was required, however. It should also be observed that, before taking office, Allende signed an agreement with the Christian Democrats in which he promised not to make any changes in the hierarchy of the armed forces. Allende was for all practical purposes bound to respect the military's own decisions with respect to appointments unless he was prepared to accept an open confrontation. This promise hardly contributed to upgrading the prospects of the 'Chilean road to socialism'.

9 But the executive could – and this is what the Chilean administrations have traditionally done – evade part of this inconvenience through the utilization of Central Bank credits for the financing of public expenditures. The fact that the constitution stated that the budget must be 'balanced' hardly contributed to the enforcing of a strict orthodoxy in fiscal policies, since credits from the Central Bank were presented simply as 'capital incomes'.

The 'normal' budgetary procedure in Chile – where almost all twentieth-century governments have been either minority governments or have been sustained by rather precarious parliamentary coalitions – has been the following:

1. The government presents its budget, which already at this stage contains an appreciable amount of 'capital income' as well as the customary tax increase proposals.

2. The parliament rejects all tax rises and cuts down a more or less equivalent amount of public expenditures.

3. The executive accepts the modifications introduced by the Congress but insists in practice on its spending proposals, which are financed by Central Bank credits.

10 By the time Allende took office the UP could count on more than one-third but less than half of the seats in both the Senate and the House of Deputies. Later party splits and complementary elections did nothing to alter this fundamental relationship, and neither did the parliamentary elections of March 1973.

11 The Supreme Court openly showed its position before Allende had taken office through its sensational refusal to repeal the parliamentary immunity of an extremist senator involved in the assassination of General Schneider (see ch. 2, p. 31).

12 For a detailed compilation of ownership and control of Chile's radio stations and newspapers by 1972, see report to the Senate by Senator Valente (PC), reproduced in *El Mercurio*, 16 November 1972. Cf. also Stefan de Vylder, *From Colonialism to Dependence. An Introduction to Chile's Economic History*, 1974, 6.

13 Among these exceptions the mining workers of Chuquicamata deserve to be mentioned in particular. Here, in Chile's and the world's largest open cast copper mine, the Chilean Left had always had difficulties, presumably as a result of these miners' comparatively privileged economic position *vis-à-vis* other Chilean workers (one of many political aspects of the problems created by the huge productivity differences found between different sectors of the Chilean economy). In Chuquicamata Allende was, in fact, defeated by the right-wing candidate Jorge Alessandri in the 1970 presidential election. Early in 1973 many of the copper miners in El Teniente, till then regarded as overwhelmingly leftist dominated, carried through a prolonged strike with clear anti-UP connotations. However, in most of the copper strikes that affected Chile in 1971–3 only technical and administrative personnel participated.

14 Cf. ch. 1 above and, for more details, de Vylder, *From Colonialism to Dependence*, ch. 6.

15 ODEPLAN, 'Balance de Mano de Obra', *Nueva Economía* no. 1, September–October 1971, p. 45.

16 For an analysis of the voting pattern of Chilean men and women see *Chile Hoy* no. 34, 2–8 February 1973.

   In the 1970 election Allende got 41.6 per cent of male votes as against only 30.5 per cent of female votes, and in the April 1971 municipal election the UP's figures were 53.4 and 43.6 per cent, respectively. The trend during the UP period was unmistakable, however: more and more women integrated themselves into political work, and the Center–Right electoral hegemony among housewives was gradually being broken.

4. THE SHORT-TERM ECONOMIC PROGRAM

1 The mimeographed document that resulted from this preparatory work is dated 19 October 1970. On the circumstances under which this document, 'Orientaciones Básicas del Programa Económico de Corto Plazo', was prepared, see Sergio Ramos (who was one of the collaborators) in *Chile*, pp. 167ff and 261.

2 Cited in Ramos, *Chile*, p. 167.

3 Banco Central, *Boletín Mensual* no. 531, May 1972, p. 535.

4 Allende, *Second Message*, p. 18.

5 See Zorrilla, *First Exposition*, pp. 24ff.

6 A fact that undoubtedly worried the government, which repeatedly urged the workers to be moderate in their negotiations and to accept the governmental norms only. The following answer by Allende to an interviewer indicates how delicate the problem was.

   Interviewer: For decades the Socialist and Communist parties in Chile have encouraged the workers to demand stiff wage hikes. Now these demands hurt your government, and may well undermine your economic policies. What course of action do you plan to take in this respect?

Allende: It is not easy to persuade workers who have acquired certain habits to give them up or to explain to them that they are no longer striking against those who exploit but against a government representing their own interests. But we have undertaken an intense effort of political education. Its results have been mixed so far, and this problem remains our Achilles' heel.

Many Chileans are convinced that a socialist government is supposed to make each citizen a lottery winner.

From *Guardian*, 29 March 1972.

7 All data from Zorrilla, *Second Exposition.*

8 In Santiago the *sueldo vital* was increased to 832 escudos, but it varied slightly between different provinces. In 1972 it was made equal throughout the country.

9 The government did propose some modest tax raises, but they were all turned down by Congress.

10 On the price policy of the UP, see pp. 58ff.

11 The latter increased substantially in number during 1971, which makes comparisons with preceding years somewhat misleading.

In Chilean legislation, as well as in Chilean statistics, the public sector was composed of three sectors: the 'fiscal sector', the 'decentralized sector', and the 'sector of public enterprises'. The first and third of these require no explanations, and the 'decentralized sector' was made up of various public institutes such as CORA, CORFO, etc. With respect to the financing of these three sectors the border-lines were far from clear; they were all to a large extent financed with credits, over which the parliamentary influence was non-existent. What the Congress decided was, at the most, only the degree of deficit financing.

12 Instituto de Economía, *La Economía Chilena en 1971*, p. 161.

13 Ministerio de la Vivienda y Urbanismo, *Política Habitacional del Gobierno Popular*, pp. 22 and 45.

14 From 827.9 to 2,167.6 million escudos. See Zorrilla, *Second Exposition*, p. 82.

15 Speech given at the Alliance for Progress meeting in Washington, February 1971. Reproduced in Martner (ed.), *El Pensamiento Económico*, pp. 253–67.

16 On the nationalization of the banking system, see ch. 6, pp. 157–9.

17 See speech by the president of the Central Bank, in Martner (ed.), *El Pensamiento Económico.*

18 ODEPLAN, *Informe Económico Anual 1971*, p. 40.

19 Based on Banco Central, *Boletín Mensual* no. 537, November 1972, p. 1360. Cf. also ch. 5, table 5.3.

20 The passage on inflation in the 'Basic Program' of the UP reads as follows: 'The rising cost of living creates havoc in people's homes ... Every day the Chileans who live from the proceeds of their work are robbed of part of their wages and salaries ... Alessandri and Frei gave assurances that they would put an end to inflation. The results are there for all to see. The facts prove that inflation in Chile is basically the outcome of deeper causes related to the capitalist structure of our society and not to wage increases as successive governments, in order to justify the system and restrain the workers' incomes, have tried to make us believe.'

21 Zorrilla, *First Exposition*, p. 22.

22 The Communist newspapers particularly published almost every day small features

showing one or more Chilean *stachanovites*, and participation in voluntary work on Saturdays and vacations was stimulated.

23 There also existed a brokers' market, used for foreign tourists, for Chileans travelling abroad, and for various non-commercial external transactions. On the brokers' market the exchange rate was set at 28 escudos to the dollar, and a host of taxes were introduced on purchases of foreign exchange for tourist purposes. On the black market, which enjoyed a considerable upswing after September 1970, the price of the dollar was later to rise to between five and ten times the official brokers' rate.

24 Instituto de Economía, *La Economía Chilena en 1971*, p. 77. Figures refer to establishments employing fifty or more people.

25 By far the best employment studies were the inquiries made by the Institute of Economics at the University of Chile. However these studies covered only three urban regions in Chile: Greater Santiago, Concepción-Talcahuano and Lota-Coronel (the last two dominated by manufacturing industry and mining, respectively). If not otherwise stated all my data on the employment situation in these regions have been taken directly from the Institute of Economics, which published the results of the inquiries four times a year for Santiago and twice a year for Concepción-Talcahuano and Lota-Coronel.

26 Banco Central, *Boletín Mensual* no. 516, February 1971, p. 157. 'Net foreign exchange reserves' were calculated as the Central Bank's gross reserves minus short-term liabilities. The existence of foreign exchange in the rest of the banking system could be considered negligible – some ten million dollars in December 1970.

27 See ODEPLAN, *Resumen del Plan de la Economía Nacional 1971–76*, table 1, p. 24, and ODEPLAN, *Antecedentes sobre el Desarrollo Chileno 1960–70*, p. 43.

28 Large-scale industry also found its access to imported machinery and credit somewhat curtailed; the borderline between economic 'resistance' and simple financial problems is not easy to draw.

29 See ch. 6.

30 The notion of 'irregularities' was, in the eyes of the workers and the government, quite wide, and the 'rules of the game' in the economy were thus drastically changed. A refusal to utilize installed capacity, a decline in the purchases of raw material, or stock-piling of finished goods could, for example, often be considered worthy of sanctions.

31 Other sources indicate a slightly lower rate of growth in 1971; some 8.0–8.4 per cent.

32 In Chile a good year means a rainy winter with a lot of snow accumulating in the Andes which during the whole summer can provide the irrigated soils in the Central Valley with water. In the southern provinces, however, where every winter is rainy and a large part of the rest of the year as well, the problem is generally too much rain and too little sunshine.

33 ODEPLAN, *Informe Económico Anual 1971*, p. 97.

34 The number of housing units under construction by CORVI increased from less than 10,000 at the end of 1970 to over 40,000 at the end of 1971. Ministerio de la Vivienda y Urbanismo, *Política Habitacional del Gobierno Popular*, pp. 54–5.

35 For details on the initiation and completion of public residential construction during the period 1971–2, see Instituto de Economía, *La Economía Chilena en 1972*, pp. 374ff.

36 ODEPLAN, *Informe Económico Anual 1971*, pp. 21ff.

37 A comparison which is not quite exact, however, since the situation in December

1970 was unusually bad owing to the fact that the 1970 inflation was much higher than the general wage readjustment at the beginning of the year. The official consumer price index of 1971 also underrates the real rate of inflation somewhat, since shortages had already begun to appear, especially of certain foodstuffs, and official prices were not always kept.

The messy situation in Chile with wage and salary adjustments based on the inflation during the preceding period makes real income estimates very hazardous, and almost anything can be 'proved' with a suitable choice of months to compare (which does not, of course, prevent fairly accurate comparisons over longer periods). Data on output and consumption in physical terms are clearly preferable to calculations of nominal income and inflation when estimating changes in real income – especially in 1972, when black and grey markets by and large destroyed the INE's efforts to make the consumer price index reflect the real rise in the cost of living (some efforts were however made to weigh together official and non-official prices in the index).

38 ODEPLAN, *Informe Económico Anual 1971*, p. 26.

39 30 million dollars, according to ODEPLAN, ibid. p. 49.

40 Banco Central, *Boletín Mensual* no. 531, May 1972, p. 542. Since the figures are expressed in US dollars it should be remembered that the dollar depreciated ten per cent in 1971.

41 ODEPLAN gives the following aggregate figures on Chile's capital account 1967–71 (million dollars):

1967   + 123.9
1968   + 303.5
1969   + 238.2
1970   + 148.5
1971   − 99.7

Informe Económico Anual 1971, p. 61.

42 Vuskovic in Banco Central, *Boletín Mensual* no. 531, May 1972, p. 544.

43 For a selection of official US statements, see Banco Central, *Boletín Mensual* no. 533, July 1972, pp. 796ff and NACLA, *Chile: Facing the Blockade*, 1972.

44 In 1971 Chile paid 310 million dollars to her creditor countries in interest and amortization payments, while she escaped with only about 100 million in 1972.

45 In Banco Central, *Boletín Mensual*, no. 531, May 1972, p. 548.

46 From 79 to 71 per 1,000 live births.

47 Although it could, of course, be argued – and has been argued by many economists – that consumption of health and sanitary services as well as of foodstuffs ought to be regarded as investment in human capital in countries where a large part of the population suffers from serious physical and mental deficiencies due to lack of calories and proteins.

48 Even Allende, who was strongly against the idea of dissolving the Parliament in 1971, later regretted the decision to 'postpone' the plebiscite. See speech delivered on 19 January 1973, in *El Mercurio*, 20 January 1973.

5. 1972 AND 1973: INFLATION AND STAGNATION

1 In the March 1973 parliamentary elections the UP got 43.4 per cent of the votes, as against 54.7 per cent for the so-called CODE (*Confederación Democrática – sic*), i.e. the electoral alliance uniting the PDC, PN and a couple of minor rightist parties.

The results were in general considered very satisfactory by the UP; they signified a decline compared to April 1971, of course, but the UP figures were only insignificantly lower than in two by-elections held early in 1972 – when economic difficulties had hardly yet arisen – to fill some vacant seats in Congress. And the UP poll remained far above the 1970 percentage of 36.3 per cent. Allende's electoral performance compared very favorably to that of Eduardo Frei, whose precipitate loss of popular support was described above (cf. ch. 2, p. 24).

2 The 1972 and 1973 figures would have been even higher if Allende had not chosen to suspend beforehand two ministers against whom the Right had initiated 'constitutional accusations'.

3 Perhaps we should say run by the military. One of the very last decisions to be taken in the Chilean National Congress was the notorious declaration of 22 August 1973 which solemnly stated that the Allende government was 'unconstitutional', 'illegitimate' and 'undemocratic' and had lost its right to govern the country. This declaration was the official *carte blanche* from the rightist deputies and senators for the military take-over and subsequent closure of, among many other things, the Congress.

4 One example deserves to be given: the Chilean courts' handling of the 'Schneider case', i.e. the trial of the assassins of former Commander-in-Chief René Schneider (see ch. 2, p. 31). The professed leader of the rightist league responsible for the murder of Schneider, ex-general Roberto Viaux, was first sentenced to twenty years in prison, but after appeals to higher authorities the penalty was reduced to five and, in the Supreme Court, to two years of imprisonment and five years of exile. Viaux, who never tried to hide his guilt and who even dedicated himself to writing books about how he planned and directed the plots of October 1970, recovered his liberty and went to Paraguay to live a comfortable life while the UP was still in 'power'. Minor rightist terrorists had absolutely nothing to fear; they were always released on bail.

5 See interview in *El Mercurio*, 2 April 1972.

6 The role played by the associations of technicians, doctors, dentists, nurses, etc. cannot be dealt with in detail here, but it must be stressed that political strikes by these groups contributed a great deal to weakening the Allende government's position. The cynical sabotage on the part of the physicians deserves to be mentioned in particular, and the following remark made by the then president of the Chilean Medical Association, Eduardo Cruz Mena, in August 1973 is quite representative: 'Of course people will be dying for lack of medical assistance – in a war one has to kill.' (Answer to a question asked by a television interviewer, wondering whether the Medical Association's decision to cancel even emergency duties in all hospitals would result in many people dying.) Cited in *Chile Hoy* no. 64, 31 August–6 September 1973.

7 The 'October crisis', which lasted for more than three weeks, was solved in two different ways. First by a truly impressive mobilization of the whole Left, in particular of the industrial workers (including many Christian Democratic workers) who kept production up in addition to helping to solve the serious distribution problems that arose. Huge contingents of students, housewives, unemployed, etc. also participated in the emergency works organized by the Left, and to the great disappointment to the opposition the rightist forces proved incapable of 'paralyzing Chile' against this mobilization. The crisis was also solved by conciliation. At the request of Allende, three high military officials (including the then Commander-in-Chief,

Carlos Prats) entered the cabinet when the Right's offensive was already in a stage of complete disintegration.

8 Cf. ch. 2, pp. 38—40.

9 'La Clase Obrera en Condiciones del Gobierno de la Unidad Popular'. *El Siglo*, 5 June 1972.

10 A somewhat extreme position in this respect was taken by *El Siglo*, the PC's official daily, which could, for example, assert that 'the most revolutionary task of the moment is the Battle of Production of Copper. Victory or defeat in our revolutionary process depends on this battle.' (Editorial, 2 February 1972).

11 *Chile Hoy* no. 27, 15—21 December 1972.

12 Published in *El Mercurio* 12 and 13 March 1972. See ch. 2, n. 49.

13 Speech published in *Posición* no. 37, 18 January 1973. Cf. also interview in *Punto Final* no. 177, February 1973, where Altamirano, when asked whether a 'confrontation' (understood as armed confrontation) was 'likely', 'possible to avoid' or 'inevitable', gave the simple answer 'inevitable'.

14 As pointed out by Arghiri Emmanuel (*Unequal Exchange, A Study of the Imperialism of Trade*, 1972, p. 180), exactly the opposite is characteristic of periods of relative tranquility.

15 *El Mercurio*, 2 May 1971, reproduced in the same paper on 17 January 1973.

16 The INE did try to take prices on the 'parallel' markets into account on several items which were traded mostly outside the official channels, but in spite of these efforts the INE index undoubtedly underrated the rate of inflation more and more. In September—October 1973, when the military junta abolished almost all price controls, prices of foodstuffs increased more than five times on the average, and the true rise in the consumer price index probably exceeded 800 per cent for the whole year.

17 In order to 'absorb liquidity', as the UP economists sometimes put it, the prices of passenger cars were, for instance, raised far above the general index. For example, in November 1970 a Fiat 600 cost 48,000 escudos, and two years later the official price had gone up to 490,000 escudos: on the black market a Fiat 600 would be sold for even more.

18 The Millas—Matus price policy was also part of the general strategy of conciliation; the rightist opposition had long been exacting 'fair prices' in order to stimulate profits and production.

19 Cf. ch. 4, p. 53.

20 For details of the budgetary development, see Banco Central, *Boletín Mensual* no. 542, April 1973, pp. 354ff.

21 Cf., for example, Zorrilla, *Second Exposition*, pp. 28ff.

22 *Chile Hoy* no. 17, 6—12 October 1972.

23 Interview in *Chile Hoy* no. 37, 23 February — 1 March 1973.

24 Representative statements along these lines were given by Altamirano in interviews in *Punto Final* no. 177, 13 February 1973, and in *Ultima Hora*, 28 February 1973.

25 This was also recognized by the Tribunal Constitucional which in April pronounced a judgement supporting the administration's interpretation.

26 These were the Treasury's own, very approximate estimates. See *Ultima Hora*, 13 September 1972, or *Ercilla* no. 1940, 20—26 September 1972.

27 The new tax rates accepted in Congress are shown in the table on p. 233.

Income bracket (number of *sueldos vitales*)[a]	Marginal tax rates (per cent)	Estimate of share of wage and salary earners within each income group[b]
0–5	10	85.4
5–10	15	10.2
10–15	20	
15–20	30	3.6
20–30	40	
30–40	45	0.8
40–50	50	

[a] One *sueldo vital* equalled 2,033 escudos per month in Oct. 1972.

[b] Extremely rough estimates.

SOURCES: Tax tables: *Ultima Hora*, 2 Oct. 1972. Income distribution: *Panorama Económico* no. 272, Oct. 1972 (based on inquiries made in 1971).

NOTE: From the above tables we can see that since income taxation was based not on nominal wages but on multiples of *sueldos vitales* the system lacked the 'automatic stabilizers' existing in countries with progressive tax scales based on nominal wages.

28 *El Mercurio*, 23 March 1973.

29 The cries 'Chile sí, Cuba no!' indicated another target for the women's attacks: Fidel Castro was just about to leave Chile after a long visit as Allende's guest.

30 A small and unpretentious poll made by the Christian Democratic magazine *Ercilla* in September 1972 gives a clear indication of the differences of opinion that existed between wealthy and poor Chileans with respect to the scarcity-of-goods problem. A sample of 300 people were asked: 'Is it, in your opinion, easy or difficult to obtain goods of prime necessity?' In reply, 99 per cent of the upper class respondents claimed that it was 'difficult' to get such goods, a judgment with which 77 per cent of the middle class but only 19 per cent of the lower class sample concurred. See *Ercilla* no. 1939, 13–19 September 1972. The poll comprised one hundred individuals, all from Santiago, from each of the vaguely defined 'upper', 'middle', and 'lower' classes.

31 Cf. ch. 4, p. 61.

32 The Santiago buses were crowded and slow for other reasons besides cheap fares. Many of the vehicles were out of action because of depleted supplies of spare parts and tires. See *Chile Hoy* no. 9, 11–17 August 1972, for data on the deficient collective transportation system of Santiago and the import problems that affected it.

33 ODEPLAN, *Informe Económico Anual 1971*, p. 175.

34 Literally 'guilds', in Chile used to designate the rightist controlled federations of small and medium-sized entrepreneurs, professionals, etc. The ideology of the *gremialismo* movement was outright fascist, with a Mussolini type of corporate state as its ideal. The *gremios* were the only kind of 'trade unions' which were not outlawed by Pinochet, and immediately after the coup in September 1973 the chief theorist of the *gremialismo*, Jaime Guzmán, was appointed member of the commission which should work out a new, 'modern' Chilean constitution.

35 In October 1972 several truck owners and taxi drivers publicly admitted that they were being offered dollars as a reward for their participation in the lockouts and strikes. A large inflow of dollars was also recorded on the black market where the dollar – in the midst of a serious political crisis – *fell* over 30 per cent against the escudo in a couple of weeks.

'Subversion against Allende was surprisingly cheap', a Brazilian businessman told a reporter from the *Washington Post* early in 1974. 'The money we sent would go a long way on the black market.' For further information on Brazilian involvement in the overthrow of Allende, see Marlise Simon's article 'The Brazilian Connection' in *Washington Post*, 6 January 1974.

According to testimonies given by the Chief of the US Central Intelligence Agency, William Colby, some eight million dollars were also spent between 1970 and 1973 by the CIA in its eventually successful campaign to install a military dictatorship in Chile.

36 See ch. 4, p. 75.

37 Estimate by *El Mercurio* (International Edn), 11–17 June 1973.

38 See, for example, Allende's 'Los Cambios Revolucionarios y el Desarrollo Económico Chileno', speech given in July 1972, printed in *Revista de la Universidad Técnica del Estado* no. 9, July–August 1972. In the first and second priority categories Allende placed 'goods of popular consumption, foodstuffs in particular' and 'transportation'.

39 Unless the dollars could be exchanged on the black market, of course; all kinds of smuggling flourished. Cf. ch. 7.

40 In current prices, as usual; early in 1973 the US dollar was devalued by some ten per cent against the industrial world's major currencies.

41 Allende, *Third Message*, p. 137.

42 Quotation taken from *El Siglo*, 29 February 1972.

43 An overview of these different agreements is found in an article by Enrique Sierra and María Cristina Germany in Banco Central, *Boletín Mensual* no. 541, March 1973.

44 CORFO, Departamento de Créditos Externos.

45 See *Chile Hoy* no. 43, 6–12 April 1973, for details of the composition of these debts.

46 In *Chile Hoy* no. 29, 29 December 1972 – 4 January 1973, the head of the Chilean renegotiation delegation, Orlando Letelier, sets out the Chilean position.

47 Millas, *Third Exposition*, p. 14.

48 These credits, given to compensate Chile for the low price of copper, in fact became very important; according to *El Mercurio* (24 December 1972) IMF lending to Chile amounted to 187.8 million dollars in 1971–2.

49 Cited in *El Mercurio*, 6 June 1972.

50 See ch. 6 and 7 respectively.

51 Some provisional indicators of the stagnation of residential construction are given in Instituto de Economía, *La Economía Chilena en 1972*, pp. 373ff, and in *Panorama Económico* no. 278, July 1973.

52 See *Panorama Económico* no. 276, April 1973.

6. THE FORMATION OF THE SOCIAL AREA OF THE ECONOMY

1 It deserves to be mentioned that the UP in no way rejected all cooperation with foreign capital interests. Several important projects with mixed foreign–Chilean

capital were in fact initiated, usually with CORFO holding a 51 per cent majority interest. The agreements thus reached tended to be quite favorable to the foreign investor who was, for example, often guaranteed a minimum annual rate of return of five per cent on invested capital (a maximum rate of twelve per cent was sometimes also established). Among industries of importance where such mixed companies were created were the automobile industry (Citroen, Peugeot), the commercial vehicles industry (Spanish PEGASO), the rubber and tire industry (General Tire Co.), and the electrical industry (RCA International).

2 *Vía Chilena* no. 2, November 1971.

3 Allende, *Second Message*, p. xiii.

4 Zorrilla, *First Exposition*, p. 33.

5 Cf. ch. 2, pp. 33–4.

6 This particular quotation is taken from Gonzalo Martner, head of ODEPLAN, in 'Lineamientos de la Estrategia de Desarrollo', *Revista de la Universidad Técnica del Estado* no. 11–12, November/December 1972–January/February 1973, p. 27.

7 *Basic program.*

8 In Debray's interview with Allende in *Punto Final*, 16 February 1971, p. 54.

9 Instituto de Economía, *La Economía de Chile en el Período 1950–63*, vol. 2, table 216, p. 176, and ODEPLAN, *Antecedentes*, table 309, p. 423.

10 Clark Reynolds in Mamalakis & Reynolds, *Essays*, p. 297.

11 Some 19,000 altogether, as against 17,000 in Gran Minería. Liliana Múñoz, *Estado Ocupacional de la Minería del Cobre*, 1971, p. 134.

12 Exhausted in 1959 and replaced by El Salvador.

13 In 1886, José Manuel Balmaceda was elected president on a nationalistic program which included promises to nationalize all foreign mineral companies and to raise taxation of the domestic ones. Five years later, when trying to put the election program into practice, Balmaceda was overthrown in a military coup financed by foreign and domestic mineral and commercial interests. It took, however, more than a traditional *coup d'état* to eliminate Balmaceda. A bloody, though short, civil war broke out, in which British naval ships (ignoring the Monroe doctrine) aided the rebels. See, especially, Hernán Ramírez-Necochea, *Balmaceda y la Contra-revolución de 1891*, 1958.

14 See 'La Situación del Cobre', *Panorama Económico* no. 31, 1951, pp. 10–14. A brief review of the losses Chile suffered due to the American price policy is also found in Salvador Allende, *Porque se Nacionaliza*, In Martner (ed.), *El Pensamiento Económico*, pp. 127–47.

15 Cited in *Panorama Económico* no. 46, 1951, where this year's parliamentary debate on copper is summarized.

16 The results of this arrangement were partly successful, but a boycott from American customers and the copper companies' drastic reduction of output made the Chilean government abandon this strategy in 1955, when a new agreement was signed. Through this 'new deal' (*nuevo trato*) the control over export sales was handed back to the American owners, who in turn had to promise to invest and increase production.

17 Salvador Allende in Martner (ed.), *El Pensamiento Económico*, p. 133.

18 *Ibid.*

19 According to the companies' own bookkeeping, gross investment in Gran Minería between 1930 and 1960 amounted to 359 million dollars, little more than 10 million a year, or hardly enough to keep the equipment intact. During the same

period net profits amounted to 849 million dollars, and net transfers abroad in the form of depreciation allowances, repatriated profits, interest and other payments in foreign exchange to 1,539 million. Based on Max Nolff, 'Los Problemas Básicos del Cobre', in Martner (ed.), *El Pensamiento Económico*, table 1, pp. 184–5.

20 Chilean sources on the details of the agreements are, of course, abundant. Among those I have utilized for the exposition below the following should be mentioned. ODEPLAN, *Antecedentes*, pp. 127–89; Lucio Geller & Jaime Estévez, 'La Nacionalización del Cobre', in Instituto de Economía, *La Economía Chilena en 1971*, pp. 565–8; *Panorama Económico* no. 246, July 1969; *Posición* no. 13, July 1972 and no. 23, September 1972, and various publications from the Central Bank of Chile. The best exposition of the 'Chileanization' program written in English, to the author's knowledge, is ch. 4 in Keith Griffin, *Underdevelopment in Spanish America*, and ECLA, *Economic Survey of Latin America 1969*.

21 Kennecott's main reasons are summarized in an exposition made in 1969 by one of its top executives, G. D. Michaelson – a document which is partly reproduced as an appendix in Martner (ed.), *El Pensamiento Económico*, pp. 187–9. The idea of suggesting a majority share for the Chilean state was based primarily upon political considerations. Kennecott hoped that such an arrangement would reduce the risk of labor disputes, heavier taxation and pressure for nationalization, and also expected the Chilean state to contribute capital for future investments more willingly if it were made majority owner.

22 See Griffin, *Underdevelopment*, pp. 153–4. 'No matter which procedure we use,' Griffin concludes, 'Kennecott was overvalued.'

23 Griffin, *Underdevelopment*, p. 164.

24 Based on Banco Central, *Balanza de Pagos de Chile*, various issues.

25 The only liability that Chile refused to take over was the 92.7 million dollar credit granted by Braden/Kennecott in 1967. The credit corresponded to the compensation paid to Braden/Kennecott for the sale of 51 per cent of its share capital to the Chilean state.

26 For example, the Under Secretary of the Treasury, John Petty, when he explained the reasons behind Nixon's earlier announcements of a 'hard line' against Chile on 19 January 1972: 'We hope that it [the US government's retaliation policy] will make any other government contemplating such steps [the expropriation of American property] think twice before taking them.' NACLA, *Chile: Facing the Blockade*, January 1973, p. 12, where a large number of similar statements can be found.

27 In the words of the World Bank: 'The report of the economic mission which returned 15 October stated clearly that Chile's economic policies would prevent the effective utilization of Bank lending even if the country were somehow deemed capable of servicing its debt ... While nationalization of and compensation for foreign held assets was a concern of the Bank, particularly in late September and early October [1971], the report of the economic mission in mid-October that Chile could not use development funds effectively under current economic policies was the decisive reason for the suspension of new lending.' IBRD, 'Chile and the World Bank', 1973, in which the World Bank attempts to justify the position it took *vis-à-vis* the Allende government.

28 Millas, *Third Exposition*, p. 58.

29 Interview in *Chile Hoy* no. 5, 14–20 July 1972, with Jorge Arrate, then Vice

President of CODELCO. Cf. also speech by Clodomiro Almeyda in the Chilean Senate, reproduced in *El Mercurio*, 28 December 1972.

30 *Time Magazine* (6 November, 1972): 'Kennecott officials are determined to keep the threat on Chile. The Manhattan office of General Counsel Pierce McCreary, who is directing the campaign, has the air of a war room. His desk is strewn with shipping reports, and on one wall hangs a large map for plotting ships' courses. From here, McCreary keeps a close watch on vessels entering or leaving the Chilean port of San Antonio, the only place from which El Teniente copper is shipped. At present he is monitoring the movements of at least six ships headed for Europe, loaded with El Teniente metal; when they arrive he wants his agents to be there to greet them with court orders.'

31 'The Appeal of Confiscation in Economic Development', in Bronfenbrenner & Randall (Eds.), *Economic Development – Evolution or Revolution?*, p. 55. Bronfenbrenner's article was first published in *Economic Development and Cultural Change*, vol. 3, no. 3, April 1955.

32 Figures from document written by Jorge Arrate, published in *Ultima Hora*, 22 February 1973.

33 Salvador Allende, speech delivered on 19 January 1973. See *El Mercurio*, 20 January 1973.

34 This was almost the first time that the UP did not cede to the miners' wage demands, and only after the abortive military coup on 29 June did the striking miners go back to work.

35 For details on these deals, see Ramos, *Chile*, pp. 48–9 and Allende, *First Message*, p. xvi.

36 A complete list of nationalized mining companies is found in ODEPLAN, *Nueva Economía* no. 2, January–April 1972, pp. 23–4.

37 *First Message*, p. xxi.

38 At that time the brokers' rate of exchange was about ten escudos to the dollar.

39 The latter bonds would undoubtedly have been the most common; in 56 per cent of all companies with 14 million escudos or more in share capital the ten largest shareholders owned more than 20 per cent of the shares, and in only 12 per cent of the cases did their share fall below 50 per cent. For further data on the concentration of shareholding in the 253 companies liable to expropriation according to the government's bill, see CEREN, *Cauadernos de la Realidad Nacional*, no. 11, January 1972.

40 *Ibid.*

41 *El Mercurio*, 19 November 1971.

42 *Ibid.*

43 The sectoral distribution and relative importance of the ninety enterprises was as shown in the table on p. 238. Fifty-two of the ninety corresponded to the social area, the remaining thirty-eight to the mixed area.

44 Renán Fuentaelba and Juan Hamilton, representatives of the left and right wing, respectively.

45 In July 1973 this court, especially assigned (during the Frei administration) to settle conflicts between the executive and legislative powers, declared itself 'incompetent' to deal with the matter.

46 For a detailed analysis of different legal proceedings concerning the social area of the economy see articles by Eduardo Novoa, the UP's first and foremost legal

Sector	Number of companies	Shares of gross value of production within each sector (percentage)
Manufacturing	74	18
Commerce	6	9
Electricity, gas, water	4	18
Transportation and communications	6	18
Total	90	

SOURCE: ODEPLAN, *Nueva Economía no. 2, January–April 1972, pp. 132ff.*

expert. Of special interest are 'Vías Legales para Avanzar hacia el Socialismo', *Revista de Derecho Económico*, vol. 9, no. 33–4, and 'El Difícil Camino de la Legalidad', *Revista de la Universidad Técnica del Estado* no. 7, April 1972.

47 The role played by the *Contraloría General* (CG) deserves a brief explanation. Formally the function of the CG was one of supervision, to see that the government acted in accordance with existing legislation, and each intervention and requisition was to be accepted and signed by the CG. When, as often happened, the CG refused to do so the executive could enforce its own will only through the issuing of a so-called insistency decree (*decreto de insistencia*) signed by every member of the cabinet. In general it was no problem – though politically a little embarassing – to get the signatures of all the ministers, but in periods of military presence in the government this expedient was more or less closed; a circumstance of which the CG was quick to take advantage by ordering the return to their owners of a large number of companies at the end of 1972.

48 These inconveniences were not confined to strong political opposition and conflicts with the CG and with the courts only. The undetermined legal status of industries kept under intervention or requisition created uncertainty among both workers and management and was a serious obstacle to all investment planning. How could one make correct decisions for the future when nobody knew who would become the owner of the plant? Another difficulty was that according to the legislation certain important decisions could not be taken by the state manager alone, since they required the approval from a representative of the legal owners. It sometimes happened that state appointed *interventores* were fined or even thrown in jail after accusations from the owners.

49 The strategy of trying to 'buy capitalism' might sound absurd and alien to all Marxist tradition, but it has sometimes been practised. In China, for example, many private industries were gradually nationalized in this way during the 1950s. And both Marx and Lenin refused to rule out this procedure in principle. Writing in 1918, Lenin argued that under certain conditions it could be more expedient to 'buy out the whole lot of them' (that is, landlords, industrialists, bankers, etc.) and continued: 'Marx taught that – as an exception, and Britain was then an exception – the idea was conceivable of *paying the capitalists well*, of buying them off, *if* the circumstances were such as to compel the capitalists to submit peacefully and to come over to socialism in a cultural and organized fashion, provided they were

238

paid.' '"Left Wing" Childishness and Petty-Bourgeois Mentality', here cited from Lenin, *On Socialist Economic Construction*, Moscow 1967, p. 149.

50 4 April 1972.

51 A salient manifestation of these different strategic concepts within the UP was the debate that arose after the presentation early in 1973 of the so-called Millas Project which promised the return to their owners of about 50 small and medium-sized industrial establishments that had been intervened or requisitioned. The project, named after the chief exponent of the conciliatory line, Orlando Millas, then Minister of Economy, provoked violent reactions from the PS and MAPU and from the workers affected, who immediately went on strike to express their indignation. The conflict, which threatened to break the already weakened unity within the government, was settled by Allende who this time supported the Left: the project was withdrawn, and the companies remained under state control.

52 *El Mercurio* (International Edition) 16–22 July 1973, and *Chile Hoy* no. 54, 27 July–1 August, 1973.

53 *El Mercurio* (International Edition) 19–25 November 1973.

54 After the last wave of interventions and requisitions in June–July 1973, for example, 22 of the 74 large companies that stood on the 'list of the 90' remained in private hands. *Chile Hoy* no. 59, 27 July–2 August 1973.

55 Sergio Bitar & Arturo MacKenna, 'Impacto de las Areas Social y Mixta en la Industria Chilena'. A preliminary version of this study was presented in *Panorama Económico* no. 278, June–July 1973, from which all information below has been taken.

56 Although the discussion of worker participation deals with the situation within manufacturing proper, much of what is said was true for state-owned companies in other sectors as well.

57 Within private industry no democratic experiments were undertaken. Relations between management and workers were characterized by conflict and tension and the so-called vigilance committees formed by the workers to supervise the owners were the only form of workers' control that became widespread.

58 To be exact, three representatives were elected by the directly productive workers, one by the clerical staff and one by the technical staff.

59 This particular quotation is taken from Allende's *First Message*, p. 52.

60 Zorrilla, *Second Exposition*, p. 24.

61 Instituto de Economía, *La Economía Chilena en 1971*, p. 447. Employment increased by 8.5 per cent, thus indicating a rise in labor productivity during 1971.

62 Instituto de Economía, *La Economía Chilena en 1972*, p. 433.

63 Claes Croner, 'Area Social. Una Evaluación Necesaria', in *Chile Hoy* no. 59, 27 July–2 August 1973.

64 For comparison, almost one-third of the sum total of fiscal expenditures in 1972.

65 Perhaps the most spectacular of these cases was the prolonged conflict over wages in the El Teniente copper mine, when virtually all rightist trade union leaders, senators and journalists rallied to the support of the miners' stiff demands and of the almost two-month long strike that followed. Only a minority of the workers participated in the strike, however. It was mainly a strike by the technical and white-collar staff.

66 This point is emphasized by Ruy Mauro Marini and Christián Sepúlveda in their excellent article 'La Política Económica de la "Vía Chilena"' in *Marxismo y Revolución* no. 1, July–September 1973. The authors argue convincingly that much of

the UP's price and credit policy tended in practice to favor the monopolistic sectors of the Chilean bourgeoisie rather than the medium- and small-scale enterpreneurs.

67 Cf., ch. 3, pp. 41–42.

68 Vuskovic, 'Dos Años de la Política Económica de la Unidad Popular', *Revista de la Universidad Técnica del Estado* no. 11–12, November/December 1972 – January/February 1973, p. 57.

69 Allende's speech presenting the bank nationalization project can be found in Martner (ed.) *El Pensamiento Económico*, pp. 245–52.

70 Especially for minor holdings – compensation was paid according to a differentiated scale, and the UP stuck rigorously to its old commitment to protect all small-holders.

71 Only in a few cases was the entire share capital purchased by the state. Private interests generally maintained minority holdings, and in the boards of directors these minority interests were guaranteed a proportional representation.

72 Zorilla, *Second Exposition*, p. 15.

73 Interview in *Chile Hoy* no. 31, 12–18 August 1973.

74 It was in no way characterized by free competition, however. About 50 per cent of all trucks and an ever higher percentage of buses and 'micro-buses' were owned by a few very large companies upon which many of the small hauliers were dependent through a complicated system of subcontracting. For an analysis of ownership and control in Chilean road transportation, see *Chile Hoy* no. 60, 3–9 August 1973.

75 ITT's refusal to extend its network to certain distant provinces had forced earlier Chilean governments to create a new telephone company, ENTEL, which worked exclusively in isolated regions. Altogether there were only some 33,000 telephones in Chile in 1970, or about three per one hundred inhabitants.

76 Data given by the President of DINAC in *Ultima Hora*, 2 Feburary 1973.

77 Cf. ch. 7, pp. 193ff.

78 For a statistical overview of Chilean retail trade see *Chile Hoy* no. 31, 12–18 January 1973.

79 Not all tradesmen who closed their shops did so out of ideological conviction or in protest against the UP's economic policies. Fear of reprisals from the strike leaders, who closely supervised (often with the help of para-military groups from 'Fatherland and Freedom') which shops were closed and which were not, forced a lot of UP adherents into joining the actions.

80 A number of artisans and small industrialists also began to sell their products directly to consumers; all kinds of fairs and outdoor markets flourished. To speak of 'elimination' of intermediaries is perhaps not quite accurate. It was more a question of a lot of petty producers' own transformation into middlemen in order to reap for themselves the speculative type of profits that arose in commerce. These initiatives were naturally felt to be threats to established retail trade. Cf. also ch. 7 for a discussion of the distribution of foodstuffs.

81 See the interview with Luis Inostroza, ex-director of DINAC, in *Punto Final* no. 179, 13 March 1973.

7. THE AGRARIAN SECTOR

1 Aranda & Martínez in Chonchol *et al.*, *Chile Hoy*, 1970, p. 142.

2 Ricardo Lagos & Kurt Ullrich, *Agricultura y Tributación – dos Ensayos*, 1965, p. 11.

3 Solon Barraclough, 'Notes on land tenure', p. 67.

4 Various data on living standards in rural Chile and on socio-economic differences between urban and rural areas can be found in Comité Interamericano de Desarrollo Agrícola (CIDA), *Chile: Tenencia de la Tierra y Desarrollo Socio-económico del Sector Agrícola*, 1966, and in Frederick S. Weaver, *Regional Patterns of Economic Change in Chile 1950–64*, 1968. ODEPLAN's *Antecedentes* also contains much useful information.

5 Net urban immigration in Chile between 1950 and 1960 is estimated at some 685,000 people (Barraclough, 'Notes on land tenure', p. 154), a figure approximately equivalent to the increase of inhabitants in the *poblaciones callampas* ('mushroom settlements') surrounding Santiago.

6 In the early 1960s only a tiny minority of the farm workers had the legal right to organize themselves in trade unions, and the informal power structure in the countryside was sufficiently rigid to prevent this type of activity even when permitted. For various aspects of power relations in rural Chile, see Chonchol's article 'Poder y Reforma Agraria', in Chonchol *et al.*, *Chile Hoy*.

7 Cf. Solon Barraclough, 'Agricultural policy and land reform', *Journal of Political Economy*, July–August 1970.

8 Charles T. Nisbet, 'Interest rates and imperfect competition in the informal credit market of rural Chile', *Economic Development and Cultural Change*, vol. 16, no. 1, 1967.

9 Cf. Solon Barraclough, 'Agricultural policy and land reform', pp. 912–13. In view of the agricultural sector's low and falling share of total tax revenues (1.2 per cent in 1964) and the existence of a wide range of subsidies to the large producers (cheap credit, technical assistance, export subsidies, etc.) it seems safe to assume that the Chilean agriculture's net fiscal contribution was in fact *negative*.

10 Marvin Sternberg, *Investment and Consumption Patterns of Large Landowners*, 1961, cited by Solon Barraclough, 'Notes on land tenure', p. 62.

11 Oficina de Planificación Agrícola (ODEPA), *Plan de Desarrollo Agropecuario 1965–80*, vol. 1, pp. 1–2.

12 −91.7 million dollars as a yearly average during 1960–64, as against −57.3 million during 1950–54 and −9.8 million in 1942–4. Kurt Ullrich in Lagos & Ullrich, *Agricultura y Tributación*, p. 35.

13 *El Siglo*, 27 April 1972.

14 Consumption of beef and veal *per capita* amounted to 32.8, 23.4 and 20.2 kilos in 1946–50, 1960, and 1964, respectively. Consumption of pork, lamb and mutton also declined. Figures from ECLA, *La Economía de Chile 1957*, 1958, p. 287; and *El Siglo*, 27 April 1972. Cf. also FAO, *Production Yearbook 1970*, table 116, p. 354.

15 René Dumont, *Lands Alive*, 1965, p. 66.

16 See especially CIDA, *Chile: Tenencia de la Tierra*.

17 That is, the Conservative and the Liberal Parties, which in 1966 merged to form the National Party (*Partido Nacional*).

18 Figures on the agrarian reform 1965–70 are found in, among others, D. Alaluf *et al.*, *Reforma Agraria Chilena: Seis Ensayos de Interpretación*, 1970; and Alaluf, *et al.*, 'El Sector Agrario . . .' in Instituto de Economía, *La Economía Chilena en 1971*.

19 ECLA, *Economic Survey of Latin America 1969*, p. 155.

20 Jorge Godoy & Manuel Krants, 'La Corporación de la Reforma Agraria y su Gestión – Análisis Financiero para el Período 1965–70,' 1971, table 14, p. 164.

21 Article in CEREN, *Cuadernos de la Realidad Nacional*, June 1970, pp. 77–78.

22 The average *asentamiento* comprised about 40 families and was managed jointly by CORA and a committee elected by the members. For a brief description, see Solon Barraclough, 'Alternative land tenure systems resulting from agrarian reform in Latin America,' *Land Economics*, August 1970.

23 This was undoubtedly the opinion of Jacques Chonchol, too, although hardly of Eduardo Frei and his rightist followers among the Christian Democrats. The legislation favored the splitting up of the land. Article 65 of the Land Reform Law stipulated that unless the *campesinos* decided otherwise, 'the land acquired by CORA will be assigned to the *campesinos* as private property'.

24 An *inquilino* usually had usufruct right to cultivate a small plot of land for his own consumption, paying for this right with labor obligations to the landowner. In early 1960s the number of *inquilino* families amounted to slightly more than 80,000.

25 Solon Barraclough, 'Agrarian reform and structural change in Latin America: the Chilean case,' *Journal of Development Studies*, January 1972, p. 168. It should be pointed out, however, that real wages of permanent agricultural workers almost doubled between 1965 and 1970 due to the equalization of legal minimum wages of agricultural and industrial workers. Since the landowner was free to fire the workers he now found unprofitable, a large number of permanent workers were turned into unattached day-laborers as a result of the new legislation.

26 Whether 'in spite of' or 'because of' the agrarian reform I dare not say, but the index of agricultural output developed as follows between 1965 and 1970: 1965 = 100, 1966 = 111.8, 1967 = 116.4, 1968 = 117.0, 1969 = 109.2, 1970 = 114.7 (1965 prices used). Source: ICIRA, 'Diagnóstico de la Reforma Agraria' (hereafter referred to as 'Diagnosis'), p. iv-30.

27 See especially Alaluf *et al.*, *Reforma Agraria Chilena*, and ICIRA, 'Diagnosis'.

28 See Instituto Nacional de Estadística, *Encuesta Nacional Agropecuaria*, various issues.

29 Allende interviewed by Regis Débray, *Punto Final*, 11 March 1971, pp. 48–9.

30 See Jacques Chonchol, 'La Política Agraria en una Economía de Transición al Socialismo: el Caso Chileno' in Martner (ed.), *El Pensamiento Económico*, p. 229, or Chonchol's speech *The Agrarian Policy of the Popular Government* in Ann J. Zammit (ed.), *The Chilean Road to Socialism*, 1973, pp. 107ff.

31 Cf. Chonchol, 'La Política Agraria ...' The crops which Chonchol mentioned as especially favorable for Chile to specialize in were wine, fruit, and horticultural products; elsewhere (in *Panorama Económico* no. 265, December 1971, p. 31) he suggested that Chile ought to be able to export between 300 and 400 million dollars worth of these products a year.

32 Later on, in 1973, the parliamentary opposition enforced a completely new land reform legislation all of its own, but being a step back even in comparison with existing legislation the bill was vetoed by Allende.

33 We recall that 80 'basic hectares' corresponded to 80 hectares of the very best land available in Chile – irrigated, good soil in the Central Valley – and in some provinces the equivalent was set as several hundred hectares of cultivatable land and far above one thousand hectares of unimproved pasture. This is a lot of land. The legal definition is quite arbitrary, and many large estates below 80 b. ha ought to be called *latifundios*. To make one comparison: when Mao Tse-Tung once

discussed his father's economic status he classified him as a 'middle peasant' since he owned as much as fifteen *mu*, or one hectare, of arable land.

34 Cf. Chonchol's own explanation in Zammit (ed.) *The Chilean Road*, pp. 107ff.

35 ICIRA, 'Diagnosis', p. v-20.

36 Figure taken from the Communist daily *El Siglo*, 30 April 1972.

37 The maximum the landowners could hope to get in cash was ten per cent of the assessed value of the land. The remainder they received in long-term bonds, running up to 30 years. The values of these latter bonds were readjusted to take account of only 70 per cent of each year's inflation.

38 In many cases the landowners did accept *reservas* smaller than 80 b. ha, but the value of the difference then had to be paid in cash. The struggle over conversion coefficients was especially intense in the south, where antagonisms were most pronounced and where, furthermore, West Germany intervened – under the threat of blocking the renegotiations over Chile's foreign debt – in order to guarantee 'fair' estimates of the *reservas* of the numerous German landowning colony. In the south there were German descendants with *reservas* covering 2,000 hectares of good land.

39 From some 12.8 to 27.3 per cent of all productive land, a difference which can only partially be explained by the existence of some 4,000 *reservas* in 1972. See 'Diagnosis', pp. iii-2ff.

40 Chonchol 'La Reforma Agraria y la Experiencia Chilena', in CESO–CEREN, *Transición al Socialismo y Experiencia Chilena*, p. 152.

41 The fast but unmeasured increase in this sector's capital intensity was to a large extent a consequence of the way the agrarian reform was carried through and of the tense political situation in general. I have already mentioned the expropriated *latifundistas*' concentration of cattle and machinery to their *reservas*, and the landowners' fear of conflicts with their workers also acted as a strong incentive for a further replacement of labor with capital.

42 Estimated from table 7.5. The average amount of land per family in the whole reformed sector amounted to about 20 b. ha.

43 Interview in *Que Pasa?* no. 51, 6 April 1972.

44 It deserves to be mentioned that Chonchol, who had conducted the expropriative phase of the land reform almost to its end, resigned in November 1972, threatened (together with three other ministers) by impeachment for 'violation of the Constitution' by the parliamentary opposition. Chonchol was also subject to criticism from various groups within the UP who wanted to make him the scapegoat for the agrarian problems. In the period that followed trial-and-error characterized the appointments of agricultural ministers, and three more (Rolando Colderón, Pedro Hidalgo and Ernesto Torrealba) were for different reasons forced to resign within ten months.

45 With the noticeable exception of the MIR, the Movement of the Revolutionary Left, which, although rather small on a national scale, had one of its strongholds among agricultural workers and Mapuche Indians in the south.

46 Both the Communists' and the *campesinos*' hostility towards the CERAs gradually wore off, however, and in 1972 both the PC and the large pro-UP *campesino* organizations gave their full support to the CERAs while rejecting the *asentamiento* system.

47 *Revista Agraria* no. 5, May 1973, p. 11.

48 There were some minor differences in this respect between the *asentamientos* and

the CERAs. On the former the *campesinos* were free to distribute all net profits among themselves if they wanted to, but on the CERAs 10 per cent of profits should go to a 'social fund', 50 per cent to finance new investment, and the remaining 40 per cent should be distributed among the members. Very few cooperatives made any net profits, however, and the practical importance of this difference was thus very small.

49 *Revista Agraria* no. 2, January 1973, p. 3.

50 Literally 'those who are outside', i.e., those who used to be unattached day-laborers on the large *fundos* and whose status thus prevented them from becoming integrated as *socios* in the cooperatives.

51 The amount of manpower needed per hectare varied greatly between different crops. It was estimated that cereals, with existing production techniques, required only some 10–30 man-days per hectare year, as against 45–110 for industrial crops (oil seeds, sugar-beet, etc.), 80–180 for fruits and 100–300 for vegetable products.

52 Several reasons for this 'competitiveness' are given in *Revista Agraria* no. 2, January 1973, which contains an analysis of the role of the private plots in the reformed sector.

53 In *Chile Hoy* no. 25, 1–7 July 1972, p. 15.

54 Figures from Allende, *Second Message*, p. 248, and *Third Message*, p. 298.

55 ICIRA, 'Diagnosis', p. iii-18.

56 The minimum wage was 20, later in 1971 30, escudos per day.

57 ICIRA, 'Diagnosis', p. iv-38. In nominal terms the rate rose to 40 per cent in 1972, which, however, signified a stabilization in real terms.

58 The reformed sector was, furthermore, exempted from all kinds of taxes.

59 Allende, *Third Message*, p. 247.

60 ODEPLAN, *Cuentas Nacionales de Chile 1960–71*, 1973, p. 23.

61 The tractor is used as an example only; imports of other forms of agricultural machinery rose in an almost parallel way. (See ICIRA, 'Diagnosis', and Allende, *Third Message*, for figures.)

62 Allende, *Third Message*, pp. 282ff.

63 Speech given in Valdivia, see *La Nación*, 2 August 1972.

64 The effects on the balance of payments would, strictly speaking, be equally negative even if domestic heavy industry and oil production were sufficiently developed to be able to satisfy the demand from agriculture (which is not the case in Chile), since the potential surplus could then be exported.

65 One example can be enough: 'CHILE: WORSE THAN BIAFRA'. Headline on the front page of the Christian Democrats' official daily *La Prensa*, 11 February 1972. We recall that the total supply of foodstuffs was much larger than in 1970 – not to mention 1974 – and its distribution more egalitarian than earlier.

66 The law permitted state-owned purchasing agencies, the most important of which were ECA (cereals) and SOCOAGRO (meat) to take over the buying of agricultural products in times of general shortage of food. This possibility was used, in the face of violent protests from the opposition, on some occasions by the UP, but results were poor. The only significant achievement was the puchase of slightly over 300,000 tons of wheat, or about one-third of the whole harvest, in 1973.

67 Many truck owners did, for example, abandon their normal activities in order to

engage in direct distribution of agricultural products for the black market. This 'smuggling' was illegal, but flourished nevertheless. A serious consequences of the existence of parallel markets was that many products were channeled to uses other than the 'normal' ones. Much foodgrain was, for example, sold to the breeders of cattle, pigs, poultry, etc., since all kinds of meat commanded very high prices on the black market. While bread for human consumption was short, many pigs and chickens thus got an excellent diet.

68 The Mapuches are the most important indigenous people living in Chile, but apart from them there are some minor groups of precolonial origin, *quechuas, aymarás, changos, huillinques,* etc., who altogether number some 140,000–160,000 people. Deprived of their land – a process which continued up to World War I – the indigenous peoples have been constantly discriminated against in all economic, political, social and cultural matters, and constitute the poorest of all Chilean poor. The indigenous population has long claimed the right to vast areas of land which have been stolen from them, and in 1971 and 1972 they did regain some of their lost land – about 70,000 hectares, as against 1,400 during the whole preceding decade. Their right to recover lost land was recognized 'in principle' by law in 1961.

69 Since priority was given to collective forms of working the land when credit or technical assistance was provided the above figure should be taken with some caution; it sometimes happened that the cooperatives were cooperatives only nominally, and many committees acted as mere intermediaries of state credits.

70 From some 900 to over 10,000 between 1970 and 1972 (Allende *Third Message,* p. 312).

71 The private sector was more difficult to supervise, of course, but the *medianos* were given some economic incentives (e.g., easier access to credits and imported machinery) if they fulfilled their obligations to the workers.

72 See *La Nación,* 12 November 1972.

73 These and the other data below are based on ICIRA, 'Diagnosis' or obtained directly from the Central Bank of Chile.

74 We recall that Chile's earlier development from a net exporter to a larger and larger net importer was the consequence of stagnating *per capita* production and not of a rise in average food standards.

75 Only products destined for consumption – immediately or after further processing in Chile – are included here. Seeds, fertilizers, tractors, oil for the tractors, reproductive cattle, etc. should thus be added if we were to estimate the value of all imports related to the agrarian sector.

76 ICIRA, 'Diagnosis', p. iv-13. This figure is provisional and possibly slightly exaggerated.

77 That smuggling was a profitable activity might sound surprising in view of the high prices that foodstuffs commanded on the black market in Chile. But it was, to begin with, only very few products that were really scarce and thus expensive. Overall prices of foodstuffs were very low. There was, furthermore, a black market in foreign exchange, where dollars were sold for increasingly fantastic amounts of escudos. To bring dollars to Chile, change them there and buy Chilean cigarettes, razor blades, coffee, tea, records, beef, etc. was a both rewarding and much practiced business.

78 Especially as from 1971 this was also true for the *campesinos'* adversaries, who in

many regions formed para-military 'white guards' which terrorized the poor peasants.

79 Figures refer to the typically agrarian provinces of Colchagua, Curicó, Muale, Linares, Ñuble, Malleco, Cautín and Chiloé.

80 The central confederation of *asentados* in fact turned openly pro-DC. The description below of a Chilean *asentamiento* is a good illustration of the reasons behind this stand:

'On *El Cerillo* in Chile the *asentados* did less than one-third of all work themselves. They made twice as much money as their workers. They lived in houses built for them by the Agrarian Reform Corporation, while their workers had taken over the old, decrepit houses they used to live in themselves. They defended the privileges they had only recently received just as doggedly as the old landowner had earlier defended his privileges. In only a few years one of Molina's most militant groups of workers had, in short, changed position and gone over to the side of the employers.' Sven Lindquist, *Jordens Gryning. Jord och Makt i Latinamerika*, 1974, p. 203.

FINAL REFLECTIONS

1 See ch. 6, p. 115.

2 Cf. ch. 3, note 1, for a brief summary of criteria often applied in the 'transitional debate' over definitional questions. It should be observed that the UP's Basic Program of 1970 referred to 'socialism' only once, and then by stating that the UP government intended to 'initiate the construction of socialism'.

3 Distributed approximately as follows: 35,000 agricultural workers (the additional beneficiaries of the agrarian reform during the Allende government; altogether some 55,000 families were given land in individual or collective forms between 1964 and 1973), 100,000—120,000 industrial workers, 50,000—70,000 mining workers and, perhaps, 30,000—50,000 workers in miscellaneous sectors.

4 Friedrich Engels, *The Peasant War in Germany*, 1969, p. 115.

Works cited

BOOKS

Alaluf, D., Barraclough, S., Corvalán, A., Echenique, J., Mattelart, A. & Sampaio, P., *Reforma Agraria Chilena: Seis Ensayos de Interpretación*, Santiago 1970.

Althusser, Luis & Balibar, Etienne, *Lire le Capital*, Paris 1968.

Amin, Samir, *L'Accumulation à l'Echelle Mondiale. Critique de la Théorie du Sous-développement*, Dakar 1970.

Bettelheim, Charles, *La Transition vers L'économie Socialiste*, Paris 1968.

Cerda, Carlos, *El Leninismo y la Victoria Popular*, Santiago 1971.

Chonchol, Jacques, *et al.*, *Chile Hoy*, Santiago 1970.

Dumont, René, *Lands Alive*, New York 1965.

Emmanuel, Arghiri, *Unequal Exchange. A Study of the Imperialism of Trade*, London, New York 1972.

Engels, Friedrich, *The Peasant War in Germany*, Moscow 1969.

Frank, Andre Gunder, *Capitalism and Underdevelopment in Latin America*, 2nd edn, London, New York 1969.

Godoy, Hernán (ed.), *Estructura Social de Chile*, Santiago 1971.

Griffin, Keith, *Underdevelopment in Spanish America*, London 1969.

Labarca, Eduardo, *Chile al Rojo*, Santiago 1971.

Lagos, Ricardo & Ullrich, Kurt, *Agricultura y Tributación – dos Ensayos*, Santiago 1965.

Lange, Oscar, *On the Economic Theory of Socialism*, London, Minneapolis 1938.

Lenin, V. I., *On Socialist Economic Construction*, Moscow 1967.

Lindquist, Sven, *Jordens Gryning. Jord och Makt i Latinamerika*, Stockholm 1974.

Mamalakis, Markus & Reynolds, Clark, *Essays on the Chilean Economy*, Homewood Illinois 1965.

Manns, Patricio, *Las Grandes Masacres de Chile*, Santiago 1972.

Múñoz, Liliana, *Estudio Ocupacional de la Minería de Cobre*, Santiago 1971.

Petras, James, *Politics and Social Forces in Chilean Development*, Berkeley 1969.

Ramírez-Necochea, Hernán, *Balmaceda y la contra revolución de 1891*, Santiago 1958.

247

Works cited

Ramos, Sergio, *Chile: Una Economía de Transición?*, Santiago 1972.

Véliz, Claudio (ed.), *Obstacles to Change in Latin America*, New York, Toronto 1966.

Vera Valenzuela, Mario, *La Política Económica del Cobre en Chile*, Santiago 1962.

Weaver, Frederick S., *Regional Patterns of Economic Change in Chile 1950–64*, Cornell University, 1968.

Zammit, Ann J. (ed.), *The Chilean Road to Socialism*, Brighton 1973.

ARTICLES AND MONOGRAPHS

Ballesteros, Marto & Davis, Tom, 'The growth of output and employment in basic sectors of the Chilean economy 1908–1957', *Economic Development and Cultural Change*, vol. XI, no. 2, 1962.

Barraclough, Solon, 'Notes on land tenure', ICIRA, Santiago (Collected articles, mimeographed).

Barraclough, Solon, 'Agrarian reform and structural change in Latin America: the Chilean case', *Journal of Development Studies*, January 1972.

Barraclough, Solon, 'Agricultural policy and land reform', *Journal of Political Economy*, July–August 1970.

Barraclough, Solon, 'Alternative land tenure systems resulting from agrarian reform in Latin America', *Land Economics*, August 1970.

Blest, Clotario, 'Los trabajadores: su organización sindical', *Punto Final*, no. 108, July 1970.

Bronfenbrenner, Martin, 'The appeal of confiscation in economic development', *Economic Development and Cultural Change*, vol. 3, no. 3, April 1955.

Chonchol, Jacques, 'La política agraria en una economía de transición al socialismo: el caso Chileno' in Martner (ed.), *El Pensamiento Económico del Gobierno de Allende*, Santiago 1971.

Giusti, Jorge, 'Political participation in Chile. Three types of *pobladores* organization', Escuela Latinoamericana da Ciencia Política y Administración Pública, Santiago 1972 (mimeographed).

Godoy, Jorge & Krants, Manuel, 'La Corporación de la Reforma Agraria y su Gestión – Análisis Financiero para el Período 1964–70', Universidad de Chile, Santiago 1971 (mimeographed).

Magdoff, Harry & Sweezy, Paul, 'Chile: peaceful transition to socialism?', *Monthly Review*, vol. 22, no. 8, January 1971.

Marín, Juan Carlos, 'Las tomas', *Marxismo y Revolución* no. 1, July–September 1973.

Marini, Ruy Mauro & Supúlveda, Christián, 'La Política Económica de la "Vía Chilena"', *Marxismo y Revolución* no. 1, July–September 1973.

Nisbet, Charles, 'Interest rates and imperfect competition in the informal credit market of rural Chile', *Economic Development and Cultural Change*, vol. 16, no. 1, October 1967.

Works cited

Novoa, Eduardo, 'Vías Legales para Avanzar hacia el Socialismo', *Revista de Derecho Económico*, vol. 9, no. 33–4, October 1970 – May 1971.

Novoa, Eduardo, 'El Difícil Camino de la Legalidad', *Revista de la Universidad Técnica del Estado* no. 7, April 1972.

Vuskovic, Pedro, 'Dos Años de Política Económica de la Unidad Popular', *Revista de La Universidad Técnica del Estado*, no. 11–12, November/ December 1972–January/February 1973.

de Vylder, Stefan, *From Colonialism to Dependence: An Introduction to Chile's Economic History*, Stockholm 1974.

DOCUMENTS AND OFFICIAL PUBLICATIONS

Chilean public agencies

Banco Central de Chile, *Boletín Mensual* (monthly).

Banco Central de Chile, *Memoria* (annual).

Banco Central de Chile, *Balanza de Pagos* (annual).

CORFO, *Programa Nacional de Desarrollo 1961–70*, Santiago 1970.

CORFO, *Inversiones Extranjeras en Chile*, Santiago 1971.

Instituto Nacional de Estadísticas (INE), *XIII Censo Nacional de Población*, Santiago 1960.

INE, *XIV Censo Nacional de Población y III de Vivienda*, Santiago 1971.

INE, *Encuesta Nacional Agropecuaria* (annual).

INE, Statistical Bulletins on Specific Subjects.

Ministerio de la Vivienda y Urbanismo, *Política Habitacional del Gobierno Popular*, Santiago 1972.

Oficina de Planificación Agrícola (ODEPA), Ministerio de Agricultura, *Plan de Desarrollo Agropecuario 1965–80*, Santiago 1968.

Oficina de Planificación Nacional (ODEPLAN), *Cuentas Nacionales de Chile 1960–71*, Santiago 1973.

ODEPLAN, *Nueva Economía* (half-yearly).

ODEPLAN, 'Vía Chilena' (bi-monthly).

ODEPLAN, *Antecedentes sobre el Desarrollo Chileno 1960–70*, Santiago 1971.

ODEPLAN, *Resumen del Plan de la Economía Nacional 1971–76*, Santiago 1971.

ODEPLAN, *Resumen del Plan Anual 1972*, Santiago 1972.

ODEPLAN, *Informe Económico Anual 1971*, Santiago 1972.

UN and other international organizations

ECLA, *La Economía de Chile 1957*, Santiago 1958.

ECLA, *Algunos Aspectos de la Industria de Cobre en América Latina*, Santiago 1968.

Works cited

ECLA, *Economic Bulletin for Latin America (half-yearly)*.

ECLA, *Economic Survey of Latin America* (annual).

Food and Agricultural Organization (FAO), *FAO Production Year-book* (annual).

International Bank of Reconstruction and Development (IBRD), 'Chile and the World Bank', 30 November 1973 (mimeographed).

Organización de los Estados Americanos (OEA), *América en Cifras* (annual).

Universities and research institutes

Centro de Estudios de la Realidad Nacional, Universidad Católica (CEREN), *Cuadernos de la Realidad Nacional* (bimonthly).

Centro Latinoamericano de Demografía (CELADE), *Chile*, Santiago 1969.

Comité Interamericano de Desarrollo Agrícola (CIDA), *Tenencia de la Tierra y Desarrollo Socio-económico del Sector Agrícola: Argentina, Brazil, Chile, Colombia, Ecuador, Guatemala y Peru*, Washington DC 1966.

Instituto de Capacitación e Investigación en Reforma Agraria (ICIRA), 'Diagnóstico de la Reforma Agraria Chilena', Santiago 1972 (mimeographed).

Instituto de Economía y Planificación de la Universidad de Chile, *La Economía de Chile en el Período 1950–63* (2 Vols.), Santiago 1963.

Instituto de Economía y Planificación de la Universidad de Chile, *La Economía Chilena en 1971*, Santiago 1972.

Instituto de Economía y Planificación de la Universidad de Chile, *La Economía Chilena en 1972*, Santiago 1973.

Instituto de Economía y Planificación de la Universidad de Chile, *Ocupación y Desocupación en Gran Santiago* (quarterly).

Instituto de Economía y Planificación de la Universidad de Chile, *Ocupación y Desocupación en Concepción-Talcahuano y Lota-Coronel* (half-yearly).

Miscellaneous

Allende, Salvador, *El Primer Mensaje del Presidente Allende ante el Congreso Pleno* 21 May 1971, Santiago 1971.

Allende, Salvador, *El Segundo Mensaje del Presidente Allende ante el Congreso Pleno* 21 May 1972, Santiago 1972.

Allende, Salvador, *El Tercer Mensaje del Presidente Allende ante el Congreso Pleno* 21 May 1973, Santiago 1973.

Allende, Salvador, 'Los Cambios Revolucionarios y el Desarrollo Económico Chileno', speech published in *Revista de la Universidad Técnica del Estado* no. 9, July–August 1972.

Centro de Estudios Socio-Económicos (CESO) – Centro de Estudios de la Realidad Nacional (CEREN), *Transición al Socialismo y Experiencia Chilena* (based on a symposium held in Santiago in October 1971), Santiago 1972.

Complida, Fransisco & Medina, Cecilia (eds.), *Constitución Política de la República de Chile*, Santiago 1971.

Works cited

Documentos Secretos de la ITT, Santiago 1972.

Garcés, Juan (ed.), *Nuestro Camino al Socialismo – la Vía Chilena* (excerpts from speeches and articles by Salvador Allende), Buenos Aires 1971.

Jobet, Julio César & Chelén, Alejandro (eds.), *Pensamiento Teórico y Político del Partido Socialista*, Santiago 1972.

Martner, Gonzalo (ed.), *El Pensamiento Económico del Gobierno de Allende*, Santiago 1971.

Millas, Orlando, *Exposición sobre la Política Económica del Gobierno y del Estado de la Hacienda Pública, 16.11.1972*, Ministerio de Hacienda, Dirección de Presupuestos, Folleto no. 122, Santiago 1972.

North American Congress on Latin America (NACLA), Latin America & Empire Report, *Chile: Facing the Blockade*, New York 1973.

Unidad Popular, *Programa Básico del Gobierno de la Unidad Popular*, Santiago 1970.

Zorrilla, Amérigo, *Exposición sobre la Política Económica del Gobierno y del Estado de la Hacienda Pública, 27.11.1970*, Ministerio de Hacienda, Dirección de Presupuestos, Folleto no. 118, Santiago 1970.

Zorrilla, Amérigo, *Exposición sobre la Política Económica del Gobierno y del Estado de la Hacienda Pública 16.11.1971*, Ministerio de Hacienda, Dirección de Presupuestos, Folleto no. 120, Santiago 1971.

MAGAZINES AND NEWSPAPERS

Chile Hoy
Diario Oficial
El Mercurio
El Rebelde
El Siglo
Ercilla
La Nación
La Prensa
La Segunda
Panorama Económico
Plan

Posición
Punto Final
Que Pasa?
Revista Agraria
Survey of Current Business
The Guardian
Time Magazine
Ultima Hora
US News and World Report
Washington Post